SACRAMENTO PUBLIC LIBRARY
828 "I" Street
Sacramento, CA   95814
11/09

Additional Praise for Billions of Drops in Millions of Buckets

"In *Billons of Drops*, Steve Goldberg offers a thoroughly researched and extremely well reasoned analysis of important developments within the social sector and its capital markets. This fascinating book is a much-needed contribution to the literature of the field and a must read for all thoughtful leaders of social change."

James L. Weinberg
Founder & CEO, Commongood Careers

"I thoroughly enjoyed this eye-opening and provocative book. It offers not only a penetrating critique of philanthropy's inefficiency but also clear and realistic remedies that could benefit millions of lives. I hope its insightful ideas are implemented nationwide."

Anne Ellinger
Cofounder, Bolder Giving in Extraordinary
Times and More Than Money

"Steve Goldberg's new book, *Billions of Drops in Millions of Buckets*, is required reading for all of us who want to see the nonprofit sector perform better. It represents the latest cutting-edge thinking on the use of Web 2.0 techniques for philanthropy. His cogent critique of the holy grail of SROI analysis, pricing nonprofit outcomes, will certainly put the kibosh on all those naysayers who think it can't be done. If you've never understood why the nonprofit sector can't get better outcomes for the money, read this book. And if you want to do something about it, make sure others around you read it too. I know I will."

Allan Benamer
Executive Director, socialmarkets

"A must read for anyone that wants to better understand how capital flows in the nonprofit sector and more importantly how it can flow better."

Andrew Wolk
Founder and CEO, Root Cause
Senior Lecturer, Social Entrepreneurship, MIT
Gleitsman Visiting Practitioner, Social Innovation,
Harvard Center for Public Leadership

Billions of Drops in Millions of Buckets

Billions of Drops in Millions of Buckets

Why Philanthropy Doesn't Advance Social Progress

Steven H. Goldberg

WILEY

John Wiley & Sons, Inc.

This book is printed on acid-free paper. ∞

Copyright © 2009 by Steven H. Goldberg. All rights reserved.

Published by John Wiley & Sons, Inc., Hoboken, New Jersey.

Published simultaneously in Canada.

No part of this publication may be reproduced, stored in a retrieval system, or transmitted in any form or by any means, electronic, mechanical, photocopying, recording, scanning, or otherwise, except as permitted under Section 107 or 108 of the 1976 United States Copyright Act, without either the prior written permission of the publisher, or authorization through payment of the appropriate per-copy fee to the Copyright Clearance Center, Inc., 222 Rosewood Drive, Danvers, MA 01923, 978-750-8400, fax 978-646-8600, or on the Web at www.copyright.com. Requests to the Publisher for permission should be addressed to the Permissions Department, John Wiley & Sons, Inc., 111 River Street, Hoboken, NJ 07030, 201-748-6011, fax 201-748-6008, or online at www.wiley.com/go/permissions.

Limit of Liability/Disclaimer of Warranty: While the publisher and author have used their best efforts in preparing this book, they make no representations or warranties with respect to the accuracy or completeness of the contents of this book and specifically disclaim any implied warranties of merchantability or fitness for a particular purpose. No warranty may be created or extended by sales representatives or written sales materials. The advice and strategies contained herein may not be suitable for your situation. You should consult with a professional where appropriate. Neither the publisher nor author shall be liable for any loss of profit or any other commercial damages, including but not limited to special, incidental, consequential, or other damages.

For general information on our other products and services, or technical support, please contact our Customer Care Department within the United States at 800-762-2974, outside the United States at 317-572-3993 or fax 317-572-4002.

Wiley also publishes its books in a variety of electronic formats. Some content that appears in print may not be available in electronic books.

For more information about Wiley products, visit our Web site at www.wiley.com.

Library of Congress Cataloging-in-Publication Data:

Goldberg, Steven H., 1954–
  Billions of drops in millions of buckets: why philanthropy doesn't advance social progress/Steven H. Goldberg.
    p. cm.
  Includes index.
  ISBN 978-0-470-45467-1 (cloth : acid-free paper)
  1. Endowments–United States–Economic aspects.   2. Endowments–United States–Management.   3. Nonprofit organizations–United States–Management.   I. Title.
  HV91.G564 2009
  658.15$'$224–dc22

Printed in the United States of America

10 9 8 7 6 5 4 3 2 1

To my sister, Missy, from whom so many good things flow

About the Author

Steven H. Goldberg is a latecomer to the nonprofit sector after a 30-year career in government, law, and business. He practiced constitutional and administrative law before state and federal courts and agencies; helped keep the Boston Harbor cleanup project on schedule as Associate and Acting General Counsel of the Massachusetts Water Resources Authority; and lectured across the country on preventing Year 2000 computer lawsuits. As Executive Vice President for Business Development and General Counsel for Imagitas, Inc., a venture-backed marketing services company in Waltham, Massachusetts, Steve managed privacy compliance and public contract acquisition for strategic alliances with federal and state government agencies. Beginning in 2005, he has provided consulting services to New Profit, Inc. and Root Cause, where he remains a Senior Fellow, and served as Chief Operating Officer to Cradles to Crayons, a Boston- and Philadelphia–based nonprofit that provides "everyday essentials" to more than 40,000 poor and low-income children annually through more than 300 social service agency partners. He coauthored *Y2K Risk Management: Contingency Planning, Business Continuity, and Avoiding Litigation* (Wiley, 1999) and wrote *The Federal Y2K Act Guidebook* (Thompson, 2000). Steve earned B.A.

and M.A. degrees in economics from the University of Massachusetts, Amherst (1975, magna cum laude), and Northwestern University (1980), respectively, and he received his J.D. degree, magna cum laude, from Boston College Law School in 1982. He and his wife, Janet Klein, have two sons and live in Needham, Massachusetts.

The core problem is that our education and training systems were built for another era, an era in which most workers needed only a rudimentary education. It is not possible to get where we have to go by patching that system. There is not enough money available at any level of our intergovernmental system to fix this problem by spending more on the system we have. We can get where we must go only by changing the system itself.

—*"Tough Choices or Tough Times," The New Commission on the Skills of the American Workforce*

The financial system [for nonprofit enterprises] we have put in place and support is the worst enemy, not only of the improvements everyone is trying to make, but of the socially critical programs and services this system is meant to sustain. All efforts to improve the sector will be merely palliative without essential, systemic reform of the way the rules of finance work.

—*Clara Miller, "The Looking-Glass World of Nonprofit Money: Managing in For-Profits' Shadow Universe"*

Many organizations with the potential to grow are unable to do so because they cannot tap into an easy-to-access capital market... There are not enough organizations able to systemically expand and strengthen their work in order to really resolve social issues.

—*Arthur Wood and Maximilian Martin, "Market-Based Solutions for Financing Philanthropy"*

The forecast is for hundreds of billions, if not trillions, of philanthropic dollars to be dropped into our industry, but given the current scattered nature of our efforts, the chances of effectively channeling these resources to substantial public good is like trying to direct the floods of the Nile River by building sand castles along its banks.

—*Lucy Bernholz,* Creating Philanthropic Capital Markets: The Deliberate Evolution

Any serious discussion of nonprofit capital market deficiencies has to start with an acknowledgement that there is no obvious way out of this maze. Expanding social needs are being addressed by nonprofits with very limited funding options. Grant seekers put extensive resources into navigating unclear and unpredictable restrictions. This fragmented funding landscape weakens the sector and ultimately limits impact, detracting from the very community efforts that the funds are meant to support.

—Cynthia Gair, *"Out of Philanthropy's Funding Maze: Strategic Co-Founding"*

. . . incremental changes in a system's parts would not alter the whole. As long as the deep structure is intact, it generates a strong inertia, first to prevent the system from generating alternatives outside its own boundaries, then to pull any deviations that do occur back into line.

—Connie J. Gersick, *"Revolutionary Change Theories: A Multilevel Exploration of the Punctuated Equilibrium Paradigm"*

Contents

Prelude: "The Great Recession"

We're in the middle of a financial crisis, but most economists say there is a broader economic crisis still to come. The unemployment rate will shoot upward. Companies will go bankrupt. Commercial real estate values will decline. Credit card defaults will rise. The nonprofit sector will be hammered.
                                    —*David Brooks, "Big Government Ahead"*

The last quarter of 2008 is either the best or the worst time to finish a book heralding our current "Golden Age of Philanthropy." As I write, President-elect Barack Obama has just held his third press conference in as many days to explain how his economic team will "hit the ground running" on January 20, 2009, and federal bailout efforts have passed the $1 trillion mark. "The worst financial crisis since the Great Depression" has all but forced the current officeholder off the stage, and no one is accusing Mr. Obama of jumping the gun.

Meanwhile, the nonprofit sector trembles. *The Chronicle of Philanthropy* answers the question foremost in everyone's mind, "How bad is it?" this way:

> The cataclysm in the nation's financial industry poses an uncharted set of challenges for nonprofit organizations. The downturn could potentially affect not just private giving, but money charities get from government sources—and it is hitting at a time of year when many charities get the bulk of their donations. What's more, for groups that serve the needy or others harmed by the economy, demand for aid is on the rise.[1]

At a time when *cataclysm* is not too strong a word to describe the state of the American economy, this book advances an incongruous proposition: record-setting levels of philanthropy have created an unprecedented opportunity for sophisticated financial intermediaries to orchestrate billions of dollars of nonprofit growth capital to produce substantially greater social impact. When I began the book three years ago, the economic outlook was distinctly sunnier; now that the storm has arrived, a brief acknowledgment of the current scene and its potential implications is in order.

As I discuss in Chapter 1, four factors have combined to create a pressing need for more effective allocation of nonprofit capital: (1) the growth of philanthropic contributions; (2) high-engagement philanthropy; (3) more capable social entrepreneurs; and (4) the foreclosure of the American Dream for millions of families. Current economic conditions are likely to affect all four to varying but uncertain extents. Poor and low-income families will almost certainly face even more difficulties, while social-sector innovation on the part of both funders and entrepreneurs should become even more prized, albeit under more hostile conditions.

This also might be a good time to slow the proliferation of new nonprofits, which exacerbates the problem of nonprofit capital fragmentation, the villain of this story. In 2007, the *Christian Science Monitor* reported that Des Moines, Iowa, had 330 nonprofits working on education issues, San Francisco had more than 125 organizations addressing homelessness, and Portland, Maine, had more than 450 children-focused charities. If, as the *Monitor* reported, Hank Goldstein, the CEO of Giving USA, is correct when he says that only one nonprofit in ten is well run, the financial collapse might well impose Darwinian discipline on what he calls a "cottage industry."[2]

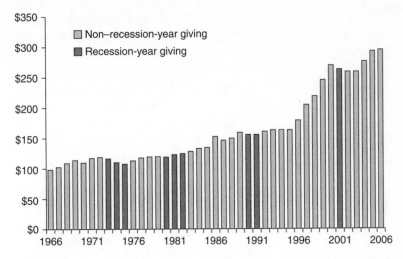

Exhibit P.1 Total Giving, Adjusted for inflation, 1966–2006, Billions of Dollars
Source: Giving USA Foundations, "Charitable Giving during Recessions Doesn't Keep Up with Inflation," press release, Figure 1, 11 Feb. 2008, http://127.0.0.1:9180/open?url=%2FUsers%2FSteve%2FDownloads%2FPR_021108.pdf&action=1&info=16&s=OG4Tx1WQEWpygYwtSCtbbmquopA.

The social sector is in an understandable panic these days about the anticipated reduction in charitable donations during what is expected to be a long and deep recession. You can't open a newspaper or a nonprofit Web site without seeing articles with titles such as "Navigating through Tough Times" and "Foundations Scale Back Grants." I don't pretend to know whether those fears are justified, but, as shown in Exhibit P.1, a recent Foundation Center study reported that, during the last four downturns, "U.S. foundation giving in inflation-adjusted dollars did not decline and, in fact, increased slightly."

It is fair to say that 2008 has been and 2009 (at least) will likely be singularly difficult years for private and institutional funders and their nonprofit grantees. I do not for a moment gainsay the seriousness of the situation.

At the same time, the problems considered in this book are structural in nature, relating to systems and institutions that are no longer up to the tasks for which they were created. Matt Miller, a senior fellow at the Center for American Progress, recalled how the virtues of "local control of schools" devolved over time:

In the early 19th century, the property tax was considered the fairest way to pay for schooling. Property was the main form of wealth, and rich and poor people didn't live in separate taxing communities. The wealthy paid more than the middle class and the poor paid nothing, yet all enjoyed access to the same public schools.[3]

Today, with the federal government providing less than 10% of public school funding, "local financing means we systematically assign the greenest, least-qualified teachers in America to the children who need great teachers the most."

Columnist Thomas Friedman makes a similar point about failing to confront enduring national challenges:

> How many times do we have to see this play before we admit that it always ends the same way? Which play? The one where gasoline prices go up, pressure rises for more fuel-efficient cars, then gasoline prices fall and the pressure for low-mileage vehicles vanishes, consumers stop buying those cars, the oil producers celebrate, we remain addicted to oil and prices gradually go up again, petro-dictators get rich, we lose. I've already seen this play three times in my life. Trust me: It always ends the same way—badly.[4]

The problems I discuss here long predate the current financial and economic crises and will endure indefinitely unless bold corrective measures are taken. Just as transitory reductions in gas prices don't obviate the need for the United States to curb its dependence on Middle East oil, cyclical changes in philanthropy don't diminish our dire need for more intelligent allocation of nonprofit capital.

In this book, I argue that, in the case of philanthropy, "more intelligent" means performance-based: more effective nonprofits should receive more funding and less effective ones should receive less. But in today's U.S. social sector, results-driven philanthropy is an embarrassingly small exception to the rule of loyalty-based giving.

Notwithstanding the staggering failures of the financial stock markets in 2008, I maintain that market-driven intermediation remains the most promising toolset for performance-based philanthropy. By harnessing the "wisdom of crowds" to gather the most basic intelligence about relative nonprofit performance, the virtual nonprofit stock market

I propose—the "Impact Index" or "IMPEX"—could produce essential information that is now wholly unavailable to social investors. Although I use language and concepts adapted from financial markets, I assure you that I am not suggesting anything that would start the nonprofit sector down a path of "Enron accounting" or exotic securities that Wharton MBAs can't understand. Even Al Gore doesn't think the internal combustion engine should never have been invented just because Detroit never got around to fixing that little problem with the exhaust.

Hard times might well encourage the advent of "smart money" in the social sector, a possible silver lining of an otherwise menacing dark cloud. As the leaders of the Andrea and Charles Bronfman Philanthropies observed in July 2008—months before things got really bad: "In an economic downturn such as the one we are experiencing, the need for philanthropic leverage is even more crucial because the relative value of a foundation's gift is diminished."[5] While I readily acknowledge the precarious situation in which we find ourselves, as well as its potential impact on factors relevant to the discussion at hand, I do not believe it undermines the argument in any significant way. To the contrary, performance-based philanthropy could magnify the impact of tens of billions of donated dollars.

Intrepid readers are invited to plunge ahead.

Notes

1. Holly Hall, "How Bad Is It?" *Chronicle of Philanthropy*, 2 Oct. 2008, http://philanthropy.com/premium/articles/v20/i24/24004701.htm.

2. Jeremiah Hall, "Too Many Ways to Divide Donations?" *Christian Science Monitor*, 20 June 2005, www.csmonitor.com/2005/0620/p13s01-wmgn.html.

3. Matt Miller, "Nixon's the One—to Imitate on Education," *New York Times*, 27 Dec. 2008, www.nytimes.com/2008/12/28/opinion/28miller.html?_r=2.

4. Thomas L. Friedman, "Win, Win, Win, Win, Win. . ." *New York Times*, 28 Dec. 2008, www.nytimes.com/2008/12/28/opinion/28friedman.html?em.

5. Charles Bronfman and Jeffrey Solomon, "Pull the Right Levers for Maximum Effect," *Financial Times*, 12 July 2008, www.ft.com/cms/s/0/67b9151e-4faa-11dd-b050-000077b07658.html?nclick_check=1.

Preface

This book addresses a set of debilitating financial constraints that I believe are preventing many nonprofit organizations from producing substantially greater social impact. Contrary to most discussions of nonprofit funding, my focus concerns the *distribution* of available funds rather than their total *amount*. I do not contend that nonprofits have sufficient funding—they clearly don't—but the misallocation of existing funds among nonprofit organizations greatly exacerbates the problem of underfunding.

There's no silver bullet for the financial challenges facing the nonprofit sector, and I certainly don't make that claim for the proposals I advance in this book. Instead, I make the case for a new approach I believe could increase social impact for certain kinds of funding (third-stage capital), provided by certain kinds of donors (social impact investors), for certain kinds of nonprofits (mid-cap social enterprises), working to achieve certain kinds of results (transformative social impact), on certain kinds of social issues ($100 million problems). I have expanded on what I mean by each of these terms, in part to make clear that my approach is a targeted rather than a universal one. I believe that a set of achievable financial innovations can produce dramatic increases in nonprofit performance in the important segment of the social sector marked by those five boundaries.

These are concurrent conditions, so all five criteria must be met for my thesis to apply. The most obvious counterexample would be a young nonprofit pursuing an interesting entrepreneurial approach to social innovation with a current annual budget of, say, less than $1 million. Such a "small-cap" organization probably has to increase its baseline funding using traditional fundraising techniques before it would make sense to consider my suggestions for marshaling significant amounts of longer-term growth capital from sophisticated social impact investors. It's unlikely that such an early-stage nonprofit could convince even risk-tolerant philanthropists to make the kinds of big bets I think need to be made to move the needle of social and economic opportunity.

When it comes to funding social change organizations, I do not think that small is bad and big is good. I do contend, however, that for certain kinds of social problems, our collective progress has been strangled by structural and systemic limitations of the nonprofit capital market so that our best nonprofits can't grow much larger and develop the horsepower needed to produce that systemic change. I hope that the approach suggested here will facilitate the connection of certain kinds of funders to certain kinds of organizations in ways that are better suited to solving major social problems.

Nor do I advocate that social impact investors adopt some hyper-rational, algorithmic approach to their philanthropy that drains all emotional considerations from their giving decisions. Charitable donations have always been, and to a significant extent always will be, personal expressions of civic engagement guided by each donor's convictions about how to make the world a better place.

Indeed, when it comes to civic generosity, "high-net-worth individuals" are pulled in a thousand different directions. Their choice is not between, say, a literacy program and the opera; often choice has little to do with it. When your college roommate, your longtime neighbor, or a close colleague at work asks for help or calls in a debt from the favor bank, philanthropists need to spread their support around. More money is not the only difference between the rich and the rest of us: the wealthy also have more obligations. I hope that my approach will inform whatever part of their charitable portfolios is truly discretionary and reserved for maximizing social impact.

A Word about Scope

One easy way to start an argument is to ask a roomful of nonprofit enthusiasts what "social entrepreneurship" means. Professor J. Gregory Dees was probably the first out of the gate:

> Social entrepreneurs play the role of change agents in the social sector, by: adopting a mission to create and sustain social value (not just private value), recognizing and relentlessly pursuing new opportunities to serve that mission, engaging in a process of continuous innovation, adaptation, and learning, acting boldly without being limited by resources currently in hand, and exhibiting heightened accountability to the constituencies served and for the outcomes created.[1]

Jerr Boschee and Jim McClurg focused on the importance of "earned income" for achieving sustainability:

> A social entrepreneur is any person, in any sector, who uses earned income strategies to pursue a social objective, and a social entrepreneur differs from a traditional entrepreneur in two important ways: . . . their earned income strategies are tied directly to their mission . . . [and] social entrepreneurs are driven by a double bottom line, a virtual blend of financial and social returns.[2]

Roger L. Martin and Sally Osberg countered:

> We define social entrepreneurship as having the following three components: (1) identifying a stable but inherently unjust equilibrium that causes the exclusion, marginalization, or suffering of a segment of humanity that lacks the financial means or political clout to achieve any transformative benefit on its own; (2) identifying an opportunity in this unjust equilibrium, developing a social value proposition, and bringing to bear inspiration, creativity, direct action, courage, and fortitude, thereby challenging the stable state's hegemony; and (3) forging a new, stable equilibrium that releases trapped potential or alleviates the suffering of the targeted group, and through imitation and the creation of a stable ecosystem around the new equilibrium ensuring a better future for the targeted group and even society at large.[3]

Rather than weighing in on this fractious debate, I'll just note that this book focuses on three dimensions of "social entrepreneurship:"

1. *Funding.* I will be addressing issues related to donated money only. Some nonprofits rely entirely on philanthropy, while others add myriad sources of cash (including earned revenue and debt) and in-kind resources. I don't exclude the latter organizations from the discussion, but I do limit my analysis and recommendations to the donated portion, without expressing any opinion about the relative merits of other funding sources or methods.

2. *Innovation.* Rather than trying to come up with a comprehensive definition of what is and is not a social innovation, I'm satisfied with the broad reference that Clayton M. Christensen and some colleagues made to "organizations that are approaching social-sector problems in a fundamentally new way and creating scalable, sustainable, systems-changing solutions."[4] My concern is with the propagation of important social innovations: the funding and growth of nonprofits that have figured out new and potentially transformative ways of solving our most difficult social problems.

3. *Organization.* We'll never know how many potentially great business innovations fell by the wayside simply because they never found fertile soil in which to grow. As I'll explain more fully, the funding problem and my proposed solution set relate to nonprofits that have advanced beyond the start-up phase and, in almost all cases, even beyond the early entrepreneurial stage. I focus on social enterprises that have reached a point of organizational development in terms of staffing, planning capability, financial management, technology adoption, and so on, that would enable them to increase their productive capacity by a factor of, say, three to ten, if only they had access to the right kinds and amounts of funding.

Again, I make no judgments about funders or organizations that don't fit within these boundaries. I just don't have anything to say about them in this book.

A Style Note

It would be an understatement to say that this book makes extensive use of block quotes containing verbatim excerpts from the works of other authors. Having written legal briefs for 25 years, in which the use of block quotes is *de rigueur*, they are a stylistic tic that I neither can nor want to relinquish. But there's also an important rhetorical purpose in this particular book.

For the millions of people devoted to nonprofit work and charitable giving, questioning traditional fundraising practices is like trying to get fish to notice water. For those good folks, the fundraising system is a given, like gravity. It is not merely one option among many available alternatives. And here I come, a nonprofit tenderfoot, suggesting that a significant part of this established reality doesn't make any sense and needs to be radically transformed. Who am I to assert such an outlandish proposition?

I hope that my arguments are convincing on their own merits. But in the course of my research, I was surprised to discover how many respected nonprofit veterans agree with my assessment of the situation and at least some of my proposals for change. Indeed, they have been both lighting candles and cursing the darkness for years. Here, for example, is a simple observation from economist David K. Smith:

> Private-sector companies have ready access to a gargantuan capital market of tens of trillions of dollars globally. Nonprofit organizations, by contrast, are crippled by capital-raising efforts that are minuscule, inefficient, and badly organized. As a result, nonprofits that have developed solutions for critical and growing challenges—in fields like education, health care, housing, economic development, and environmental sustainability—often struggle to grow.[5]

Moreover, many of these people—like those quoted in the front of this book—offer better explanations than I could.

Inasmuch as I'm trying to make an argument that is counterintuitive at best, I hope it will help readers if I call upon authoritative voices in their own words to help me lay convincing bricks for this new edifice I propose we build. In fact, in addition to the original ideas I offer, I hope that one of the contributions of this book is to pull together in a comprehensive and compelling way the many scattered pixels that I believe form a compelling picture of the need for, and the possibility of, a new funding paradigm.

A Case to Be Made

In addition, this book is neither a criticism of the millions of people who work and volunteer for the U.S. nonprofit sector nor a disparagement of their accomplishments. Although I am critical of certain philanthropic practices that are widely accepted today—the absurdly low 5% payout rule for charitable foundations established by the federal tax code comes to mind—there are many others that I think could be improved but I certainly don't mean to condemn.

For example, the foundation system of grantmaking, for all its shortcomings, has produced an enormous amount of social value over the course of many decades, and many foundations are themselves great founts of innovation. While I believe that institutional funding has developed in ways that are sometimes self-defeating, I don't propose to throw out the baby with the bathwater, nor do I mean to speak ill of the baby or the bath. I hope that my ideas might be taken up by grantmakers frustrated by the lack of progress resulting from their dedicated efforts.

The structural deficiencies I examine are a natural part of evolving social systems. Today's American social sector emerged from the benevolence of altruistic individuals who ventured out from their own comfortable lives to help the sick, the poor, and the deprived. It has evolved over the course of decades to the point that some now lament the extent to which philanthropy has become a professionalized field of endeavor. Now, with the confluence of several important developments, we find ourselves facing broad institutional and systemic failures in economic and educational opportunity, but also with the financial means and imagination to make meaningful progress against seemingly intractable problems.

Like stamping and scratching a piece of paper with an empty pen to make sure it has really run out of ink, creative and determined people persevere against the limitations of their available resources long past the point of futility and denial. It's almost always the case that society will wait too long before recognizing geological shifts and understanding their implications. Until the disconnection between social problems and the means to address them becomes sufficiently grave, a critical mass of interest and support for dramatic changes simply cannot be achieved.

It follows that the path to social progress is rarely smooth or incremental. In 1962, Thomas S. Kuhn observed in "The Structure of Scientific Revolutions" that "the successive transition from one paradigm to another via revolution is the usual developmental pattern of mature science."[6] In 1972, paleontologists Niles Eldredge and Stephen Jay Gould postulated the evolutionary concept of "punctuated equilibrium": "change occurs in large leaps following a slow accumulation of stresses that a system resists until it reaches the breaking point."[7] In 1993, Frank R. Baumgartner and Bryan D. Jones extended the biological concept of punctuated equilibrium to the political realm, which they saw as highly resistant to fundamental change until conditions deteriorated well past the breaking point:

> If we put together the limits of human information processing and the characteristics of democracies that encourage error correction, we get a model of politics that is very static but reluctantly changes when signals are strong enough. The system resists change, so that when change comes it punctuates the system, not infrequently reverberating through it.[8]

I contend that the prevailing means for raising money has outlived its usefulness for mid-cap nonprofits working on solving "$100 million problems" such as educational inequity and economic incapacity. The conditions for "third-stage funding" have ripened to a point that it is now time to build information engines of sufficient power to drive better-informed and more concentrated funding. If we want to multiply the performance of a resurgent social sector, I believe we must punctuate the equilibrium of an underpowered nonprofit capital market. I am not alone in thinking there is "a confluence of social and economic factors encouraging this growth of the market system in philanthropy."[9]

Some of the concepts I explore, such as information markets, "power law distributions," and the life cycles of technological innovations, will seem exotic and impractical. Please bear with me. At this point, I cannot say with conviction that the ideas offered here will work. Instead, I try to convince thoughtful readers that they should be put to the test. I hope that I've visualized a more intelligent system for channeling charitable donations that at least crosses the threshold of plausibility.

The nonprofit sector is quintessentially a social institution that springs fundamentally from the goodness of millions of people's hearts as they've tried to help others who are less fortunate than themselves. The world is a much better place because of what they've done, and they're constantly striving to do better against formidable obstacles. I have nothing but admiration for them, and I hope that they will find ways to test the ideas presented here and, if they work, put them to good use.

It is the keepers of the flame to whom those of us who seek to challenge established institutions owe the deepest respect and to whom a convincing and sound case for a new way of doing things must be made. With full recognition of all that philanthropy has accomplished to date, and as someone who, until quite recently, has never raised a single dollar or run the smallest social program, I offer this book for their earnest consideration.

Notes

1. J. Gregory Dees, "The Meaning of 'Social Entrepreneurship,'" Center for the Advancement of Social Entrepreneurship (CASE), Duke University's Fuqua School of Business, original draft: 31 Oct. 1998, reformatted and revised: 30 May 2001, www.caseatduke.org/documents/dees_sedef.pdf.

2. Jerr Boschee and Jim McClurg, "Toward a Better Understanding of Social Entrepreneurship: Some Important Distinctions," 2003, www.se-alliance.org/better_understanding.pdf.

3. Roger L. Martin and Sally Osberg, "Social Entrepreneurship: The Case for Definition," *Stanford Social Innovation Review*, (Spring 2007): 35, www.skollfoundation.org/media/skoll_docs/2007SP_feature_martinosberg.pdf.

4. Clayton M. Christensen, Heiner Baumann, Rudy Ruggles, and Thomas M. Sadtler, "Disruptive Innovation for Social Change," *Harvard Business Review* (December 2006): 2, https://harvardbusinessonline.hbsp.harvard.edu/b02/en/common/item_detail.jhtml?id=1683.

5. Douglas K. Smith, "Market Magic: Nonprofits Could Access Needed Capital by Turning Donors into Investors," *Slate*, 13 Nov. 2006, www.slate.com/id/2152801.

6. Thomas S. Kuhn, *The Structure of Scientific Revolutions* (Chicago: University of Chicago Press, 1962), p. 12.

7. Stephen Jay Gould, "The Episodic Nature of Evolutionary Change," in *The Richness of Life: The Essential Stephen Jay Gould* (New York: W. W. Norton, 2007), p. 266.

8. Bryan D. Jones and Frank R. Baumgartner, *The Politics of Attention: How Government Prioritizes Problems* (Chicago: University of Chicago Press, 2005), p. 19.

9. Katherine Fulton and Andrew Blau, "Cultivating Change in Philanthropy," Monitor Group, 2005, www.futureofphilanthropy.org/files/workingpaper.pdf.

Chapter 1

The Disheartening Problem of "Scale"

Philanthropy today generates a world in which experiments multiply but very little sums.

—*Katherine Fulton and Andrew Blau, "Cultivating Change in Philanthropy"*

Anyone in search of the very model of the modern social enterprise need look no further than Teach For America (TFA). Wendy Kopp founded TFA in 1990, and the title of her book about that adventure, *One Day, All Children...*, encapsulates in just four small words what is so important about the social movement TFA represents:

> As a college senior, I happened upon an idea that would put me in the middle of an incredible movement. The idea was to create a corps of top recent college graduates—people of all academic majors and career interests—who would commit to teach two years in urban and rural public schools and become lifelong leaders dedicated to the goal of educational opportunity for all.[1]

Just 21 years old at the time, the estimable Ms. Kopp didn't just want to help a lot of kids in underperforming public schools, she wanted to help *all* of them. She envisioned creating "an enduring American institution" that would "eliminate educational inequality," the socioeconomic and racial disparities that "severely limit the life prospects of the 13 million children growing up in poverty today."[2] And so TFA dedicated itself to the proudly audacious proposition that "one day, all children in this nation will have the opportunity to attain an excellent education."

The problem of educational inequity is no small matter, as virtually all recent studies confirm. Douglas Harris of Arizona State University's Education Policy Studies Laboratory calibrated the differences among high-performing schools for different socioeconomic cohorts:

> The achievement gap between students of various racial, social, and economic groups is large and growing. For example, between whites and African-Americans, the size of the achievement gap ranges from 29 to 37 percentile points. Between whites and Hispanics, the gap is 16 to 34 percentile points. Strong signs suggest these gaps have worsened recently after decades of improvement.[3]

Such pervasive and enduring disparities do not originate from simple or ephemeral causes. Rather they reflect the corrosive effects of long-term institutional and systemic failures:

> All parts of the political spectrum seem to agree that these educational inequities represent a significant problem. There is also strong evidence and agreement that students' social and economic disadvantages are substantial causes of the problem. Poor nutrition and illness cause students (a) to miss school more often and (b) to be less prepared to learn when they attend. Within the disadvantaged home, parents often have relationships with their children that are, emotionally and physically, less healthy. These unhealthy relationships are reinforced in part by economic pressures that induce conflicts between parents and children. The combination of these factors and other effects is shown to be worse as students remain in poverty for longer periods of time. Of course, many parents living in poverty are able to successfully navigate and avoid these potential problems, and some parents with high incomes are not great parents, but the general patterns described here are quite strong.[4]

Andrew Sum, director of Northeastern University's Center for Labor Market Studies, puts it more simply: "Declining economic fortunes of young men without college degrees underlie the rise in out-of-wedlock child-bearing, and they are creating a new demographic nightmare for the nation."[5]

The gravity of the situation makes TFA's accomplishments over the past 17 years all the more extraordinary. A 2004 independent research report found that "even though Teach For America teachers generally lack any formal teacher training beyond that provided by Teach For America, they produce higher test scores than the other teachers in their schools—not just other novice teachers or uncertified teachers, but also veterans and certified teachers."[6] Another study concluded that "nearly three out of four principals (74 percent) considered the Teach For America teachers more effective than other beginning teachers with whom they've worked" and "the majority of principals (63 percent) regarded Teach For America teachers as more effective than the overall teaching faculty, with respect to their impact on student achievement."[7] Most recently, a 2008 study found: "TFA teachers tend to have a positive effect on high school student test scores relative to non-TFA teachers, including those who are certified in-field. Such effects exceed the impact of additional years of experience and are particularly strong in math and science."[8]

More than 17,000 "corps members" have joined TFA since 1990, and they've reached more than 2.5 million kids in more than 1,000 public schools nationwide. TFA plans to more than double the number of corps members from the year 2005 to 2010, from 3,500 to 7,500, and to increase its placement sites by 50%, from 22 to 33.[9]

Remarkably, TFA recently eked out tenth place in *Business Week*'s "The Best Places to Launch a Career," and it recruits more college seniors than Microsoft, Procter & Gamble, Accenture, or General Electric.[10] The once famously shy Ms. Kopp is so dedicated to her cause that she not only appeared on Comedy Central's *The Colbert Report*, but she mopped the floor with the pugnacious satirist.[11]

Notwithstanding these impressive achievements, there is one measure of success that TFA has not met: its own. TFA's success is impressive except in comparison to the universe of need embodied in the phrase, "one day, all children." After 17 years of perseverance, the 425,000 students TFA plans to reach in 2008 represent just 3.3% of the 13 million kids who face "educational inequity."

As far as I know, TFA has no specific plans by which it will reach 13 million disadvantaged students. Nor, for that matter, does any other social change organization of which I'm aware.

For example, the NewSchools Venture Fund, another proud flagship of the nonprofit entrepreneurial fleet, is dedicated to "promoting high academic achievement for every child by attracting, preparing, and supporting the next generation of outstanding leaders for our nation's urban public schools."[12] Since 1998, NewSchools has raised and deployed tens of millions of dollars for educational innovation at dozens of charter-management and school-support organizations. It states that "over the next several years, the organizations we support will run more than 200 charter schools and serve nearly 75,000 students, making NewSchools' national portfolio comparable in scale to a mid-sized urban district."[13] After 10 years of exceptional work and highly sophisticated financial management, the aggregate result (at least of the charter school portion of its portfolio) amounts to one school district that performs at the level to which the entire country aspires.

"All Children"

Social entrepreneurs "carry out innovations that blend methods from the worlds of business and philanthropy to create social value that is sustainable and has the potential for large-scale impact."[14] But for all that social entrepreneurs such as TFA and NewSchools have accomplished, they have yet to come to grips with the implications of their worthy goal of helping "all children" in need. While quite a few successful and innovative nonprofit organizations (NPOs) aspire to serve millions of people who need their services, I've yet to see even one strategic growth plan that explains how the organization will address anywhere close to even 20% of the need.

A comparison of what social entrepreneurs call "scale" and what I'll be calling "transformative social impact" puts things into perspective. Social entrepreneurs (and their "venture philanthropy" funders) appropriately identify organizational growth as one of their fundamental strategic objectives, and after a decade or so of hard slogging, they take justifiable pride in what they've accomplished.

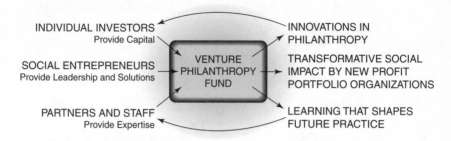

Exhibit 1.1 New Profit, Inc. Model of Venture Philanthropy
Source: "Our Model of Venture Philanthropy," New Profit, Inc., 14 Apr. 2008, www.newprofit.org/about_model.asp.

For example, New Profit, Inc. (NPI) in Cambridge, Massachusetts, was one of the original venture philanthropies that adopted a funding approach modeled after venture capitalism in order to alleviate many of the shortcomings inherent in traditional foundation financing. NPI devised a novel funding and support model (see Exhibit 1.1) that integrated the efforts of investors, social entrepreneurs, business consultants, and other experts to nurture and grow portfolio NPOs to an extent that had not been possible under the more passive foundation model.

Venture Philanthropy Partners (VPP) in Washington, DC, also provided innovative social entrepreneurs with funding tailored to their more businesslike approach to social change (see Exhibit 1.2). Like NPI,

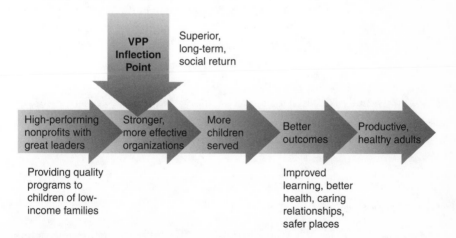

Exhibit 1.2 Venture Philanthropy Partners' Value Chain for Institution Building
Source: "Future Impact," Venture Philanthropy Partners, 17 Sept. 2007, www.vppartners.org/impact/future.html.

VPP made larger, longer, and more flexible grants to carefully selected nonprofits and provided in-kind management consulting to help their portfolio NPOs enhance organizational capacity and effectiveness.

The traditional model of nonprofit finance that venture philanthropy sought to reinvent is deceptively simple: foundations collect charitable contributions and bequests from individuals, corporations, and institutions, and they administer systems of grant application, review, and funding to NPOs that the foundations believe will advance their social missions. But entrenched historical, practical, and structural problems have come to plague foundation funding:

Fragmentation and Undercapitalization

Traditionally, "[f]oundations saw their role as funding a large number of small programs for a short time, hoping that a few would enjoy some initial success."[15] As a result, it has become a regrettable fact of nonprofit life that "[f]oundations generally spread their resources—both money and people—too thin."[16] "The average grant among the 100 largest foundations is roughly $50,000."[17] Such grant sizes are simply too small to support the development of robust and enduring nonprofits capable of achieving scale and consequential social impact, and foundation employees are responsible for too many grant applications to provide active or sustained engagement with recipients beyond simple financial support. More than 90% of U.S. nonprofits have annual budgets of less than $1 million, and fewer than two dozen social entrepreneurs have annual operating budgets exceeding $20 million.[18] As a result, "a foundation grant covers only a small proportion of a nonprofit's costs."[19]

As one trenchant example, *Business Week* reported that the $1.6 billion Annenberg Challenge was "widely viewed as a crushing disappointment." The reason: "The five-year grants, sprinkled across a range of initiatives in New York, Chicago, and 16 other cities, were too diffuse to have much impact."[20]

Time Horizons

Compounding the grant-size problem, foundations generally assess their own grantmaking performance on a quarterly basis, and 95% of all foundation grants are for just one year (subject to reapplication for subsequent funding).[21] The duration of grants is driven primarily by institutional guidelines, rather than collaboration with applicants or an assessment of whether the length of the grant is commensurate with the time required to accomplish the nonprofit's objectives.[22] The system "has led to foundations' time horizons being out of sync with those of their grantees, which are trying to build organizations that can sustain programs."[23]

Distraction

The inevitable result of the size and duration constraints is the "tyranny of the grant cycle":[24] nonprofit executives devote an absurd amount of essentially unproductive time to continual and unrelenting fundraising. Clara Miller, CEO of the Nonprofit Finance Fund, observes that "nonprofits, almost by definition, run two businesses—the core, mission-oriented business, and a second 'subsidy' business or businesses." The length and breadth of such activities that have nothing directly to do with achieving the NPO's objectives would sap the strength of the most lion-hearted private-sector CEO: "[s]ubsidy businesses include fundraising, dinner dances, special events, bingo, the capital campaign, for-profit related and unrelated businesses (bookstores, gift shops, parking lots), donated services, wine and cheese parties, endowment management, and any number of creative fundraising ideas long a staple of the sector."[25] In fact, fundraising diverts management attention from mission-related activities to such an extent that it has become a primary source of burnout and excessive turnover among experienced nonprofit leaders.[26]

Grant Restrictions

Traditional foundations have an anaphylactic aversion to paying administrative overhead expenses, viewing them as "costs that divert precious resources from the real work of delivering programs."[27] To insure that grants benefit disadvantaged populations directly, rather than the nonprofit equivalent of "bureaucrats" in what foundations perceive as uncertain start-ups, funders "prefer working with well-established organizations or restrict their giving to programmatic support."[28] Not only do such restrictions deprive NPOs of needed support for the enterprises through which nonprofits carry out their work, but restricted grants and contracts that fund program expansion often create additional expenses or cash requirements that the funding does not fully cover.[29]

Transaction Costs

As a result, nonprofit financial markets are highly disorganized, with considerable duplication of effort, resource diversion, and processes that "take a fair amount of time to review grant applications and to make funding decisions."[30] It would be a major understatement to describe the resulting capital market as inefficient. McKinsey & Company found that, while for-profit companies spend only $2 to $4 for every $100 of capital raised, nonprofits spend between $10 and $24 to acquire the same $100. When the administrative costs of foundations, federated givers such as the United Way, and government grantors are factored in, "the cost of raising capital consumes roughly 22 to 43 percent of the funds raised."[31] Such a system significantly reduces potential social impact well before charitable contributions find their way to NPOs.

In June 2008, REDF (formerly the Roberts Enterprise Development Fund) published a brilliant paper by Cynthia Gair, "Strategic Co-Funding," the first of three that will comprise a series entitled "Out of Philanthropy's Funding Maze."[32] Gair's comparison of two hypothetical investment scenarios, one for-profit and one nonprofit, perfectly captures the absurd carnival that passes for the social capital market:

> Three years ago, Janet Schmidt started her solar energy company, Solar-Jay. She and her team have developed a unique product and a growing customer base. What they're doing works and it's time to expand. Janet contacts Fred Malcolm at Green Cap LLP, a venture capital firm known for its investments in early-stage, green-technology companies. Fred reads the Solar-Jay business plan, meets with Janet, and decides the business has great promise. He assesses the potential for a high-return acquisition of the firm and estimates that Solar-Jay may need twice the $5 million investment it seeks, to reach its profit targets. Since Green Cap can only commit to a $3 million investment, Fred calls up two friends who are partners at nearby VC firms. Three months later, after discussions, due diligence, and some business plan revisions,

Green Cap and Solar-Jay agree on final terms for the investment. Fred joins the company's board, Solar-Jay receives its initial cash infusion, and expansion plans are set in motion.

A few miles away, Ed Baker runs StepUp to Solar, Inc., a nonprofit that helps runaway teens stabilize their lives by engaging them in environmental education and jobs in the growing solar panel installation field. In the eight years since Ed founded the organization, the program has developed a good track record with the teens it serves and with community funders. It has demonstrated tangible, positive outcomes. Solar panels are catching on and more youth need jobs, so Ed and his board would like to expand. They calculate that it will take a one-time, $1 million upgrade of infrastructure plus an annual $300,000 increase in operating costs. Ed and his development manager start contacting potential funders. After six months—and 36 phone calls, 13 funding proposals, six meetings with commercial banks, 18 conversations with local and national foundations and city government departments—two foundations have committed to grants totaling $55,000. Proposals are on hold with two foundations that are undergoing strategy changes. Five foundations have rejected StepUp's proposal because the program is not new. A city department is eager to refer youth to StepUp's expanded program, but will not be able to fund the expansion unless it takes on a technical training focus. Ed calculates that in a best-case scenario, StepUp may receive $700,000 of the $1 million needed, but the expanded reporting requirements from these funding sources will add $50,000 to StepUp's annual operating costs, which no one appears ready to fund. Given these results, StepUp's board is uncertain about approving any expansion at all, but Ed and his team go back to the drawing board to calculate the costs of a reduced plan.

To overcome these serious and long-standing deficiencies, both NPI and VPP borrowed heavily from venture capital approaches to selecting, funding, and supporting promising nonprofits that they believed could achieve the "one day" visions they all shared (see Exhibit 1.3).

The venture philanthropy model has amply demonstrated its ability to significantly accelerate nonprofit growth trajectories. For example, from 1999 through 2005, the NPI portfolio achieved 29% compound annual revenue growth and 42% compound annual growth in "lives touched." Both figures substantially exceeded rates for comparable

Exhibit 1.3 New Profit, Inc. Graduation Standards

Attribute	Standard
Organizational Competencies	Robust, strategically focused management team.
	Key leadership positions have a succession plan in place.
	Performance-based culture is in place throughout the organization.
	Results are quantified using Balanced Scorecard.
Mission and Social Impact	Proven results tell a compelling social impact story.
	Growth model of the organization is sustainable.
	The organization is mission-focused and able to prevent mission drift.
	The organization is recognized as a leader in the field.
Financial Sustainability	Performs regular, effective forecasting of revenue and expenses.
	Distinguishes between growth capital and revenue.
	Maintains ample working capital and contingency funds.
	Diversified funding base with major funders aligned around growth priorities.
	The organization has a clear understanding of cost per incremental life touched.

Source: Robert S. Kaplan and David P. Norton, *The Balanced Scorecard: Translating Strategy into Action* (HBS Press 1996). Adapted from "Citizen Schools' Growth with High-Engagement Funders," New Profit, Inc., 2004

nonprofits.[34] Likewise, Venture Philanthropy Partners estimates that the number of children its investment partners serve will increase from 44,000 in 2007 to more than 80,000 by 2010.[35]

Consider the year-over-year growth of two organizations in the New Profit portfolio. College Summit, which helps low-income students matriculate and succeed in college, has multiplied the number of students reached by about 700% in five years, and it hopes to nearly double in size in 2007–2008.[36] Jumpstart, which helps poor and low-income children enter school prepared to succeed, has also increased the number of children served to about six times the level it achieved just six years ago.[37]

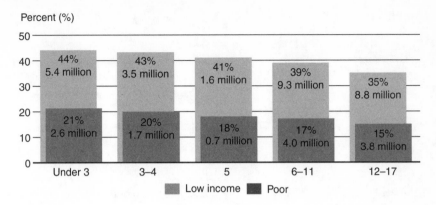

Percent (%)

Exhibit 1.4 Children Living in Low-Income and Poor Families, by Age Group, 2006
Source: Ayana Douglas-Hall and Michelle Chau, "Basic Facts About Low-Income Children: Birth to Age 18," National Center for Children in Poverty, Mailman School of Public Health at Columbia University, 14 Apr. 2008, www.nccp.org/publications/pub_762.html.

"One Day"

Regrettably, the national dimensions of the problems on which these intrepid entrepreneurs focus their considerable energies dwarf their genuinely impressive accomplishments. As a sobering baseline, consider that in 2006 there were 28.3 million low-income children aged 17 and below in the United States (comprising 39% of the total 73 million children), of whom 12.8 million were poor (see Exhibit 1.4).[38]

Viewed from this humbling perspective, the absolute numbers of children helped by these admirable organizations barely comprise, to use a familiar metaphor, a drop in the bucket (see Exhibit 1.5).

As we consider the current state of American social progress, we need to recognize just how far away "one day" really is likely to be under the most optimistic assumptions. Even at double-digit annual growth rates, it will take many years for social entrepreneurs and their funders to address even 10% of the populations in need. While we rightly celebrate the advancements that social entrepreneurship and venture philanthropy represent, the eminent nonprofit scholar Peter Frumkin reminds us that we have to look to the horizon with a clear eye:

It remains very difficult, however, to see how the many small and isolated success stories of donors around the country ever amount

Exhibit 1.5 Percentages of Need Served by Leading Social Enterprises.

Organization	Focus	Served per Year	Total Need	% of Need
BELL	Out-of-school time	8,000	10,800,000	0.07%
College Summit	College access	1,300	200,000	0.65%
Jumpstart	School readiness	13,000	3,300,000	0.39%
Raising a Reader	Infants to 5-year-olds	200,000	10,100,100	1.98%
Teach For America	"Educational inequity"	425,000	13,000,000	3.30%
Year Up	"Disconnected youth"	350	3,800,000	0.09%

Source: Based on data from Web sites of organizations listed.

to anything vaguely resembling a meaningful response to any of the major social problems—be it economic development in the inner city, access to health care, reduction in youth violence, or reform of public schools—that private philanthropy has long targeted.[39]

Transformative Social Impact

This is not a knock on social entrepreneurs or any other nonprofit. To the contrary, successful social entrepreneurs, venture philanthropies, and other funders have accomplished something extraordinary. They have figured out real solutions to long-standing social problems of the most serious kind, including:

- Helping disadvantaged kids reduce the educational achievement gap
- Placing disconnected youth in entry-level technology jobs with major corporate employers
- Bringing nontraditional leaders into failing public schools
- Increasing college enrollment and graduation rates
- Enhancing parental involvement in their children's education

- Increasing minority participation in top MBA programs
- Creating thousands of homegrown small businesses in developing countries to reduce poverty

Just as important, they have built enduring organizations to deliver those solutions over an extended period of time, replicated those delivery systems at multiple sites while maintaining high levels of quality, and accomplished rates of organic growth that most private sector companies would envy.

These are not small accomplishments. In fact, figuring out and delivering the core solution to our most stubborn social problems, such as reducing dropout rates and increasing teaching effectiveness, just might be the hardest part of the puzzle. But while social entrepreneurs have established thriving base camps, it must be acknowledged that something fundamentally different will be required to extend their impacts by the orders of magnitude needed to transform their small-scale successes into transformative solutions to national problems.

Turning those drops into rivers won't be easy, but I believe it can be done. Now that these pioneers have begun to unlock these previously unyielding obstacles, it would be unforgivable for others of us not to step up to help on this next set of challenges.

I certainly do not fault social entrepreneurs for thinking about how to help "only" tens of thousands of disadvantaged people, rather than millions. If anything, the growth plans they've crafted are a testament to the seriousness of purpose and level-headedness of the leadership teams of these business-minded organizations. While the new wave of nonprofit leaders are certainly tenacious, they haven't taken leave of their senses altogether. It is one thing to plan, say, 25% annual growth, or even tripling or quadrupling in size in, say, five years; it is quite another to announce your intention to become 10, 20, or 100 times bigger in the foreseeable future than you are today. How could anyone explain—with a straight face, anyway—how and where they would find the money and the people to build and manage all the programs and sites that would be needed to accomplish such a bizarrely audacious objective?

However, social entrepreneurs do sometimes indulge in what I consider unrealistic and amorphous notions about avenues for growth, such as other nonprofits emulating and extending their work, and increased government funding. Such thinking reminds me of a favorite *New Yorker* cartoon in which two academic types stand in front of a blackboard on which two batches of complex equations are separated by the phrase "then a miracle occurs." One says to the other, "I think you should be more explicit here in step two."[40]

Although expectations of emulation and increased government funding undoubtedly have some validity, neither faces up to the nature or difficulty of the problem realistically:

> Being effective means more than just carrying out an initiative well and meeting the needs of a small group of people. Effectiveness also involves reaching many people and taking the social leverage that an intervention creates and amplifying it even more broadly. Given the interest in having a real impact, donors speak variously of taking programs to scale, going to scale, and scaling up. The idea of scale focuses on creating a lasting and significant impact. Beyond the broad idea of greater impact, the idea of scale becomes more enigmatic when it is subject to sustained scrutiny.[41]

I do not mean to suggest that Teach For America's mission to help "all children" is grandiose or unreachable. To the contrary, I think the scale of its ambitions is exactly right, and I have every confidence that TFA can fulfill its mission. As a nation, we can't accept anything less. However, I don't think TFA or any of the other pioneering nonprofits that have galvanized the sector in recent years can do so within the growth models that are currently available to nonprofit organizations.

The Funding/Performance Disconnection

An often-heard and wholly justified complaint in the nonprofit sector is that "funding is not tied to performance." Even when they accomplish their objectives and demonstrably increase their impact, NPOs encounter great difficulty in raising the funds they need to grow. It is a frustrating and debilitating experience for all concerned that burns out its most talented practitioners and causes unacceptably high levels of turnover that sap the strength of the sector. Consider how one exasperated leader recently vented his frustration:

> Another challenge of performance measurement has been how little it is valued or used by the funding community in the nonprofit sector. The connection between Jumpstart's success at demonstrating impact and its ability to fund raise is at best tenuous. Fund raising success comes primarily from building relationships based on trust and reputation—which can be completely disconnected from the actual performance of the organization. Furthermore, continued funding from philanthropic sources, other than venture philanthropists, is not contingent on achieving specific performance milestones. I've grown incredibly frustrated by the total disconnect between performance and access to capital in the nonprofit world. We double every single year, we get better impact measurements, and still no one ever comes back to us and says, "Hey, you guys are doing so great, we want to give more. We want to invest more."[42]

Nonprofit performance doesn't have clear financial consequences, whether in the form of incentives or penalties. Harvard professor Allen Grossman has contended that philanthropy "actually discourages management from pursuing performance as a primary objective":

> The conversation must begin with an analysis of how and why the philanthropic capital markets, for the most part, fail to encourage high performance in nonprofit organizations. Ironically, nonprofit executive directors, in numerous interviews, consistently reported that excellent performance of a nonprofit organization is rarely systematically rewarded with an increased flow of philanthropic capital. In fact, an opposite situation prevails. As programs were proven effective and the nonprofit organizations developed plans to grow, foundations (even those currently funding their organizations) were less receptive to their requests for funding. Nor is there a systematic reduction of philanthropic funds for mediocre performance. Examples abound of low performing nonprofit organizations that are kept afloat by sympathetic donors willing to contribute without objective data.[43]

The efforts to identify and reward high-performing nonprofits have been numerous, diverse, and, broadly speaking, unsuccessful.

Tremendous strides have been made in recent years in strategic planning, goal-setting, disciplined management, and performance measurement within not only individual NPOs, but also the entire investment portfolios of enlightened funders committed to accountability and performance enhancement. However, the nonprofit sector as a whole still is not structured in ways that connects dollars to impact. As one discouraged executive director put it,

> Everyone says they want to be data-driven in their decision-making. But now we have all of this robust data, and it doesn't seem to have any effect on funders' decisions. . . . From the viewpoint of financial sustainability, we are no better off than before.[44]

The chief operating officer of the Better Business Bureau's Wise Giving Alliance confirms that "the unfortunate fact is the public doesn't in general do research. People base their decision on the appeals they receive, and they respond accordingly."[45]

There are many explanations for this generally accepted reality, having to do with myriad factors such as the complex missions of social organizations, their historical roots in volunteerism and charity, and the limited resources available to them for enhancing organizational capacity. And if performance and funding were connected, poor performance would have consequences: "Ineffective nonprofits would come under attack, and some of them would shrink . . . and some of them would cease to exist. Stale old models would change, or they would die."[46]

All of these considerations bear on the issue in significant ways, and the mismatch between impact and funding is not amenable to easy solutions. If it were, any number of intelligent and dedicated nonprofit professionals would have figured it out by now.

Small Caps and Large Caps

As we look more closely, though, we can see that the problem is not homogeneous. Across much of the nonprofit world, the disconnection between funding and impact doesn't matter all that much. The vast majority of the more than 2 million NPOs in the United States are quite small volunteer and community-based organizations that do good and noble work locally with budgets substantially below seven or even six figures. Let's call them the "small caps," referring, of course, to their financial capitalization.

This is a vast and diverse constellation of small stars that enriches American life and does much to ameliorate the cultural and social deprivations that fall haphazardly upon the unlucky. From local food pantries to arts councils and blood drives, from sports leagues to literacy programs and voter registration drives, there are hundreds of thousands of voluntary groups and associations that emerge spontaneously from the goodness of people's hearts and make small but important differences in millions of lives. Significant growth is not an important objective of such organizations, so the fundraising burden is a tiresome but accepted fact of life.

At the other end of the spectrum—the "large caps"—we find the brand-name behemoths of the social sector: the Red Cross, the United Ways, the Boys and Girls Clubs, and the universities, hospitals, and leading cultural institutions found in every large metropolis. An entirely different calculus drives the funding of these mainstream organizations, starting with the fact that most of them were founded with substantial endowments.

But large-cap nonprofit organizations also mount massive and coordinated capital campaigns raising tens or hundreds of millions of dollars that are managed by financial professionals as expert as any found on Wall Street. They rely on six-, seven-, eight-, and even nine-figure bequests, institutional constituencies, social elites, and celebrity supporters. In this rarified atmosphere, growth is a paramount driving force, but the large caps have perfected the art and science of Olympian fundraising.

These mighty NPOs do not suffer from any supposed mismatch between performance and funding. Yes, fundraising is an insatiable beast that must be fed constantly, but there is no shortage of nourishment. Yes, it takes enormous amounts of time, effort, and money to meet everincreasing fundraising targets, but the large caps have the wherewithal to exceed their goals year after year. In 2006, for example, the United Ways raised a staggering *$4.14 billion*.[47] Whatever fundraising challenges the large caps face, the lack of a system for rewarding performance is not part of the problem.

Mid-Caps and $100 Million Problems

Between these two extremes, however, there is an important and sizable segment of NPOs for which the absence of a reasonably direct and reliable connection between performance and funding is surpassingly important. I've been talking about the "large caps" and the "small caps" in terms of their total revenues, but there's another important dimension that distinguishes the "mid-caps."

Many of our most innovative mid-caps work on our most serious and widespread social problems, the kinds that consign millions of people to life in a largely permanent and stubbornly inescapable underclass. As I discuss in Chapter 2, the members of the underclass often remain stuck there from one generation to the next, and almost always for extended periods of time measured in years and even decades. Leading social entrepreneurs concern themselves with problems endemic to the underclass that are similar in scope, complexity, and consequence to matters handled by federal, state, and local government agencies, such as education, employment, health care, public safety, and housing.

Two renowned pioneers of the nonprofit world, Mario Marino of Venture Philanthropy Partners and Bill Shore of Community Wealth Ventures, have observed a similar trichotomy of small-, mid- and large-cap organizations:

> At the outset we should clarify to which part of the nonprofit world our observations apply. The nonprofit sector is composed of large and complex institutions like health care systems, universities, art museums, and cultural organizations, as well as tens of thousands of small, local human service providers that perform with compassion, effectiveness, and efficiency. Many of the former have characteristics that enable them to achieve both scale and sustainability. Many of the latter are volunteer-based with appropriately no agenda or ambition beyond their neighborhood and the immediate tasks before them, nor should they. The strategies of highly engaged philanthropy might not be relevant or useful to either broad category. But they may be relevant to a specific subsector of nonprofit community-based organizations that—by virtue of size, ambition, need, resources, geography, and experience—do break through to another level and find themselves facing challenges associated with scale and sustainability, as well as for

aspiring social innovators working to affect large, and in many cases, public systems. Certainly the challenge of the inadequacy of both operating and growth capital, which we discuss, faces the whole sector and not just those organizations dealing with the delivery of social services. However, most of the high-engagement strategies appear to be more applicable to the specific subsector mentioned above.[48]

By "transformative social impact," I mean substantially and permanently reducing structural barriers to educational and economic opportunity to enable poor and low-income people to become self-sufficient. In their very fine book, *Philanthrocapitalism: How the Rich Can Save the World*, Matthew Bishop and Michael Green offer an apt illustration of a British charity, the Children's Investment Fund Foundation:

> After CIFF exits a project, says [founder] Jamie Cooper-Hahn, the children it has worked with should be healthy and have the ability to protect themselves and their families from disease. They should be equipped to provide for themselves and their families' nutrition, education, and health.[49]

Another example (this time from a small cap) is the work of Ron Rivera, who died in 2008 after completing his thirtieth "factory"—really, a small rural business—for the production of special clay-pot water filters that make contaminated water safe to drink. Rivera wanted to "put a dent" in the tragedy of 5 million people dying each year from drinking unclean water.[50] Surely he succeeded, having built the capacity to produce potable water for approximately 1.5 million desperate people in Colombia, Honduras, El Salvador, Mexico, Burma, Bangladesh, Nigeria, Kenya, Cambodia, Cuba, the Dominican Republic, Darfur, Ghana, and Sri Lanka.

At the national level, the United Way has set transformational goals to be achieved by 2018: "cut by half the number of young people who drop out of high school, cut by half the number of lower-income families that lack financial stability, increase by a third the number of youths and adults who are healthy and avoid risky behaviors."[51]

The achievement of lasting and decisive social changes will require nonprofits to conduct much bigger field experiments than they normally undertake. NPOs will have to align themselves, both vertically and horizontally, with complementary organizations, as well as with business and governmental organizations, to see if they can deliver results on a much larger playing field with many more clients. Doing this will require significantly larger and more capable staffs, management teams, support systems, and infrastructure, all of which will require substantially more money and organizational horsepower than mid-caps handle today.

How much will it cost to demonstrate the potential to achieve transformative social impact? Many successful mid-caps have annual budgets of $10 million to $20 million, which they're using to reach levels of growth that, although large on a relative scale, fall well short of national or even regional impact. For purposes of our discussion, I think we need to consider what levels of funding would be needed to serve at least 5 to 10% of the total population in need, rather than the less than 1 to 2% that even excellent social enterprises are reaching today. Until such organizations can increase their impact by five or ten times, I don't think we can say that we're on the path to transformative impact. That translates into annual budgets in the very pricey neighborhood of $100 million or so.

Keep in mind that I'm referring to large-scale, integrated programs that can demonstrate success at the level of a state or a large urban or metropolitan area. I anticipate that several complementary mid-caps would have to coordinate their efforts for such an ambitious undertaking, so that "$100 million" would represent a very round number of the total cost of their combined effort to mount large-scale pilot projects that could make a convincing case for potential systemic change.

For example, the Edna McConnell Clark Foundation organized a $120 million "Growth Capital Aggregation Pilot" with 19 foundations, corporations, and individuals after "funding experiences over the past seven years convinced the Foundation that its most successful grantees required more support than EMCF alone could provide if they were to help solve at sufficient scale some of the nation's most intractable social problems."[52] Funders Together to End Homelessness was formed to "generate the philanthropic commitment necessary to transform political will and policies, by leveraging at least $100 million in funding from other national and locally-based foundations, financial institutions and businesses."[53] The MacArthur Foundation, recognizing that "only broad, concerted strategies will bring lasting solutions," started a $100 million "Models for Change" initiative that hopes to reduce juvenile incarcerations by "screening young offenders for mental health problems, identifying those who have been involved with child welfare services, and providing earlier intervention by schools [to] divert a large proportion to community services."[54] Clara Miller believes that growth-capital grants intended to scale organizations should be "typically in the tens of millions of dollars."[55]

Now, $100 million is a lot of money, but it's not as stratospheric as you might think. TFA is trying to build an annual funding base of that size by 2010. As of 2007, the total amount of grants to organizations working on global warming was nearly $100 million,[56] and the Doris Duke Charitable Foundation recently committed that amount for climate change research over five years.[57] The Ford Foundation is contributing $100 million to 18 organizations in 13 countries working on local poverty solutions,[58] and the Gates Foundation made an initial investment of $100 million in the Alliance for a Green Revolution in Africa. The Omidyar Network has started a $100 million microfinance fund with Tufts University, although they've "discovered that a hundred million dollars might be difficult to place."[59]

In the private sector, $100 million will buy Kleiner Perkins's "iFund" investment in iPhone-related start-ups;[60] IBM's annual investment in campus computing;[61] a house, if you're the founder of Microsoft or Oracle Corporation;[62] a six-year contract to play baseball, if you're Houston Astros' left fielder Carlos Lee;[63] Ivan Boesky's insider trading fine;[64] gifts to Stanford and Brown universities, if you're real estate developer John Arrillaga[65] or convenience store owner Warren Alpert;[66] or former New York Stock Exchange chairman Richard Grasso's legal bills (as of early 2007) to defend himself (successfully, as it turned out) from an excessive compensation suit by the state attorney general.[67]

So I'll use the term "$100 million problems" as shorthand for this new and considerably more ambitious level of effort, complexity, and scale. Of course, full-scale implementation for any nationwide effort will cost billions of dollars, but I hope "$100 million problem" is a useful way to illustrate the steepness of the climb that must be made to achieve the next stage of American social progress. The renowned thought leaders at REDF might agree:

[W]hen funders seek to solve a long-term problem, Strategic Co-Funding is called for. A group of funders aiming to improve the economic health of Latino communities, for example, would need to take a Strategic Co-Funding approach. The result might be a $100 million, 10-year plan for revitalizing 10 communities.[68]

I can understand why some people might balk at "throwing" such large sums of money "at" social problems that have long resisted well-intentioned efforts at reform. But we should learn from past failures, not submit to them. Nor should we lose heart when there is so much to be gained.

Consider the example of hunger in the United States. Some 35 million Americans live in families that don't have enough to eat. According to a study commissioned by the Sodexho Foundation and conducted by researchers at Harvard, Brandeis, and Loyola universities, the total "economic burden" of hunger, including charitable contributions, impaired educational outcomes, and related physical and mental illnesses, is more than $90 billion annually. But the estimated cost to strengthen existing federal nutrition programs to virtually eliminate hunger would be about $10 to $12 billion.[69]

Of course, the $90 billion annual expenditure is an estimate derived from myriad direct and indirect costs that are so diffused as to be virtually nonexistent, while a $12 billion increase in federal outlays would (and should) be the subject of sharp debate among nearly innumerable contending stakeholders. Moreover, as the authors concede, "[T]here is more to ending hunger than providing food for those in need." Ample experience has proved there isn't a linear relationship between public expenditures and the diminution of social problems. But the extent of the apparent overspending relating to inadequate nutrition and its consequences, combined with the unrealized potential from such underfunded innovations as the National Anti-Hunger Organizations' "Blueprint to End Hunger" should embolden philanthropists and policy-makers alike to consider more sophisticated approaches to funding.[70]

Nurse-Family Partnership provides a singular example of the potential power of growth capital. Founded more than 30 years ago, NFP is "an evidence-based, nurse home visiting program that improves the health, well-being and self-sufficiency of low-income, first-time parents and their children."[71] Extensive independent studies confirm that NFP reliably produces improved prenatal health; fewer childhood injuries; fewer subsequent pregnancies; increased intervals between births; increased maternal employment; and improved school readiness for children born to mothers with low psychological resources. Financial performance is equally impressive: every dollar NFP spends on higher-risk families saves $5.70 in government expenditures and other social costs; every dollar NFP spends on the average participating family saves taxpayers $2.88.

EMCF chose NFP as one of the first three grantees (along with Youth Villages and Citizen Schools) of its Growth Capital Aggregation Pilot in order to:

> Demonstrate that a large infusion of philanthropic capital, committed in full before the implementation of a sound business plan, can propel the growth of a nonprofit organization with evidence-based programs and leverage the additional, more reliable funding, public as well as private, that can sustain the organization at its new, greater scale.

In the case of NFP, EMCF set out to tackle the same market penetration problem discussed earlier:

> Clearly, NFP had developed a program with impressive, proven outcomes for the 12,700 poor, first-time families it served in 2007. But 650,000 such families are formed in the United States every year. How could EMCF help NFP achieve the scale that would make a significant national impact? NFP's business plan set a goal of expanding enrollment to 100,000 families annually by 2017, yielding a social return of over $5.4 billion. Implementing the plan would require an initial investment of $50 million in growth capital.

Under the NFP plan, the percentage of families served would increase from 2% in 2007 to 15% in 2017, a nearly eightfold increase. The $5.4 billion value of the social return produced would represent a 1,080% return on the $50 million co-invested by the Bill and Melinda Gates Foundation, the Robert Wood Johnson Foundation, the Kresge Foundation, the Picower Foundation, and NFP's board of directors.

But EMCF is the exception that proves the rule. Simply put, "[T]he [foundation] field has not developed an approach that supports long-term solutions to the long-term problems it seeks to address."[72] Hence our collective dilemma: foundations provide only about 12% of all charitable giving, but they could—but generally don't—leverage their resources by co-investing. Individuals contribute more than 75% of all donations, but they aggressively defragment their funding, precisely the opposite of strategic investing.

The point is this: for mid-cap nonprofits with "one day, all children" visions that want to solve $100 million problems, exponential growth is vital. The gulf between performance and funding is one of the most profound and frustrating obstacles they face, and the narrowing of that gulf requires consideration of entirely new approaches to financing growth that is five or ten times higher than today.

Making the Most of a New "Golden Age"

It has become something of a cliché—albeit a well-founded one—that we are now in a "golden age of philanthropy"[73] in terms of the unprecedented amount of money gushing into the nonprofit sector. The bursting of the Internet bubble appears to have been just a temporary setback for the American economy, and the upper ranks of wealth continue to swell in both numbers and size of fortunes. (As of this writing, it is too soon to say whether and for how long "the Great Recession" of 2008 might reverse or slow these trends.) Philanthropy has increased as a direct result, well beyond the media fascination with the likes of Bill Gates, Warren Buffett, and Oprah Winfrey. The U.S. nonprofit sector now collects more than $300 billion each year.[74] In $100 bills, that would be a stack more than 200 miles high.

But the unprecedented growth in both the aggregate amount of donations and the burgeoning number of NPOs clamoring for their share—*2 million*—has only attenuated further the relationship between funding and performance. Paradoxically, the fact that the social sector as a whole is not short of money makes the disconnection between funding and performance more acute for mid-cap NPOs.

By itself, the unprecedented increase in the total amount of dollars donated to charitable causes would not require the creation of new capital market structures. Rather, the need for more effective capital allocation systems arises from the confluence of increased funding with three other important trends:

- High-engagement philanthropy
- More capable social entrepreneurs
- The foreclosure of the American Dream for millions of families

High-Engagement Philanthropy

Mario Marino of Venture Philanthropy Partners and Bill Shore of Community Wealth Ventures coined the phrase "high-engagement philanthropy" to describe "an approach in which the funders or 'investors' are directly and personally engaged and involved with their investment partners (in traditional terms, the grantees) beyond providing financial support." Important nonfinancial support can include such value-added strategic activities as "long-term planning, board and executive recruitment, coaching, help in raising capital, assuming board roles, accessing networks, and leveraging relationships to identify additional resources and facilitate partnerships."[75] Katherine Fulton and Andrew Blau of the Monitor Group have neatly summarized just how much high-engagement philanthropy differs from traditional models (see Exhibit 1.6).

In the financial sector, it's not just the money that venture capitalists, investment banks, and other intermediaries provide to fledgling businesses that helps the economy to flourish and the stock markets to set new records (2008–2009 reversals notwithstanding). It's also the expertise that comes into play when significantly larger tranches of money are made available for investment with potentially high payoffs. In fact, major investors have a lot to say about how the money will be used and who will be hired in senior posts to help their companies grow.

In the nonprofit sector, the funding architecture is quite different. Typically, it starts with rather informal "first-stage" donations in the hundreds and thousands of dollars from friends, family, and local community groups, and then progresses to more formal "second-stage" funding of five- and six-figure grants by foundations, institutions, and venture philanthropies.

Exhibit 1.6 What Are the Patterns in the Innovation?

Old Patterns or Habits	Seeds of Change
Giving primarily late in life	Giving throughout life
Foundation as the key institutional form	Foundations as one form among many
Social benefit equals the nonprofit sector	Social benefit can come from any sector
Philanthropy corrects for the market, because the market is part of the problem	Philanthropy connects to the market, because the market is part of the solution
Older, white, male leadership	Diversifying leadership
Donors focus on the communities where they live or have a connection	Donors focus both close to home and on systemic global problems with equal ease
Donors set general goals	Donors set specific targets
Donors make gifts	Donors make investments, award contracts, and gifts
Money is the resource, grants the tool	Influence is the resource, money is one tool
Donors keep grantees at arm's length	Donors highly engaged with partners
Donors give independently	Donors give independently and give together
Donors content to do good	Donors try to assess impact
Donors learn from their own work	Donors learn from their work and share what they learn with others

Source: Katherine Fulton and Andrew Blau, "Looking Out for the Future: An Orientation for Twenty-First Century Philanthropists," Monitor Institute, 2005. Future of Philanthropy, Monitor Company Group, LLP, 3 Aug. 2007, www.futureofphilanthropy.org/files/finalreport.pdf.

After the second-stage funding, the nonprofit capital market runs out of steam, at least for mid-caps. There is almost no "third-stage funding" of capital in the form of (1) long-term six- and seven-figure grants pooled from multiple sources; (2) coordinated to support integrated projects;

(3) to be undertaken by one or more successful mid-cap NPOs; (4) for the purpose of attacking $100 million problems.

So high-engagement philanthropy holds considerable promise for third-stage funding to address $100 million problems, but its realization requires something more. A three-tiered financing system makes sense for mid-caps in the nonprofit sector. I will attempt to describe what such a system might look like and how its development can be fostered.

More Capable Social Entrepreneurs

One of the defining characteristics of the new wave of innovative non-profit organizations is the strategic and multidisciplinary approaches they take. The causes of social and economic disadvantage are many and varied, so disadvantaged children and adults have quite a variety of needs, many of which don't fall within the narrow boundaries of traditional NPOs.

For example, educational entrepreneurs define their domains of responsibility with unprecedented breadth: stability in the home, parental involvement, homework completion, academic remediation, safety at home and in school, transportation, truancy and tardiness, and even sound nutrition. Great "out-of-school-time" programs like the Breakthrough Collaborative, Citizen Schools, and BELL (Building Educated Leaders for Life) have figured out what's preventing their students from succeeding in school and they fill as many of those gaps as they can.

Charter and other innovative public schools like Knowledge Is Power Program (KIPP) and Green Dot teach their students about such essential but generally overlooked skills as punctuality, attentiveness, public speaking, expectations-setting, long-term thinking, and planning for college. Consider the impressive outcomes for KIPP students:

> In the 2005–2006 school year, more than half (59 percent) of KIPP fifth grade classes outperformed their local districts in reading/English language arts at the end of their first year in KIPP schools, as measured by state exams. Nearly three-fourths (74 percent) of KIPP fifth grade classes outperformed their districts in mathematics. In the 2005–2006 school year, 100 percent of KIPP eighth grade classes outperformed their district averages in both mathematics and reading/English language arts, as measured by state exams.[76]

Even some traditional large caps are taking a page from the social entrepreneurs' playbook and have begun exploring more strategic and disciplined approaches. For example, in May 2007, the United Way of Massachusetts Bay and Merrimack Valley announced a new funding strategy that abandoned the old "something for everyone" approach (my term, not theirs) to focus on four strategic areas: healthy child development; youth opportunity; family-sustaining employment; and safe and affordable housing:

> With this change, United Way is pioneering an approach that combines the flexibility of providing unrestricted operating support to agencies with the accountability of expecting them to achieve specific contributions to measurable community goals.[77]

Social entrepreneurs and venture philanthropies have not only broadened the vision of what kinds of primary and secondary services people need to overcome structural barriers to self-sufficiency. They are also redefining the capabilities and resources organizations must have to deliver them broadly and effectively. Such thinking has worked before. One example is the reduction in youth violence attributed to the "Boston Miracle" of the 1990s:

> The Boston Miracle was about more than just law enforcement and lengthy imprisonment. It was a balanced approach to crime: a strong and genuine partnership among law enforcement agencies, the active support and involvement of the communities most victimized, and the availability of meaningful alternatives to those youth tempted to commit crimes. It understood the important role of the schools, the social service departments, businesses, and the community in addressing long-ignored problems.[78]

Foreclosing on the American Dream

I will address this issue at some length in Chapter 2, "The American Underclass," but let me preview three themes of that discussion:

1. The $100 million problems that I believe necessitate new capital-driving institutions share certain common characteristics: they are

massive and pervasive; they seem intractable; and they are incapacitating. By *incapacitating*, I mean they impede access to the tools
for achieving basic economic opportunity (such as an effective
education) that those of us who are more privileged consider an
American birthright. All $100 million problems share these chal-
lenging attributes.

2. The combination of these factors makes the indefinite continuation
   of these $100 million problems simply untenable not only for the
   people who face them directly, but for the economic mainstream
   as well. We cannot allow the United States to have a permanent
   underclass that numbers in the tens of millions. It is not merely unjust,
   but a real danger to our domestic tranquility and global competitiveness.

3. These problems no longer lend themselves to purely governmental, or even government-centric, solutions. Systemic change and
   transformative social impact will not be possible without significantly more purposeful, effective, and sustained involvement by the
   nonprofit sector.

In the United States today, there are tens of millions of people in this
country to whom the American Dream is simply not available. They
cannot fend for themselves because the problems they face are too big
and too impervious to existing government responses, and they lack the
most basic resources needed to achieve self-sufficiency.

Our inability to put this unacceptable state of affairs right results
not from the amount of money available for NPOs but rather from its
distribution and deployment:

> Nonprofit enterprises suffer not so much from a lack of money (though
> reliable revenue is scarce in some subsectors and unevenly distributed
> throughout), but from a lack of something more fundamental—equity
> capital, as well as a lack of the managers, board members, and philan-
> thropic investors who know what nonprofit equity capital is and how
> to deploy it successfully.[79]

Charitable donations find their way to grantees through a haphazard
combination of luck, charisma, and razzmatazz that is poorly suited to
the importance of their work. Consideration of which organizations can

use the money most effectively plays only a small part, in large measure because there are so few cause-and-effect signals to which donors can respond.

When tens of billions of dollars can't find their way to their best uses, there is a massive but unquantifiable opportunity cost to society. The misallocation of funding represents not just "inefficiency" or even "waste" as those terms are commonly used, but a loss of potential impact of enormous proportions. Even if every penny donated was used efficiently, there would still be massive underutilization of the available resources.

There are two related forms of such opportunity costs. First, by failing to direct donations to the most effective NPOs, society suffers a corresponding loss of beneficial impact. Second, the diversion of staff energy to relentless fundraising is a crippling distraction that the sector cannot afford.

Of Drops and Buckets

WARNING! EXTENDED METAPHOR ALERT!

If the impact of social entrepreneurs is but a drop in the bucket of national need, then fundraising today is like an unending series of downpours in which there are hundreds of billions of raindrops—donated dollars—falling into nearly 2 million nonprofit buckets. At any given time, some buckets are overflowing, some are empty, and most have some rain.

The allocation of rain into buckets isn't exactly random, but it's not entirely logical, either. That is, there's some correlation between the amount of rain that falls into particular buckets and the amount those buckets "need," but the fit between the demand for and the supply of rain is surely not the "best" one we could envision if we had better ways to gather reliable information about the weather and to use that information to allocate water more effectively.

Part of the problem is we don't know what the optimal distribution of water is, either in the aggregate or among individual buckets. In fact, we don't really know what the actual distribution is, that is, how many buckets have how much water in them (although I suppose we could examine each of more than a million buckets to find out, if we had all the time in the world, which we don't).

There's no mechanism like a common system of pipes or funnels to direct the "right" amount of rain into the "right" buckets. Rather, our metaphorical system depends on more than a million people holding more than a million buckets running around trying to catch hundreds of billions of raindrops. After the storm ends and the carriers use whatever water they've collected, they take their buckets out in search of new storms and the process of chasing raindrops begins anew. This goes on essentially forever. They cope with this problem by using larger and larger buckets and hiring more and more people to run around holding them up during storms.

This is an incredibly chaotic scene we're imagining. There are more than 100 million clouds, but it's hard to tell which ones are going to rain, when, or how much. Everyone is looking up, studying the same clouds while they're running around holding up their buckets and banging into each other, and shouting up to the clouds that look like they're going to rain, "Over here! Over here!" At the same time, the clouds are looking down at all this bedlam, trying to figure out which buckets need rain the most and which ones will make the best use of whatever water they collect.

When the storm passes and everyone looks in their buckets, some are full and the carriers are more or less content because they own many such full buckets and they really need and will make very good use (or at least pretty good use) of quite a lot of water. Many other small buckets contain just a little rain and the owners are more or less content because they don't actually need that much water and they will do the best they can with whatever they get.

But a lot of buckets will have less water than the owners need, and certainly less than they could put to good use. Those

(Continued)

owners are chronically dissatisfied with the amount of rain they get, but they doggedly persevere, constantly on the lookout for more storms. They race out whenever dark clouds appear, at least until they're so exhausted that they look for another line of work.

To improve this dismal situation, we first need to acknowledge that this "system" doesn't work for bucket holders that are neither large nor small. Those in the middle are using water for our most important social needs, such as responding to massive droughts and growing crops to feed millions of hungry people. The grim reality is that they're never going to get enough water by running around holding up buckets to catch a few drops from thousands of small storms.

Second, we need to separate the job of water-using from the job of water-gathering. Water-using is a highly challenging, full-time job that requires a certain set of skills; water-gathering is a quite different enterprise involving a quite different set of skills. When water users are forced to gather water, too, the water isn't used as productively as it otherwise could be.

If we could make the clouds smarter about where, when, and how much they rained, the water users could devote more attention to making better use of greater amounts of water. We would need to collect better information about water needs and water usage so the clouds could make better decisions about which buckets they want to fill. The result should be to make the overall distribution of rain more beneficial than it is now.

ALL CLEAR! THE METAPHOR HAS PASSED!

A Potential Inflection Point

The primitive state of the nonprofit capital market imposes an upper limit to the achievement of social progress that is substantially below what the sector is otherwise capable of achieving. We have the means and know-how to accomplish much more than we do, but the financial system does not and, indeed, cannot make the required funds available to the organizations that could best put them to productive use. For certain kinds of social problems—$100 million problems—and certain kinds of nonprofit organizations—mid-cap social enterprises—traditional methods of fundraising simply don't work. They take too much time or attract too little money, or, most often, both, and they don't connect funding to performance.

Without a much more sophisticated and intelligent capital-generation and -distribution system, successful nonprofit organizations can achieve "scale," that is, they can grow larger relative to their current baselines, but they cannot achieve "transformative social impact," that is, they cannot solve our most damaging social problems to an extent that is significant relative to the total need. Established fundraising practices will no doubt be with us for the indefinite future and they will always represent a vital part of the mix across the entire funding spectrum. If we aspire to achieve essential social progress, such as conquering educational inequity and extending economic opportunity, then we must develop new methods and institutions that are up to the task of raising much larger sums of money with much less effort, time, and cost, and distributing it in ways that increase its impact.

We now face a potential inflection point at which the nonprofit sector (working in partnership with business and government) can dramatically improve its effectiveness and make substantial headway against what have seemed like intractable problems of the first order. But we cannot take advantage of this opportunity until nonprofit professionals recognize that the financial tools available today are structurally incapable of supporting the required level and complexity of effort.

Bringing more horsepower to nonprofit capital markets will force sector leaders to face uncomfortable choices, and consider innovative approaches that will be unfamiliar. But if we agree that the time has come to achieve transformational social impacts that will actually enable large segments of the underclass to achieve self-sufficiency, we must begin by acknowledging that existing funding models won't take us there.

Just as experienced financial investors find the most lucrative investment opportunities before everyone else, we need to help "smart money" find the most capable nonprofits that are ready to take on $100 million problems. If we really want to help "all children" but we don't want to wait forever for "one day" to arrive, we need to turn the fundraising paradigm on its head:

> We need a financing system that helps highly engaged social impact investors to direct third-stage growth capital to the best mid-cap nonprofits, instead of one that forces those nonprofits to spend all their time looking for more drops to fill more buckets.

Objectives of This Book

So this book has two objectives. The first is to explain why meaningful reductions in poverty, illiteracy, violence, and hopelessness will require a fundamental restructuring of nonprofit capital markets. Such a restructuring would need to make it much easier for philanthropists of all stripes—large and small, public and private, institutional and individual—to fund nonprofit organizations that maximize social impact. It would also need to make it possible for promising mid-caps to raise much larger pools of money with substantially less time and effort.

There are encouraging signs that such a restructuring is already taking shape. NFF Capital Partners acts as a "benevolent broker" to facilitate nonprofit "capital campaigns of $5 million or greater."[80] SeaChange Capital Partners will help nonprofits with revenues in the range of $2 million to $75 million revenue "with a multimillion dollar round of financing, sized to fund a well-defined, multiyear growth plan."[81] The Edna McConnell Clark Foundation has raised $120 million for its Growth Capital Aggregation Pilot.[82]

These are singularly important experiments advanced by some of the most sophisticated financial minds the nonprofit sector has to offer. Of necessity, however, these are carefully vetted offerings for a small number of exceptional organizations. They are not designed to be broad-based innovations, nor should they be. I hope to persuade readers that this nascent development must be extended and increased by orders of magnitude if we hope to rescue the American Dream for millions of families.

Second—and this is where I'm going to have to ask you to hear me out—I make the case for a new nonprofit capital market institution, a virtual stock market, as one way to help highly engaged social investors find promising NPOs where their money can do the most good. The virtual stock market, which I call "the Impact Index," or "IMPEX" for short, would take the form of a "prediction market" designed to harness what *New Yorker* financial columnist James Surowiecki most famously called "The Wisdom of Crowds." We will explore this at some length, but for now I will just note that Surowiecki grounds his thesis in what he rightly calls a "mathematical truism":

> If you ask a large enough group of diverse, independent people to make a prediction or estimate a probability, and then average those estimates, the errors each of them makes in coming up with an answer will cancel themselves out. Each person's guess, you might say, has two components: information and error. Subtract the error, and you're left with the information.[83]

A Virtual Nonprofit Stock Market

The idea of the nonprofit virtual stock market would be to emulate market-like signals to help "smart money" find its "best" uses—however investors define "best" for themselves—with the intended side-effect of significantly reducing the cost and effort of raising funds to support both programs and organizations.

Like other free market mechanisms, the IMPEX would be "designed to solve [the] coordination problem [of] getting resources to the right places at the right cost."[84] It would increase "signals" and reduce "noise" about nonprofit performance by coalescing the views of thousands of people who follow their work into a more coherent picture.

The idea of a nonprofit virtual stock market has been mentioned by a few thought leaders, but it has not received sufficiently careful or comprehensive consideration. It would be modeled after the kinds of prediction markets (also called *information markets*) that have been used to forecast the outcomes of such diverse events as political elections, economic policy decisions, athletic competitions, box office receipts, book sales, and new product launches. Extensive academic research has confirmed the predictive accuracy of such markets when they are well designed. Indeed, a new industry is emerging to bring prediction markets inside corporations to help them make more informed decisions about such matters as what strategic direction the company should take or which new product should receive more marketing support.

The mechanism that enables these virtual markets to operate is a simple voting system that allows a sizable and diverse group of reasonably knowledgeable participants to conduct virtual "trades" when they believe that other participants are underestimating or overestimating the chances that a certain future event will occur. The market should produce a rough consensus of the true probabilities and provide an inexact but still informative ranking of the events in terms of their relative probabilities.

In the case of the nonprofit sector, prediction markets might help investors identify which approaches to, say, improving high school graduation rates or educating teens about pregnancy prevention are likely to be the most effective, as a way of informing their philanthropic choices. Such markets might also help discover overlooked organizations that deserve wider consideration, just as the stock market helped tip the balance in favor of eBay rather than its many long-gone competitors in what was then the new field of online auctions.

I hope to provide the first in-depth consideration of a nonprofit virtual stock market here, by answering three questions:

1. Why does the nonprofit sector need a capital market to achieve transformational social impact?
2. What would a nonprofit virtual stock market look like, and what would it do?
3. How could a nonprofit stock market be developed to help link funding and impact in the near term?

I will suggest both "laboratory" and field experiments to test whether an Impact Index could be developed that would provide some measure of rank-ordering of NPOs according to their perceived effectiveness.

Throughout the discussion, it will be extremely important to understand clearly what an Impact Index would and would not do, how it would differ from financial stock markets, and what its potential value and limitations might be. As an opening cautionary note, I do not contend that philanthropists would "own" nonprofit shares, that social investors would earn financial returns on their donations, that the Impact Index would be the sole or even primary source for making decisions about giving money to NPOs, or that the Impact Index would establish how much NPOs, either singly or collectively, are "worth." IMPEX rankings would be one source of information—guidance, not algorithms—that individual investors could incorporate into their decision making to whatever extent they think wise.

Nor do I delude myself into thinking that the IMPEX would magically transform the chaotic nonprofit funding circus into an exact science that would perfectly match nonprofit performance and funding. My aspirations are considerably more modest but, I hope, realistic. Given the primitive state of the nonprofit capital market as its exists today and the mystifying fundraising system under which mid-cap nonprofits labor, a tool that might improve the signal-to-noise ratio for nonprofit effectiveness could help channel funds in more intelligent ways that would enable the social sector to break through the unacceptably low ceiling of impact.

Notes

1. Wendy Kopp, *One Day, All Children* (New York: Public Affairs, 2001).

2. Teach For America, "Our Nation's Greatest Injustice," 12 Sept. 2007, www .teachforamerica.org/mission/index.htm.

3. Douglas N. Harris, "Background," in "Ending the Blame Game on Educational Inequity: A Study of 'High Flying' Schools and NCLB," March 2006, Education Policy Studies Laboratory, Division of Educational Leadership and Policy Studies, College of Education, Arizona State University, www.asu.edu/ educ/epsl/EPRU/documents/EPSL-0603-120-EPRU.pdf.

4. Ibid.

5. Bob Herbert, "A Dubious Milestone," *New York Times*, 21 June 2008, www .nytimes.com/2008/06/21/opinion/21herbert.html?hp.

6. Kane, Parsons & Associates, "Studies on Corps Member Impact: What the Research Says," Teach For America, 18 Sept. 2007, www.teachforamerica. org/mission/our_impact/studies_corps_impact.htm.

7. www.teachforamerica.org/mission/our_impact/corps_impact.htm.

8. Zeyu Xu, Jane Hannaway, and Colin Taylor, "Making a Difference? The Effect of Teach for America on Student Performance in High School," Urban Institute, 27 Mar. 2008, www.urban.org/url.cfm?ID=411642.

9. www.teachforamerica.org/about/our_growth_plan.htm.

10. Patricia Sellers, "Schooling Corporate Giants on Recruiting," *Fortune*, 27 Nov. 2006 and 17 Sept. 2007, http://money.cnn.com/magazines/fortune/fortune_archive/2006/11/27/8394324/index.htm.

11. Wendy Kopp, interview with Stephen Colbert, *The Colbert Report*, Comedy Central, 17 Sept. 2007, www.colbertnation.com/the-colbert-report-videos/81750/february-05-2007/wendy-kopp.

12. "Our Work," NewSchools Venture Fund, http://newschools.org/work.

13. "Charter Management Organizations," NewSchools Venture Fund, 14 Apr. 2008, www.newschools.org/portfolio/impact/charter-management-organizations.

14. Shirley Sagawa, "Fulfilling the Promise: Social Entrepreneurs and Action Tanking in a New Era of Entrepreneurship," pre-reading materials, Gathering of Leaders, 15–17 Feb. 2006, New Profit, Inc., Ed. Shirley Sagawa and Deb Jospin, 4 Oct. 2007, www.sagawajospin.com/Fulfilling%20the%20Promise_Sagawa_February%202006.pdf.

15. Robert S. Kaplan, "New Profit Inc.: Governing the Nonprofit Enterprise," Harvard Business School, Case Study 9-100-052, p. 1 (rev. July 3, 2001).

16. Michael E. Porter and Mark R. Kramer, "Philanthropy's New Agenda: Creating Value," *Harvard Business Review* (Nov.–Dec. 1999): 127, harvardbusinessonline.hbsp.harvard.edu/b01/en/common/item_detail.jhtml?id=99610.

17. Clara Miller, "The Equity Capital Gap," *Stanford Social Innovation Review* (Summer 2008): 45, www.nonprofitfinancefund.org/docs/2008/ssir_summer_2008_equity_capital_gap.pdf.

18. Heiner Baumann, "The Growth Capital Market in the U.S.," *Alliance* 10.1 (March 2005): 37; *Alliance Magazine*, 14 Apr. 2008, www.allavida.org/alliance/0503-pages37-39.pdf.

19. Christine W. Letts, William Ryan, and Allen Grossman, "Virtuous Capital: What Foundations Can Learn from Venture Capitalists," *Harvard Business Review* (March–April 1997), harvardbusinessonline.hbsp.harvard.edu/b01/en/ common/item_detail.jhtml?id=97207.

20. "The Reform of School Reform," *Business Week*, 26 June 2006, p. 72.

21. Porter and Kramer, "Philanthropy's New Agenda," pp. 121–130.

22. Kim Alter, Paul Shoemaker, Melinda Tuan, and Jed Emerson, "When Is It Time to Say Goodbye? Exit Strategies and Venture Philanthropy Funds" (September 2001), www.virtueventures.com/files/exitstrategy.pdf.

23. Letts et al., "Virtuous Capital," p. 5. See also Gregory M. Stanton, Jed Emerson, and Marcus Weiss, "Going Mainstream: NPOs Accessing the Capital Markets," Draft Rev., 26 Feb. 2001 ("Nonprofits often labor under the continual

cycle of annual fundraising efforts and are forced to finance their long-term operations with short-term funding strategies, such as annual grants, contracts, and subsidies"), www.redf.org/download/other/cmap_going. doc.

24. Dennis Prager, "Raising the Value of Philanthropy: A Synthesis of Informal Interviews with Foundation Executives and Observers of Philanthropy," Prepared for Jewish Healthcare Foundation, the Forbes Fund, and Grantmakers in Health, February 1999.

25. Clara Miller, "The Looking Glass World of Nonprofit Money," *Nonprofit Quarterly* 12, no. 1 (Spring 2005), www.nonprofitfinancefund.org/docs/ Looking%20Glass,%20NPQ%20website.pdf.

26. Cynthia Gair, "Stepping Out of the Maze: Aligning to Improve the Nonprofit Capital Market," www.redf.org/publications-newsletter-old.htm.

27. Letts et al., "Virtuous Capital," p. 3. See also p. 6: "Many [NPOs] have been conditioned by the existing grant-seeking process to camouflage their organizational expenses and needs."

28. Baumann, "The Growth Capital Market in the U.S.," p. 38.

29. Miller, "The Looking Glass World of Nonprofit Money."

30. "Note on Starting a Nonprofit Venture," Harvard Business School, Case No. 9-391-096, p. 7 (rev. Sept. 11, 1992); Miller, "The Looking Glass World of Nonprofit Money" (cost of raising one dollar by small social service agency might cost 50 cents while a major institution with efficient fundraising might spend "only a fraction of a cent").

31. William F. Meehan, Derek Kilmer, and Maisie O'Flanagan, "Investing in Society: Why We Need a More Efficient Social Capital Market—and How We Can Get There," *Stanford Social Innovation Review* (Spring 2004), www.ssireview.org/articles/entry/investing_in_society.

32. Gair, "Stepping Out of the Maze."

33. Robert S. Kaplan and David P. Norton, *The Balanced Scorecard: Translating Strategy into Action* (Boston: Harvard Business School Press, 1996).

34. *Our Story of Impact*, 2005–2006 Annual Report (N.p.: New Profit, 2006).

35. "Future Impact," Venture Philanthropy Partners, 14 Apr. 2008, www. vppartners.org/impact/future.html.

36. "Our Reach and Growth," College Summit, 12 Sept. 2007, www. collegesummit.org/about/results-and-metrics/our-reach-and-growth.

37. "Our Impact," Jumpstart, 11 Sept. 2007, www.jstart.org/index.php? submenu=about_us&src=gendocs&link=Our_Impact&category=Main.

38. Ayana Douglas-Hall and Michelle Chau, "Basic Facts About Low-Income Children: Birth to Age 18," National Center for Children in Poverty, Mailman

School of Public Health at Columbia University, 14 April 2008, www.nccp. org/publications/pub_762.html.

39. Peter Frumkin. *Strategic Giving: The Art and Science of Philanthropy* (Chicago: University of Chicago Press, 2006).

40. Sidney Harris, www.cartoonbank.com/product_details.asp?sid=40967.

41. Peter Frumkin, *Strategic Giving*, p. 204.

42. Allen S. Grossman, "Jumpstart," Case 9-301-037, p. 14 (rev. May 17, 2002), http://harvardbusinessonline.hbsp.harvard.edu/b02/en/common/item_detail. jhtml?id=301037.

43. Allen Grossman, "Philanthropic Social Capital Markets: Performance Driven Philanthropy," *Social Enterprise Series* 12 (Boston: Harvard Business School, 1999).

44. Alana Conner Snibbe, "Drowning in Data," *Stanford Social Innovation Review* (Fall 2006): 39–40. Stanford University Graduate School of Business, Center for Social Innovation, 18 Sept. 2007, www.ssireview.org/articles/ entry/drowning_in_data.

45. Meehan, Kilmer, and O'Flanagan, "Investing in Society."

46. Ibid.

47. Sue Hoye, "United Ways Raised More than $4-Billion Last Year," *Chronicle of Philanthropy*, 19 Sept. 2007, http://philanthropy.com/news/updates/ 3065/united-ways-raise-more-than-4-billion-last-year.

48. Mario Marino and Bill Shore, "High-Engagement Philanthropy: A Bridge to a More Effective Social Sector," Venture Philanthropy Partners, Community Wealth Ventures, 2004, 3 Aug. 2007.

49. Matthew Bishop and Michael Green, *Philanthrocapitalism: How the Rich Can Save the World* (London: Bloomsbury 2008), pp. 82–83.

50. Caroline Richmond, "Ron Rivera, Potter who developed a water filter that saved lives in the third world," Obituary, *The Guardian*, 16 Oct. 2008, www.guardian.co.uk/science/2008/oct/16/1; Sara Corbett, "Solution in a Pot," *New York Times Magazine*, 24 Dec. 2008, p. 38, www.nytimes.com/ 2008/12/28/magazine/28rivera-t.html?_r=2&ref=magazine.

51. "Goals for the Common Good: The United Way Challenge to America," www.liveunited.org.

52. Edna McConnell Clark Foundation, "An Experiment in Coordinated Investment: A Progress Report on the Edna McConnell Clark Foundation's Growth Capital Aggregation Pilot" (October 2008), www.emcf.org/pdf/ gcap_progressreportOct08.pdf.

53. "About Us," Funders Together to End Homelessness, www.endlongterm homelessness.org/about_the_partnership.aspx.

54. Jonathan F. Fanton, "Juvenile Justice Reforms," Letters, *New York Times*, 20 Aug. 2008, http://query.nytimes.com/gst/fullpage.html?res= 9905E5D91731F930A1575BC0A96E9C8B63.

55. Miller, "The Equity Capital Gap," p. 42.

56. Steve Lohr, "Foundation to Offer $100 Million to Deal with Global Warming," *New York Times*, 9 Apr. 2007, www.nytimes.com/2007/04/09/business/ 09climate.html.

57. "Doris Duke Charitable Foundation Makes First Climate Change Initiative Grants," *Philanthropy News Digest*, 6 July 2007, http://foundationcenter.org/ pnd/news/story.jhtml?id=181800021.

58. Connie Bruck, "Millions for Millions," *New Yorker*, 30 Oct. 2006, www. newyorker.com/archive/2006/10/30/061030fa_fact1.

59. Ibid.

60. Kleiner Perkins Caufield & Byers, "Initiatives: iFund," www.kpcb.com/ initiatives/ifund/index.html.

61. William J. Holstein, "And Now a Syllabus for the Service Economy," *New York Times*, 3 Dec. 2006, www.nytimes.com/2006/12/03/jobs/03advi.html.

62. Austan Goolsbee, "Why Do the Richest People Rarely Intend to Give It All Away?" *New York Times*, 1 Mar. 2007, query.nytimes.com/gst/fullpage. html?res=9B05E0D81F3EF932A35750C0A9619C8B63&scp=2&sq=austan %20goolsbee%20%24100%20million%20ellison&st=cse.

63. "Lee Signs with Houston for Six Years, $100 Million," ESPN.com news services, 24 Nov. 2006, http://sports.espn.go.com/mlb/news/story?id= 2674398.

64. Michael J. de la Merced, "Ripples from the Last Takeover Wave," *New York Times*, 4 Apr. 2007, query.nytimes.com/gst/fullpage.html?res= 9907E0DD1E30F937A35757C0A9619C8B63.

65. "Arrillaga Gives $100 Million to Stanford in Largest Single Gift Ever from Individual," *Stanford Report*, 26 May 2006, news-service.stanford.edu/ news/2006/may31/arrillaga-053106.html.

66. "Rhode Island: $100 Million Gift for Brown," *New York Times*, 30 Jan. 2007, www.nytimes.com/2007/01/30/us/30brfs-brown.html.

67. Thomas Landon Jr., "Court Rules for Grasso in Pay Case," *New York Times*, 9 May 2007, www.nytimes.com/2007/05/09/business/09grasso.html.

68. Cynthia Gair, "Roadmap #1: Strategic Co-Funding," Out of Philanthropy's Funding Maze, REDF, p. 3, www.redf.org/user/login?destination=node/ 548.

69. J. Larry Brown, Donald Shepard, Timothy Martin, and John Orwat, "The Economic Cost of Domestic Hunger: Estimated Annual Burden to the

United States," 5 June 2007, www.sodexofoundation.org/hunger_us/Images/Cost%20of%20Domestic%20Hunger%20Report%20_tcm150-155150.pdf.

70. National Anti-Hunger Organizations, "A Blueprint to End Hunger," 2008, www.bread.org/learn/us-hunger-issues/blueprint10-16-08.pdf.

71. Edna McConnell Clark Foundation, "An Experiment in Coordinated Investment."

72. Gair, "Roadmap #1."

73. Paul S. Schervish and John J. Havens, "A Golden Age of Philanthropy? The Impact of the Great Wealth Transfer on Greater Boston," Center for Wealth and Philanthropy at Boston College, 2006, www.bc.edu/research/cwp/meta-elements/pdf/goldenagephil.pdf.

74. Press release, GivingUSA Foundation, "U.S. Charitable Giving Estimated to Be $306.39 Billion in 2007," 23 June 2008, www.givinginstitute.org/press_releases/releases/20080622.html.

75. Marino and Shore, "High-Engagement Philanthropy."

76. "Results of KIPP Schools," KIPP, 15 Apr. 2008, www.kipp.org/01/resultsofkippsch.cfm.

77. United Way of Massachusetts Bay and Merrimack Valley, "Seeking Greater Positive Impact in Helping People: New United Way $100 Million Investment Plan Highlights Initiatives, New Organizations; Ties Traditional Funds to Specific Community Goals," 3 Aug. 2007, www.uwmb.org/press-room/07-Investment-Strategy.html.

78. Donald K. Stern and Nancy Gertner, "A Balanced Approach to Fighting Violence," *Boston Globe*, 21 Apr. 2007, www.boston.com/news/globe/editorial_opinion/oped/articles/2007/04/21/a_balanced_approach_to_fighting_violence.

79. Miller, "The Equity Capital Gap."

80. "About NFF Capital Partners," Nonprofit Finance Fund, 15 Apr. 2008, www.nonprofitfinancefund.org/details.asp?autoId=119.

81. SeaChange Capital Partners, 15 Apr. 2008, http://seachangecap.org/index.html.

82. Edna McConnell Clark Foundation, "$120 Million in Growth Capital Secured to Advance Opportunities for Low-Income Youth," www.emcf.org/who/presidentspage/index.htm.

83. James Surowiecki, *The Wisdom of Crowds* (New York: Random House, 2005).

84. Ibid., p. 102.

Chapter 2

The American Underclass

If America is to remain a first-class nation, it cannot have a second-class citizenship.

—*Martin Luther King Jr.*

[T]the overall situation has continued to go downhill among the poor who are mostly shut out from the mainstream of success.

—*Bill Cosby and Alvin F. Poussaint, M.D.,*
Come on People: On the Path from Victims to Victors

Why do we need better nonprofit capital markets to bring about meaningful social progress? The answer rests on two as-yet unsupported assertions advanced in Chapter 1:

1. There is both an acute need and an unprecedented opportunity for mid-cap social entrepreneurs to make real and sustained progress against our most debilitating social problems.
2. Such a vital national goal cannot be accomplished without new kinds of financial structures and systems to collect and distribute third-stage capital.

In this chapter, I address the first assertion and explain why the problems we face require fundamentally more robust solutions than the ones we have available today. In the next chapter, I defend my second contention that existing nonprofit funding institutions can't support the new solutions required.

American Social Progress: The Early Years

Henry Roger Seager's *Social Insurance: A Program of Social Reform* is believed to be the first American work on the important subject of social reform. Professor Seager opened his Kennedy Lectures for 1910 to the Columbia University School of Philanthropy with an astute observation about American character:

> Among the many characteristics which foreign observers have ascribed to Americans are two about which there has been little difference of opinion. We are good-natured, and we are individualists. Sermons have been preached against our good nature, so I need not dwell upon it. Much more important is our individualism—our absorption in individual interests and our reluctance to undertake things in combination with our neighbors or through the government. That individualism is an American characteristic is proved by a number of familiar facts. Thus, the phrase, "social reform," which, in other countries, suggests comprehensive plans of state action, is still usually associated in the United States with the welfare departments of private corporations, privately endowed schools of philanthropy, or such splendid examples of private beneficence as the Russell Sage Foundation. Again, the cooperative movement, which has made such signal progress in Europe, is in its infancy here.[1]

By "the cooperative movement," Seager was referring to what was then the heretical notion that social support should be provided to needy individuals through "state action," that is, the paternal agency of government. He acknowledged that, at a time when "abounding prosperity has been the rule," a national mind set that avidly favored individual self-reliance might well be the wise course. Seager also recognized that the circumstances necessary for such a happy state of affairs were not immutable. Virtually alone among the professoriate, Seager foresaw "an insurmountable obstacle to the realization of the individualist's millennium" comprising "the five great misfortunes to which wage earners are exposed—accidents, illness, premature death, unemployment, and old age."

Seager asserted that "these evils do not confine themselves to the families who suffer directly from them." Rather than just a coincidental increase of individual misfortune to which existing instruments of charity could be expected to respond, Seager saw, nearly 20 years before the arrival of the Great Depression, that industrial accidents, disabling illness, advancing mortality, loss of gainful employment, and elderly poverty represented an interrelated set of structural dysfunctions through which an "army of unskilled and unorganized casual labor is constantly recruited."

Seager considered it inevitable that "collective remedies must be found and applied to these evils." Drawing heavily from successful efforts adopted abroad, he proposed a "program of social reform" founded on two simple principles: "protecting wage-earning families which have developed standards of living from losing them, and helping wage-earning families without standards to gain them."

All of Seager's proposals proved enormously prescient, but consider for now just his views on the need to confront "impecunious old age." He saw that the problem had to be understood in its dynamic and systemic dimensions: "As the typical American is changing from the farmer to the factory employee, the likelihood that old age poverty will be provided against by voluntary saving is decreasing." Observing that the United States was "still in a transition stage," he warned that

> European experience . . . should leave us in no doubt that a great increase in old-age poverty lies before us. . . .

> Old age is a risk to which all are liable, but which many never live to experience. Thus, according to American life tables, nearly two thirds of those who survive the age of ten die before the age of seventy. Under these circumstances, for every wage earner to attempt to save enough by himself to provide for his old age is needlessly costly. The intelligent course is for him to combine with other wage earners to accumulate a common fund out of which old-age annuities may be paid to those who live long enough to need them.

And thus were sown the seeds of the Social Security Act.

The American Dream Arrives

Seager's insights mark the time when our shared image of a vigorous social sector first became imprinted on the American consciousness. Shirley Sagawa, a renowned expert on children's policy and philanthropy, vividly recalled the duality confronting an emerging industrial power in the early years of a young century:

> Turn the clock back 100 years, and you would find a country swirling with change. The Progressive Era, as the period from the 1890s to World War I has come to be called, was an age of optimism in the face of desperate problems. Widespread poverty, large-scale immigration, the extensive use of child labor, racial violence and ethnic divisions, and unsafe working conditions characterized the day. At the same time, new industries fueled a growing economy, created large corporations, and concentrated wealth among leading industrialists.[2]

It was in the later years of that era that historian James Truslow Adams first used the elusive term "American Dream" to refer to "[t]hat dream of a land in which life should be better and richer and fuller for everyone, with opportunity for each according to ability or achievement."[3] Scholars Joanna Schneider Zangrando and Robert L. Zangrando defined the American Dream as "a fragile agglomeration of (1) individual freedom of choice in lifestyles, (2) equal access to economic abundance, and (3) the pursuit of shared objectives mutually advantageous to the individual and society."[4] The conservative commentator William Safire described it "as a combination of freedom and opportunity with growing overtones of social justice."[5]

The four decades following the Great Depression were years of adversity and progress, seasoned by extraordinary accomplishments that gave the American Dream much of its substance as a hallmark of social advancement. It is all too easy now to take them for granted, but we have reason now to look back at past years of American glory.

1933 Tennessee Valley Authority

At the time of the Depression, the 1.3 million acres located in seven states that comprised the Tennessee Valley were beset by poverty, hunger, disease, and depleted agricultural, natural, and commercial resources.[6] A young James Agee wrote movingly that the Tennessee River ran "like blown smoke through the floodgates of Wilson Dam, to slide becalmed along the crop-cleansed fields of Shiloh."[7]

President Franklin D. Roosevelt created the Tennessee Valley Authority (TVA) as the first "corporation clothed with the power of government but possessed of the flexibility and initiative of a private enterprise."[8] Under the banner, "Electricity for All," the TVA "held fast to its strategy of integrated solutions," "whether it was power production, navigation, flood control, malaria prevention, reforestation, or erosion control." Today, TVA generates electricity at 29 hydroelectric dams, 11 coal-fired plants, 6 combustion turbine sites, 3 nuclear plants, a hydropower plant, 18 green power sites, and 17,000 miles of transmission lines serving about 8.6 million people.

1935 Social Security Act

We can begin to understand the heated response to recent proposals to "privatize" Social Security when we recall that, in the 1930s, the majority of elderly Americans lived in poverty. From that perspective, the sweeping preamble of the 1935 statute seems no less audacious today:

> AN ACT to provide for the general welfare by establishing a system of Federal old-age benefits, and by enabling the several States to make more adequate provision for aged persons, blind persons, dependent and crippled children, maternal and child welfare, public health, and the administration of their unemployment compensation laws.[9]

By 1967, the percentage of the elderly population that was poor had fallen to 30%. In 2000, just 10% of the elderly lived in poverty (see Exhibit 2.1).

1944 GI Bill

Ken Burns's searing documentary, *The War*, vividly depicts the grueling conditions that millions of soldiers endured on three continents, the prolonged sacrifices of their families, and the determined focus of the

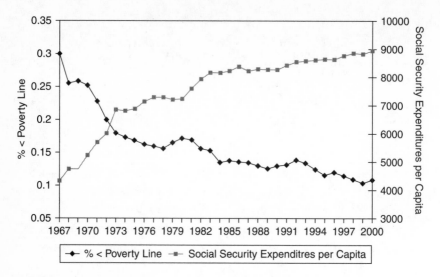

Exhibit 2.1   Elderly Poverty and Social Security Expenditures over Time
Source: www.nber.org/aginghealth/summer04/w10466.jpg.

nation. His wrenching portrayal helps later and lesser generations begin to understand, some 50 years on, the impetus for what became known as the GI Bill of Rights.

Having learned bitter lessons in the aftermath of World War I when the nation's shame was put on display as 31,000 impoverished veterans marched on Washington during the "Bonus March" of 1932, Congress passed the final piece of New Deal legislation, the GI Bill, "To provide Federal Government aid for the readjustment in civilian life of returning World War II veterans."[10] As Bill Gates, Sr., put it, "Without the GI Bill, the American Dream would have never become real for millions of Americans."[11] The program of debt-free college education and vocational training, low-interest home mortgages, and small-business loan assistance gave birth to a capacious middle class:

> A nation of renters would become a nation of homeowners. College would be transformed from an elite bastion to a middle class entitlement. Suburbia would be born amid the clatter of bulldozers and the smell of new asphalt linking it all together. Inner cities would collapse. The Cold War would find its warriors—not in the trenches or the barracks, but at the laboratory and the wind tunnel and the drafting board. Educations would be made possible for fourteen future Nobel Prize winners, three Supreme Court justices, three presidents,

a dozen senators, two dozen Pulitzer Prize winners, 238,000 teachers, 91,000 scientists, 67,000 doctors, 450,000 engineers, 240,000 accountants, 17,000 journalists, 22,000 dentists—along with a million lawyers, nurses, businessmen, artists, actors, writers, pilots, and others.[12]

1954 Polio Vaccine

As public health victories go, few can compare with the eradication of poliomyelitis in the United States. Polio wasn't just a terrible disease, it was a source of terrifying panic. Tens of thousands of once-healthy children became inexplicably paralyzed, with no known cause or cure. Victims of the epidemic were kept alive by a medieval-looking ventilator known as the "iron lung." "When polio struck, movie theaters were shut, camps and schools were closed, drinking fountains were abandoned, draft inductions suspended, and nonessential meetings were canceled."[13]

In January 1938, President Roosevelt (a polio victim himself) established the National Foundation for Infantile Paralysis, a nonprofit organization, which was later renamed the "March of Dimes" after a phrase coined by the popular comedian, Eddie Cantor. Dr. Jonas Salk used March of Dimes funding to develop a vaccine in 1948, and in 1954, nearly 2 million schoolchildren tested the vaccine in the largest peace-time mobilization of volunteers in U.S. history. Over the next four years, 450 million children were vaccinated, and the disease was eradicated in the United States shortly after the introduction of the oral vaccine in 1962.[14]

Interstate Highway System

In 1919, then Major Dwight D. Eisenhower traveled in a three-mile long caravan of Army vehicles from Washington, D.C., to San Francisco. The 3,000-mile trip took 62 days at an average speed of just five miles an hour due to the poor condition, or complete absence, of available roads.[15] Thirty-seven years after reporting to his military superiors that the country desperately needed better roads, then President Eisenhower signed the Federal-Aid Highway Act of 1956, whose impact can scarcely be comprehended today:

> The Dwight D. Eisenhower System of Interstate and Defense Highways is in place and celebrating its 40th anniversary, must surely be the best investment a nation ever made. Consider this: It has enriched the quality of life for virtually every American. It has saved the lives of

at least 187,000 people. It has prevented injuries to nearly 12 million people. It has returned more than $6 in economic productivity for each $1 it cost. It has positioned the nation for improved international competitiveness. It has permitted the cherished freedom of personal mobility to flourish. It has enhanced international security. It is not an exaggeration, but a simple statement of fact, that the interstate highway system is an engine that has driven 40 years of unprecedented prosperity and positioned the United States to remain the world's pre-eminent power into the 21st century.[16]

1964 Surgeon General's Report on Smoking

When I was a kid, it seemed that every adult smoked cigarettes, and they smoked them everywhere: in elevators, restaurants, airplanes, movie theaters, work places, hospitals, schools, libraries, you name it. Smoking in the 1950s and 1960s was as common as men wearing hats in the 1930s and 1940s, and the peculiar idea of having to go outside to smoke did not exist. When the surgeon general published the first report on the health dangers of smoking on January 11, 1964, smoking was so ingrained in American culture that 200 reporters were locked into the State Department's auditorium for security reasons. His pronouncement justified the precaution: "Cigarette smoking is a health hazard of sufficient importance in the United States to warrant appropriate remedial action."[17]

In 1965, the year after the publication of the Surgeon General's report, more than 53 million Americans—nearly 43% of the population aged 18 and above—"consumed" 71.4 million pounds of smoking tobacco in more than half a trillion cigarettes and other products. Domestic consumption peaked in 1970 at 74.6 million pounds, bottomed out at 14.2 million pounds in 1995, and stood at 18.7 million pounds in 2006.[18] Millions of lives and billions of health-care dollars have been saved in the process.

1965 Head Start

As much as any "Great Society" program, Head Start exemplified President Johnson's towering command over domestic affairs, sometimes forgotten among sadder memories of the calamitous Vietnam War. Head

Start, the longest running antipoverty program in the country, reflected LBJ's belief that "the tyranny of America's poverty cycle could be broken if the emotional, social, health, nutritional and psychological needs of poor children could be met."[19]

Head Start provides comprehensive education, health, nutrition, and parent-involvement services to poor and low-income children and their families. Over the course of more than four decades, Head Start has served more than 22 million pre-school-aged children. While program results have been mixed, Head Start has produced consistent small to moderate gains and the benefits both improved with early participation and varied among racial and ethnic groups.[20]

1968 "Seat Belts Save Lives"

There was a time when seat belts were something kids moved out of the way as they climbed into the back seat. After nearly two decades of "building partnerships, enacting new legislation, conducting strong enforcement, and expanding public information and education," we can see about as clear a demonstration of cause-and-effect between seat belt usage and lives saved as social science can produce (see Exhibit 2.2).

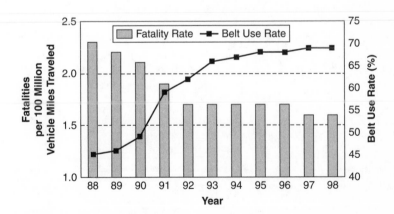

Exhibit 2.2 Rates of Seat Belt Usage and Auto Accident Fatalities
Source: "Trends in Occupant Restraint Use and Fatalities," Process and Outcome Evaluation of the Buckle Up America Initiatives, May 2001, U.S. Department of Transportation, National Highway Traffic Safety Administration, www.nhtsa.gov/people/injury/research/BuckleUp?ii_trends.htm.

The American Dream Recedes

After such a remarkable 40-year run, perhaps it was inevitable that our once-great engines of social progress began to sputter.

In April 1983, the National Commission on Excellence in Education, appointed by Secretary of Education T. H. Bell under President Ronald W. Reagan, released its eye-opening report on the state of American public education, *A Nation at Risk: The Imperative for Educational Reform*. The Commission sought to awaken the country from complacency when it concluded that "the educational foundations of our society are presently being eroded by a rising tide of mediocrity that threatens our very future as a Nation and a people." Although the report condemned the public school system in its entirety, it took special note of the central role that education plays in enabling the American Dream of equal opportunity for all:

> All, regardless of race or class or economic status, are entitled to a fair chance and to the tools for developing their individual powers of mind and spirit to the utmost. This promise means that all children by virtue of their own efforts, competently guided, can hope to attain the mature and informed judgment needed to secure gainful employment, and to manage their own lives, thereby serving not only their own interests but also the progress of society itself.[21]

Nearly 20 years later, it is difficult to keep track of the number of studies and opinion pieces published by education experts of every political stripe under the title "A Nation Still at Risk." (The phrase scores over 1,000 hits on Google.) Joel Klein, the much-admired chancellor of New York City schools, observed that "[u]rban education in the U.S. is broken and it is failing kids who really need the opportunities most."[22] Extensive academic research has demonstrated "just how deeply pervasive and ingrained are the intellectual and academic disadvantages that poor and minority students must overcome to compete with their white and middle-class peers."[23]

America is indeed a "land of opportunity." Social mobility—the ability to transcend restrictions arbitrarily imposed by the happenstance of where, when, and to whom you were born—remains an enduring part of the American saga. In a pluralistic society tied inextricably to an economy grounded in private enterprise, the notion of "winners" and "losers" is easily reconciled with our ideals of fairness by the absence of insurmountable barriers defined by class:

> Mobility is the promise that lies at the heart of the American dream. It is supposed to take the sting out of the widening gulf between the have-mores and the have-nots. There are poor and rich in the United States, of course, the argument goes; but as long as one can become the other, as long as there is something close to equality of opportunity, the differences between them do not add up to class barriers.[24]

The channels of social mobility provide the opportunities for indigent but determined Americans to become self-sufficient. Unfortunately, there is convincing evidence that inequality has increased in recent decades, while economic and social mobility have either stagnated or declined. As a result, the "bedrock American principle ... that all individuals should have the opportunity to succeed on the basis of their own effort, skill, and ingenuity" has become increasingly hollow for tens of millions of disadvantaged Americans.[25]

Education is not the only domain in which the basic tools required to achieve self-sufficiency are denied to large and discrete segments of the American public. A 2002 study published by the Federal Reserve Bank of Boston concluded that "those who are concerned about the future for families at the lower rungs of the income ladder may have cause to worry. Compared to 30 years ago, families at the bottom are poorer relative to families at the top and also a bit more stuck there."[26]

Among other findings, the study looked at the poorest 20% and the second-poorest 20% of families and tracked where they ended up on the economic ladder over the course of two separate decades, 1969 to 1979 and 1988 to 1998. As shown in Exhibit 2.3, we can pose the inequality/mobility question any way we like, but the answer always comes out the same:

- Did the poorest move up? No: In the first decade, 49.4% of the poorest families remained in the poorest quintile, but in the second decade, the percentage stuck at the bottom increased to 53.3%. (See Exhibit 2.3, bars labeled "Poorest to Poorest.")

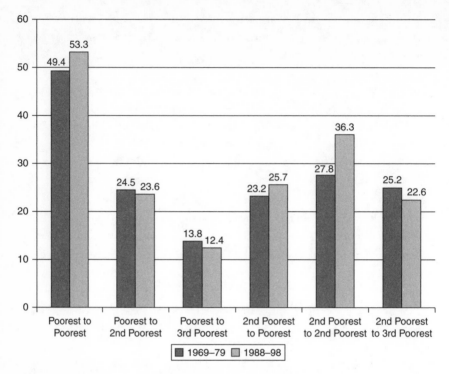

Exhibit 2.3   Income Inequality and Social Immobility
Source: Data from Katherine Bradbury and Jane Katz, Federal Reserve Bank of Boston, "Are Lifetime Incomes Growing More Unequal? Looking at New Evidence on Family Income Mobility," *Regional Review*, 3 Aug. 2007, www.bos.frb.org/economic/nerr/rr2002/q4/issues.pdf.

- Did progress advance? No: In the first decade, 24.5% of the poorest families moved up to the second-poorest group; in the second decade, only 23.6% left the poorest quintile behind. (See "Poorest to 2nd Poorest" bars.)
- Did exceptionalism endure? No: The poorest families entering the third-poorest group declined from 13.8% in the first decade to 12.4% in the second decade. (See "Poorest to 3rd Poorest" bars.)
- Did low-income families avoid poverty? No: Among those who began in the second-poorest group, 23.2% fell into the poorest group from 1969 to 1979, but 25.7% experienced similar declines from 1988 to 1998. (See "2nd Poorest to Poorest" bars.)
- Did low-income families progress? No: The percentage of the second-poorest who remained stuck in that group increased from

27.8% in the first decade to 36.3% in the second. (See "2nd Poorest to 2nd Poorest" bars.) And the percentage of the second poorest who advanced to the third-poorest group fell from 25.2% to 22.6% over the two time periods. (See "2nd Poorest to 3rd Poorest" bars.)

By any measure, compared to their counterparts in the 1970s, poor and low-income families in the 1990s were more likely to remain poor and to become even poorer, and they were less likely to move up the economic ladder. As the "Economic Mobility Project" of The Pew Charitable Trusts put it, "the up-escalator that has historically ensured that each generation would do better than the last may not be working very well."[27]

Eric Schwarz, cofounder and chief executive of Citizen Schools, has painstakingly cataloged the diffusion of educational, economic, and social opportunity over the past 30 years in his *American Dream Scorecard, 1970–2003*.[28] He began by defining the American Dream as "a dream of educational and economic opportunity; of freedom, leisure, and peace; of a secure retirement; and, perhaps most of all, of a better life for their children." After studying the available data on 28 indicators of our national creed of "life, liberty, and the pursuit of happiness," Schwarz concluded that, in marked contrast to the nation's first 200 years, "the final decades of the 20th century were especially discouraging ones for less fortunate Americans and for the American ideal of ever-expanding opportunity." Exhibit 2.4 presents his findings.

The bottom line is sobering: from 1970 through 2003, of the 28 indicia of the American Dream that Schwarz examined, 7 improved, 2 remained the same, 19 declined, and 1 had mixed progress and decline (see Exhibit 2.4).

One recent study disagrees with Schwarz about progress relating to life expectancy:

Those in less-deprived groups experienced a longer life expectancy at each age than their counterparts in more-deprived groups. In 1980–82, the overall life expectancy at birth was 2.8 years longer for the least-deprived group than for the most-deprived group (75.8 vs. 73.0 years). By 1998–2000, the absolute difference in life expectancy at birth had increased to 4.5 years (79.2 vs. 74.7 years).

Exhibit 2.4 American Dream Scorecard, 1970–2003.

Economic Opportunity and Security	
Family Income	Better
Overall Poverty Rate	Worse
Child Poverty Rate	Worse
Distribution of Wealth	Worse
Average of Net Assets (for low- to moderate-income families)	Worse
Readiness for Retirement	Worse
Home ownership	Better
Home ownership (for low-income families)	Worse
Economic Mobility	Worse
Income Gap by Race	Better
Educational Opportunity and Achievement	
Graduation Rates from Public Schools	Worse
Academic Skills	Mixed
Standardized Achievement Test Scores	Worse
Math & Science Skills (compared to other countries)	Worse
Access to College by High School Graduates	Better
College Completion (by income level)	Worse
College Matriculation in the U.S. (compared to other industrialized countries)	Worse
Public Health and Safety	
Infant Mortality	Better
Life Expectancy	Better
Health Insurance	Worse
Children Living with Two Parents	Worse
Teen Parenting Rates	Same
Asthma Rates	Worse
Obesity Rates	Worse
Smoking Rate	Better
Illicit Drug Use	Same
Population in Prison	Worse
Violent Crime	Worse

Source: Eric Schwarz, "Realizing the American Dream: Historical Scorecard, Current Challenges, Future Opportunities," Pre-Reading, A Gathering of Leaders: Social Entrepreneurs and Scale in the 21st Century, 15–18 Feb. 2005, accessed 4 Aug. 2007, www.uwmb.org/livingthedream/Realizing-the-American-Dream.pdf.

Over twenty years, the U.S. life expectancy gap between the rich and poor increased by 60%. The poorest population group had a life expectancy in 2000 that was one year shorter than the life expectancy of the richest group in 1980. There is strong reason to suspect that the widening gap in life expectancy arises from differences in economic opportunity: Increasing inequalities in life expectancy parallel the rising trend in US income inequality and may reflect increasing polarization among deprivation groups with respect to material and social conditions.[29]

Social stagnation seems to have other consequences. A study published by Northeastern University professors James Alan Fox and Marc Swatt reported that murders of African Americans between 14 and 17 years of age increased by 39% from 2001–2002 to 2006–2007, compared to a 7.4% increase in homicides overall. The *Wall Street Journal* reported comments by Professor Fox that recent cuts in youth-focused law enforcement programs that had lowered murder rates in the 1990s "disproportionately affect African-Americans because they are more likely than their white counterparts to come from communities where there is inadequate adult supervision, high rates of single-parent homes, inferior schools and widespread gang activity."[30] It is reasonable to ask whether recent increases in violence are "being perpetrated by those who have just been released from jail without any resources, jobs, or job possibilities?"[31]

At the risk of inducing compassion fatigue, let me offer one more catalog of just how dire the situation has become. In their inspiring new book, *Come on People: On the Path from Victims to Victors*, Drs. Bill Cosby and Alvin F. Poussaint "call . . . on men, all men, the successful and the unsuccessful, the affluent and the poor, the married and the unmarried, to come and claim their children."[32] Although the authors focus on personal, family, and community responsibility, they also recognize that "there are many causes of poverty among African Americans," including "institutional racism, limited job opportunities, low minimum wage, mental illness, physical disabilities, drug and alcohol abuse, lack of a high school diploma, incarceration, and a criminal record."

Their list of grim statistics makes a convincing case that "underclass" is not too strong a word:

- Homicide is the number one cause of death for black men between fifteen and twenty-nine years of age and has been for decades
- In the past several decades, the suicide rate among young black men has increased more than 100 percent
- In some cities, black males have high school dropout rates of more than 50 percent
- Young black men are twice as likely to be unemployed as white, Hispanic, and Asian men
- Although black people make up just 12 percent of the general population, they make up nearly 44 percent of the prison population
- At any given time, as many as one in four of all young black men are in the criminal justice system—in prison or jail, on probation, or on parole
- By the time they reach their midthirties, six out of ten black high school dropouts have spent time in prison
- About one-third of the homeless are black men[33]

Consequences of Social Immobility

In Chapter 1, I claimed that three factors contribute to the foreclosing of the American Dream: (1) a set of "$100 million problems" that are pervasive, incapacitating and, so far, at least, intractable; (2) the inability of the country at large, not just the underclass itself, to sustain these conditions indefinitely; and (3) the inability of government to address the situation on its own. In this chapter, we've discussed the existence of a largely static American underclass that has little or no access to the tools of economic opportunity, and we will consider shortly the barriers to effective governmental responses.

What about the third characteristic: the supposed *unsustainability* of denying basic educational, economic, and social opportunity to millions of Americans?

This contention is harder to prove for the simple reason that, unlike the other two criteria, unsustainability is a prediction about the future that, so far at least, hasn't come true. The United States remains the most powerful country in the world, and most Americans enjoy significantly higher standards of living than most other people around the world, even in many highly developed countries.

The sustainability question concerns the likely consequences of economic inequality and social immobility. If inequality is merely temporary or transitional, or if opportunities for upward mobility mitigate the effects of inequality, then our basic confidence in the fundamental fairness of American society can remain intact. But what if economic inequality becomes compounding? Would we reach a tipping point at which the American Dream became a figment of our collective imagination? Others have begun to pose similar questions:

> Is the recent burst of economic inequality nothing but a temporary consequence of the transition to a new and more productive economy? Can Americans respond to the increasing economic importance of education by going to college in greater numbers and insulating themselves from computerization and global competition? Or will inequality, once under way, prove difficult to reverse? This might happen if the families who have fallen behind economically also fall behind in other ways that will make it more difficult for them, and for their children, to compete with the more advantaged. If, for example, as economic inequality rose over the past twenty-five years, the children of families at the bottom of the income distribution were increasingly likely to live in single-parent families, grow up in distressed neighborhoods, receive substandard child care and health care, attend poor-quality schools, and have less of an opportunity to go to college, then economic inequality might become a self-reinforcing trend.[34]

The kind of untenability that should concern us is not of the cataclysmic, a-giant-meteor-killed-the-dinosaurs variety. Rather, it is more akin to the "boiled frog" problem to which Vice President and Nobel Peace Prize winner Al Gore alludes in his documentary, *An Inconvenient Truth*, in which a frog sitting in a pot of water on a stove doesn't sense danger if the heat is turned up slowly enough. More generally, "if drastic change takes place abruptly, we notice and react to it. If it takes place gradually, over a few generations, we are hardly aware of it, and by the time that we are ready to react, it can be too late."[35]

The situation is much like the new scientific field of "threshold and pattern dynamics" that focuses on "understanding when a vital threshold (to a catastrophe or major change) is crossed—and recognising patterns in the things that are driving it."[36] We're engaged in a similar kind of endeavor here: there are thoughtful voices across the political spectrum asserting that the conditions facing the American underclass cannot be considered either marginal or benign, and that these conditions cannot last indefinitely without repercussions.

On the liberal side of the ledger, *New York Times* columnist Bob Herbert has provided some of the most consistently cogent analysis of the precarious existence confronting the underclass:

> There comes a time when people are supposed to get angry. The rights and interests of black people in the U.S. have been under assault for the longest time, and in the absence of an effective counterforce, that assault has only grown more brutal.

> Have you looked at the public schools lately? Have you looked at the prisons? Have you looked at the legions of unemployed blacks roaming the neighborhoods of big cities across the country? These jobless African-Americans, so many of them men, are so marginal in the view of the wider society, so insignificant, so invisible, they aren't even counted in the government's official jobless statistics.[37]

Harvard sociology professor Orlando Patterson describes the situation in similar terms:

> The circumstances that far too many African-Americans face—the lack of paternal support and discipline; the requirement that single mothers work regardless of the effect on their children's care; the hypocritical refusal of conservative politicians to put their money where their mouths are on family values; the recourse by male youths to gangs as parental substitutes; the ghetto-fabulous culture of the streets; the lack of skills among black men for the jobs and pay they want; the hyper-segregation of blacks into impoverished inner-city neighborhoods—all interact perversely with the prison system that simply makes hardened criminals of nonviolent drug offenders and spits out angry men who are unemployable, unreformable, and unmarriageable, closing the vicious circle.[38]

Jeff Howard, founder of The Efficacy Institute, says "[b]ad public schools destroy the only hope for those left behind."[39] Amherst College president Anthony M. Marx goes a step further, finding implications for the American mainstream:

> If economic mobility continues to shut down, not only will we be losing the talent and leadership we need, but we will face a risk of a society of alienation and unhappiness. Even the most privileged among us will suffer the consequences of people not believing in the American dream.[40]

Some conservative commentators express similar concerns. David Brooks, now a *New York Times* columnist, was senior editor at the neo-conservative *Weekly Standard*, plays the conservative foil to über-liberal Mark Shields on the *News Hour with Jim Lehrer*, and edited the anthology *Backward and Upward: The New Conservative Writing* (Vintage Books 1996). Brooks recognizes "inequality is obviously increasing," and, more portentously, "Just when it needs a more skilled work force, the U.S. is getting a less skilled one. This is already taking a bite out of productivity growth, and the problem will get worse."[41]

New York Times business columnist Ben Stein, a self-described "lawyer, writer, actor, and economist" (best known for his role as the clueless teacher in *Ferris Bueller's Day Off*), was a speechwriter and lawyer for Presidents Nixon and Ford, both of whom he continues to admire. Stein is a true believer in American capitalism, but he's no blinkered apologist: "A free society with as much inequality as ours, with inequality growing as rapidly as ours, is not a society that will last, and this society is far too beautiful to lose."[42] Recalling that "one of the causes of the French Revolution was the sad truth that the aristocracy was not taxed at all, while the workers and burghers were taxed highly," Stein asks, "Is this our future?"[43] When an old-school Republican such as Ben Stein thinks that inequality is getting away from us and that current fiscal policies could lead us "down the road to the Bastille," those concerns deserve a place in our national dialogue.

Two conservative think tanks, The American Enterprise Institute and The Heritage Foundation, issued a joint report with the more liberal Brookings Institution and The Urban Institute, which found that 33% of

Americans are "downwardly mobile." For them, the report concluded, "the American Dream seems to be out of reach."[44]

Moreover, there seems to be a pronounced tinge of hostility in many news stories. Jeff Howard writes that school choice proponents "focus on winning the hearts and minds of disappointed, angry parents desperate to save their kids from lives on the margins of society."[45] Demonstrations and counterdemonstrations against illegal immigration proliferate in cities featuring "jaw-jutting shouting matches" and nervous police who "counted down the minutes on the hour-and-a-half city permit for the rally."[46] Incidents like the debacle in post-Katrina New Orleans, the racial hostilities exposed by the Jena Six explosion in Louisiana, rising murder rates in cities like Philadelphia, the appearance of armed vigilante groups at the Mexican border, and headlines such as "Colleges See Flare in Racial Incidents" and "Teens Say They're Victims of Gang Violence at School" give one pause about whether these are early warning signs of impending seismic shifts.[47]

More Complex Solutions

I grew up in Eisenhower's postwar America when a working-class father with just a high school education could earn a middle-manager's salary and feed and clothe a family of four, buy a small house with a loan under the GI Bill, help send two kids to public colleges, and have a comfortable retirement, with his wife staying home with the kids for good measure. Today, "two-thirds of new jobs being created require higher education or advanced training."[48]

Even without pretending there were "good old days" when everything was great for everyone all the time, we can still recognize that the problems we face today as an organized society are more entrenched and have more moving parts than similar problems of past decades. Consider how President Bill Clinton described what it took to make welfare reform work:

> The success of welfare reform was bolstered by other anti-poverty initiatives, including the doubling of the earned-income tax credit in 1993 for lower-income workers; the 1997 Balanced Budget Act, which included $3 billion to move long-term welfare recipients and

low-income, noncustodial fathers into jobs; the Access to Jobs initiative, which helped communities create innovative transportation services to enable former welfare recipients and other low-income workers to get to their new jobs; and the welfare-to-work tax credit, which provided tax incentives to encourage businesses to hire long-term welfare recipients. I also signed into law the toughest child-support enforcement in history, doubling collections; an increase in the minimum wage in 1997; a doubling of federal financing for child care, helping parents look after 1.5 million children in 1998; and a near doubling of financing for Head Start programs.[49]

The need for such comprehensive and multidimensional approaches to pervasive social problems is more the rule than the exception. As a rather different example of the same phenomenon, a 2006 report by the International Fertilizer Development Center summarized what it would take "[t]o bring a green revolution to Africa": "a functioning road network, credit for farmers, extension agents to teach new methods, better irrigation, as well as development of retailers to sell fertilizers and improved seed varieties in rural areas."[50] The Rockefeller and Gates foundations formed the Alliance for a Green Revolution in Africa, which focuses "on eight interconnected areas: Seeds, Soils, Water, Markets, Agricultural Education, African Farmer Knowledge, Policies, and Monitoring and Evaluation."[51]

It may be that we won't ever again see the kind of violence that shook the nation during the civil rights era of the 1960s. But can we really expect another generation of black and brown, urban and rural, or poor and low-income families to accept indefinite exclusion from the basic opportunities by which the rest of us become self-sufficient? Perhaps there won't be uprisings in the streets again, but we shouldn't delude ourselves into thinking that millions of uneducated, jobless, and hopeless Americans will accept indefinitely a status quo that serves them so poorly.

Governmental Response Mechanisms

The central concern of this book—the structural barriers that inhibit our most effective nonprofit organizations from producing transformative social impact—requires us to think about the changing capacities and roles of the public sector. For now, the salient point is that government ain't what it used to be. As Stephen Goldsmith and William D. Eggers observe in their important book, *Governing by Network: The New Shape of the Public Sector*, "New Deal-style initiatives, in which government assumes the dominant service delivery role, have become increasingly rare, especially for newly developed programs."[52] Explanations aren't difficult to come by.

Process Failures

The political process is less productive than it used to be as an instrument for reconciling competing policy interests. One noteworthy example is the inability of Congress to enact national health insurance legislation, even though seven out of ten Americans support it. The *New Yorker's* Hendrik Hertzberg explained the problem in this way:

> The Clintons blew it last time, but they weren't the first to break their picks against the unyielding granite of the American political system. Every Democratic President since Truman has been elected on a platform of national health insurance, and, in spite of public support for the idea by majorities as big as those in Europe, every one of them has failed to get it enacted. In this country, elections are just the beginning. To get to the finish line, a big reform has to run a gantlet of three independently elected "governments"—not just the Presidency but also the House and the Senate, all the members of which are elected independently of one another, too. Besides all this, the committees of Congress, where most business actually gets done, provide plenty of dark corners where determined, well-financed, well-organized special interests can make short work of an obvious but amorphous majority will.[53]

When 70% of the country wants the federal government to do something, the political system should be able to respond, but it can't. The health-care impasse is symptomatic of a larger dysfunctionality:

> Partisanship particularly increased after the 1994 elections and then the appearance of the first unified Republican government since the 1950s. Now it is tribal warfare. The consequences are deadly serious. Party and ideology routinely trump institutional interests and responsibilities.

Regular order—the set of rules, norms, and traditions designed to ensure a fair and transparent process—was the first casualty. The results: No serious deliberation. No meaningful oversight of the executive. A culture of corruption. And grievously flawed policy formulation and implementation.[54]

Ruthless Demographics

Within the next two decades, more than 70 million Baby Boomers will stop working and paying taxes, and start collecting taxpayer-funded benefits, with significant but uncertain consequences for the federal budget:

> That impending wave of retirements has become a source of concern for two reasons. First, the population of retirees will grow much more quickly than the taxpaying workforce, at a time when average benefits per retiree are expected to continue rising. Those developments will place severe and mounting budgetary pressures on the federal government. Second, some researchers have questioned whether many boomers are accumulating enough wealth to pay for an adequate retirement. Not only could inadequate saving leave boomers poorly prepared, but it could compound the government's budgetary problems by limiting the growth of investment, productivity, and wages (which drive federal revenues).[55]

Newsweek's Robert J. Samuelson envisions "a profound transformation of the nature of government: commitments to the older population are slowly overwhelming other public goals; the national government is becoming mainly an income-transfer mechanism from younger workers to older retirees."[56] Keep in mind that these governmental budgetary pressures will arise during the same decades for which the Boston College Center on Wealth and Philanthropy has projected an intergenerational transfer of *private* wealth of between $10 trillion to $40 trillion.[57]

Retrenchment on the Horizon

Looming fiscal realities will make it increasingly difficult for the public sector to meet these growing challenges. In Philadelphia, black community leaders have called for 10,000 volunteers to patrol the streets to quell unprecedented levels of violence that have overwhelmed police resources.[58] The Defense Department has had to pay over $100 million in bonuses to dissuade veteran Green Berets and Navy SEALs from decamping to corporate employers such as Blackwater USA.[59] According to investment bank Credit Suisse, state and local governments owe *$1.5 trillion* in unfunded liabilities for their workers' health-care and pension benefits, "presenting difficult challenges for the U.S. economy."[60]

In such overextended times, government is much more likely to take anemic half measures than pursue the kinds of institutional transformations that are needed to open doors of opportunity to the underclass:

> The core problem is that our education and training systems were built for another era, an era in which most workers needed only a rudimentary education. It is not possible to get where we have to go by patching that system. There is not enough money available at any level of our intergovernmental system to fix this problem by spending more on the system we have. We can get where we must go only by changing the system itself.[61]

Consider, for example, governmental support for preschool programs that prepare three- and four-year-olds to enter kindergarten ready to learn (see Exhibit 2.5). At a time when calls for "universal pre-K" are becoming widespread, and we know what it costs to provide effective

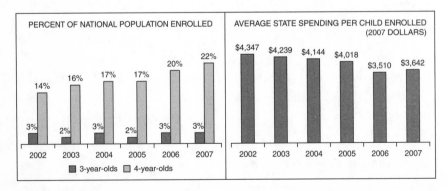

Exhibit 2.5 Preschool Spending
Source: W. Steven Barnett et al., "The State of Preschool 2007," "National Profile" chart (N.p.: The Pew Charitable Trusts, 2007), p. 4, http://nieer.org/yearbook/pdf/yearbook.pdf.

programs, higher enrollment levels have meant lower per-capita funding, with a 16.5% reduction per child from 2002 to 2006.

Peter Orszag, director of the Congressional Budget Officer (and subsequently director of the White House Office of Management and Budget), once testified that "one of the most significant risks that we as a nation are facing that every serious budget analyst looking at the long-term picture agrees with is that we are on an unsustainable fiscal path."[62]

Changing Roles

Goldsmith and Eggers foresee "a new model of government" in which public sector actors increasingly become "generators of public value within the web of multiorganizational, multigovernmental, and multisectoral relationships," notably including the nonprofit sector among government's key partners. They are not alone. Kirsten Gronjberg and Lester Salamon advocate "more sustained efforts by government to activate and modulate the network structures under which public policy initiatives are now carried out." Indeed, they go much further, urging us to find the virtue in an inevitable necessity:

> . . . a new paradigm of government-nonprofit interaction is needed, one that treats the collaboration between government and the non-profit sector not as a regrettable necessity but as a highly positive feature of a modern, pluralistic society that encourages active engagement by all sectors in the resolution of societal problems.[63]

Could federal or state government build an interstate highway system today? Eradicate a communicable disease? Rescue millions from poverty? Reflecting on the recent collapse of the Interstate 35W bridge in Minneapolis, a *Washington Post* commentator opined that "the United States seems to have become the superpower that can't tie its own shoelaces."[64]

For present purposes, we don't have to resolve the contentious questions about what the proper role of government should be or the extent to which fiscal and other taxpayer-funded resources should be devoted to social ends. It is enough for mature adults to recognize that the governmental institutions that achieved such impressive social progress in decades past are no longer capable, on their own, of doing so again in the same way or to the same extent. Instead, "U.S. nonprofits are being asked to take on an increasing share of society's most important and difficult work."[65]

As this shift gains momentum, policymakers might look more closely at the opportunity cost of charitable tax deductions. The rationale for giving tax breaks for charitable donations is based on leverage:

> When an individual contributes $100 to a charity, the nation loses about $40 in tax revenue, but the charity gets $100, which it uses to provide services to society. The immediate social benefit, then is 250% of the lost tax revenue.[66]

What if, as the current economic crisis deepens, the validity of the assumed 250% leverage is called into question? If we attribute just $1 million in donations to each of the 50,000 or so mid-cap social enterprises, that represents $50 billion in productive capacity. But at a time when the federal government is incurring extraordinary levels of debt to forestall further economic decline, we cannot afford $50 billion of funding to accomplish only, say, $25 billion of impact. The problem is not that successful nonprofits waste money but that they lack the capacity to perform to their full potential. The ordinary response of social entrepreneurs—trying to make the hamster run even faster—is hardly a promising or enduring response to the question of whether taxpayers get maximum value from charitable funding compared to alternative uses of the money.

Perhaps it is always time to look for new solutions to our most difficult and important problems, but, these days, the alignment of need and opportunity seems particularly propitious:

> Today, with government cutbacks escalating, nonprofits are more often being called on to provide many of the services that the public sector has traditionally provided, including healthcare, social services, and job training. Concurrently, the market in which nonprofits function is progressively more complex and, in some cases, populated by for-profit competitors. In addition, public and private funding priorities and levels have changed—and continue to change—very quickly, along with shifting regulatory and policy environments. The communities in

which nonprofits operate have also changed and become more diverse, while constituents expect more accountability, and technology continues to suggest new ways of working. All of these changes require that nonprofits learn and adapt quickly. This necessitates a vibrant, robust infrastructure that gathers, aggregates, and circulates information in real time.[67]

The Challenge of Producing Transformative Social Impact

Allow me to sum up the argument to this point. During the middle four decades of the twentieth century, the United States effectively subscribed to Henry Roger Seager's "program of social reform" of "protecting wage-earning families which have developed standards of living from losing them, and in helping wage-earning families without standards to gain them." The resulting accomplishments in spreading the blessings of prosperity to a vast and secure middle class exceeded anything ever seen in modern times. By contrast, the past nearly four decades have been years of stagnation for the middle class and significant decline at lower socioeconomic levels. Two distinctly American levers of change that contributed to past accomplishments—economic mobility and representative democracy—have failed to correct the situation, calling into question not only their own efficacy, but the continuing viability of the American Dream itself. The established means of attaining self-sufficiency appear to be slipping away and there may be early warning signs that the social and economic order itself is under extreme stress.

My point is not to describe a hopeless situation; rather, it is quite the opposite. We have extraordinary private means and ingenuity to bring to bear on this complex and difficult state of affairs. As President Clinton put it:

Today we have more power as private citizens to do public good, both at home and around the world, than citizens in all of human history have ever had. We have the means, we have the knowledge, and there are willing partners in unlimited numbers on every continent.[68]

However, we cannot hope to effectively deploy those resources unless we clearly understand the nature and extent of the problems before us, so that we can confront them with a response that is commensurate to the severity of the risks they pose to the country at large. And so, I submit, our search for solutions must begin with the premise that I've tried to establish here, namely that these "$100 million problems" are ones that society can no longer tolerate. Even if it isn't necessary that we take Wendy Kopp's admonition to help "all children" literally in order to reinvigorate the American Dream, a compelling case exists that we have to do a heck of a lot better than 1 or 2%.

Given the pressing need for change and the formidable difficulties we face, what is it going to take to produce systemic change to an extent that leads to transformative social impact? How will it differ from what social entrepreneurs and funders, with all their innovation and success, are already doing?

Candor requires us to concede that the answer to the question, "How can the nonprofit sector bring about systemic change?" is that we don't know yet. What we need is a way to figure it out. As Project Hope's Sister Margaret Leonard observed, "We may think we understand how to organize a more just society, but we only know by experimenting and evaluating the effects of our experiment."[69]

Transformation

Significant *organizational* change—that is, change *below* the system level—is itself extremely difficult to pull off. After analyzing more than 100 companies that tried to transform themselves into more formidable competitors, Harvard Business School professor John P. Kotter concluded that a few had been either "very successful" or "utter failures," but "[m]ost fall somewhere in between, with a distinct tilt toward the lower end of the scale."[70] Kotter isolated eight major kinds of errors that prevent organizations from accomplishing transformation:

1. Not establishing a great enough sense of urgency
2. Not creating a powerful enough guiding coalition
3. Lacking a vision
4. Undercommunicating the vision by a factor of ten
5. Not removing obstacles to the new vision

6. Not systematically planning for and creating short-term wins
7. Declaring victory too soon
8. Not anchoring changes in the corporation's culture

The potential for these kinds of errors becomes magnified when we move up to the *systems* level and complexity increases exponentially. Consider the graphical depiction (see Exhibit 2.6) developed by MIT professor Jay W. Forrester of a "world model [that] is a beginning basis for analyzing the effect of changing population and economic growth over the next 50 years."[71] The vertigo-inducing model incorporates 48 different variables covering birth rate, capital investment, death rate, food production, land area, material standard of living, natural resource extraction, population, pollution, and quality of life.

Forrester cautions that "[b]ecause dynamic behavior of social systems is not understood, government programs often cause exactly the reverse of desired results." He gives the example of a municipal program to increase low-cost housing that attracted an influx of new residents "until their numbers sufficiently exceed the available jobs that the standard of living declines far enough to stop further inflow."

More generally, he describes how "[e]motionally inspired efforts often fall into one of three traps set for us by the nature of social systems":

> The programs are apt to address symptoms rather than causes and attempt to operate through points in the system that have little leverage for change; the characteristic of systems whereby a policy change has the opposite effect in the short run from the effect in the long run can eventually cause deepening difficulties after a sequence of short-term actions; and the effect of a program can be along an entirely different direction than was originally expected, so that suppressing one symptom only causes trouble to burst forth at another point.[72]

Public health initiatives raise similar issues of transformational complexity. After the Bush administration curtailed federal funding for stem cell research, California established a $3 billion fund dedicated to "turning stem cells into cures." The flowchart depicting how the state planned to realize that vision (Exhibit 2.7) is only somewhat less forbidding than Professor Forrester's.

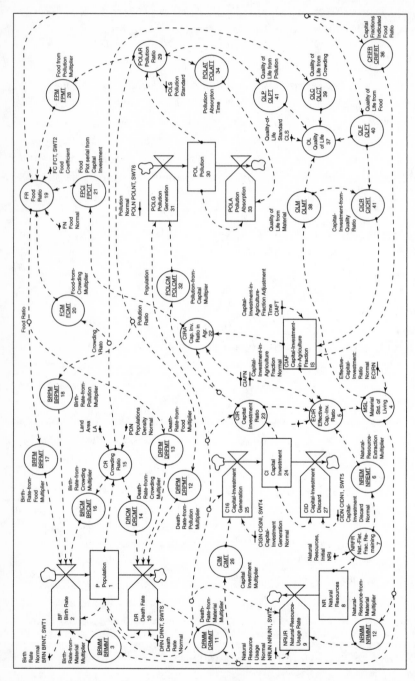

Exhibit 2.6 Basic World Model Behavior Showing the Mode in which Industrialization and Population Are Suppressed by Falling Natural Resources

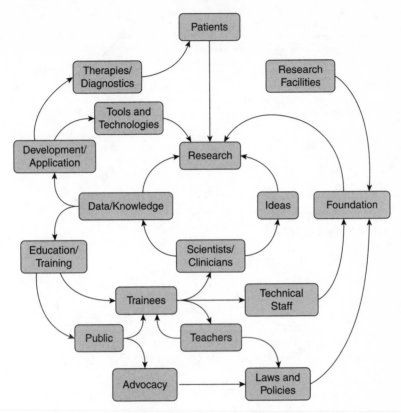

Exhibit 2.7   California Stem Cell Research Development Process
Source: California Institute for Regenerative Medicine, "Draft Scientific Strategic Plan," October 2008, www.cirm.ca.gov.

Moving Parts

Inasmuch as systems comprise the interactions of numerous constituent organizations, they generally have more elements in play than single organizations do. For example, the system of social capital markets refers to the collection of financial institutions, instruments, stakeholders, and processes by and through which funds flow to support the development, operation, and growth of nonprofits.

To understand the inherent complexity of systemic change, let's consider first the major operating units of a generic business organization. Harvard professor Michael Porter showed that business organizations create value by effectively coordinating five "primary activities" and four

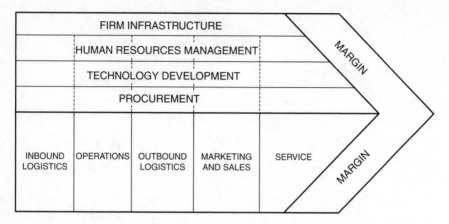

Exhibit 2.8   Value Chain Analysis
Source: Michael E. Porter, "Value Chain Analysis," Chart 1, June 1998, in *Competitive Advantage: Creating and Sustaining Superior Performance.* (New York: Free Press, 1998).

"support activities" that generate profit "margin," that is, extra value beyond the combined cost of the inputs (see Exhibit 2.8).

Dagmar Recklies extended Porter's model to show how an organization's own value chain must intersect with the value chains of its suppliers, channels, and customers (see Exhibit 2.9).

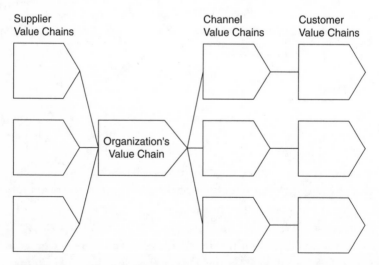

Exhibit 2.9   Whole Value System
Source: Dagmar Recklies, "The Value Chain," www.themanager.org/models/Value Chain.htm.

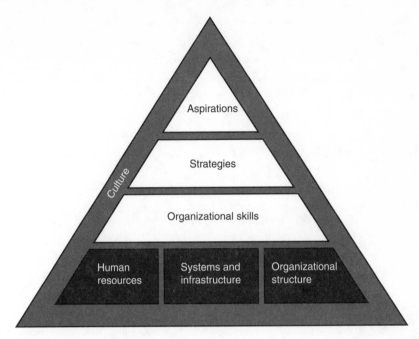

Exhibit 2.10   Nonprofit Capacity Framework
Source: McKinsey & Company and Venture Philanthropy Partners, "Effective Capacity Building in Nonprofit Organizations," 2001, www.vppartners.org/learning/reports/capacity/elements.pdf.

Although nonprofit organizations generally aren't in the business of generating "profit" margins, they are interested in creating what economists call "surplus value" in the form of improved social benefits. They do so in ways that are analogous to Porter's model. For example, when New Profit, Inc. evaluates prospective and current portfolio organizations, it considers (among other things) such "organizational competencies" as finance, recruiting and managing talent, marketing, fundraising, technology, policy, program evaluation, corporate partnerships, and innovation and business development. Venture Philanthropy Partners and McKinsey & Company have identified "seven elements of nonprofit capacity" (see Exhibit 2.10) with a detailed "capacity assessment grid".

Alignment and Synchronization

Given the similarities in the ways that business organizations and nonprofit organizations create value, it makes sense to ask if there's a model of nonprofit networks that's analogous to the kinds of value networks within which successful businesses operate. It turns out that it's rather difficult to find models for networks of nonprofits and other organizations that align their efforts to produce system-wide impacts. For a variety of reasons I'll explore in Chapter 4, this is largely uncharted territory.

When we consider the challenge of producing value with partners outside the organization's own boundaries, we can see that there are fundamental similarities between for-profit and nonprofit organizations. For example, Robert S. Kaplan and David P. Norton draw this analogy between corporate enterprises with multiple strategic business units (SBUs), government agencies, and large-cap nonprofits:

> Public-sector and nonprofit organizations face similar issues. The Department of Defense must integrate the efforts of large, powerful units (such as the Army, Navy, Air Force, Marines, and Defense Logistics Agency) that are well funded and have years of autonomous operation and trading. The Royal Canadian Mounted Police must align its diverse functional and regional units, including national police units dealing with international crime and terrorism, remote units that promote health and safety in aboriginal communities, and contract policing units that provide provinces and municipalities with localized traditional police services. The American Diabetes Association and the Red Cross must unite a multinational network of decentralized units under a common brand and philosophy.[73]

Although Kaplan and Norton focus primarily on aligning separate SBUs housed under common corporate ownership, they also identified "sources of enterprise synergy" that could inform our thinking about ways that multiple but independent mid-cap nonprofits can drive transformative social impact (see Exhibit 2.11).

In a similar vein, Goldsmith and Eggers focus on network "initiatives deliberately undertaken by government to accomplish public goals, with measurable performance goals, assigned responsibilities to each partner, and structured information flow."[74] They envision a government-as-integrator model in which "a public agency can use its positional authority and perceived impartiality to bring the different parties together, coordinate their activities, and resolve any disputes" (see Exhibit 2.12), as well as alternative models in which a lead government

Exhibit 2.11   Sources of Enterprise Synergy.

ENTERPRISE SCORECARD	SOURCES OF ENTERPRISE-DERIVED VALUE (STRATEGIC THEMES)
Financial Synergies	
"How can we increase the value of our SBU portfolio?"	Internal capital management: Create synergy through effective management of internal capital and labor markets.
	Corporate brand: Integrate a diverse set of businesses around a single brand, promoting common values or themes.
Customer Synergies	
"How can we share the customer interface to increase total customer?"	Cross-selling: Create value by cross-selling a broad range of products and services from several business units.
	Common value proposition: Create a consistent buying experience, conforming to corporate standards at multiple outlets.
Internal Process Synergies	
"How can we manage SBU processes to achieve economies of scale or value-chain integration"?	Shared services: Create economies of scale by sharing the systems, facilities, and personnel in critical support processes.
	Value-chain integration: Create value by integrating contiguous processes in the industry value chain.
Learning and Growth Synergies	
"How can we develop and share our intangible assets?"	Intangible assets: Share competency in the development of human, information, and organization capital.

Source: Robert S. Kaplan and David P. Norton, *Alignment: Using the Balanced Scorecard to Create Corporate Synergies* (Boston: Harvard Business School Press, 2006), p. 11.

agency oversees a prime contractor or a third-party private contractor acts as the integrator.

Of course, managing networks of discrete organizations is not the same thing as managing a single organization of comparable size, whether in the public, private, or nonprofit sectors. For one thing, most

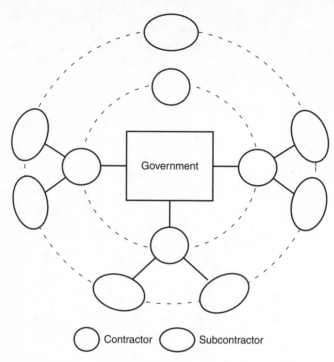

Exhibit 2.12   Government as Integrator.
Source: Goldsmith and Eggers, *Governing by Network,* p. 83.

organizations don't have the internal skills or expertise to manage strategic alignments with other organizations:

> Alignment, like the other strategy execution processes, crosses organi-
> zational boundaries. To be executed effectively, alignment requires the
> integration and cooperation of individuals from various organizational
> units. This poses a dilemma because most organizations have no natural
> home for cross-business processes.[75]

The same holds true for public sector enterprises:

> As more and more [government] agencies forge partnerships with
> third parties, agency performance will largely depend on how well
> the partnerships are managed. To achieve high performance in this
> environment, governments will need to develop core capabilities in a
> host of areas where today they have scant expertise.[76]

Exhibit 2.13 Cross-Boundary Initiatives.

Sponsor	Project
British Columbia Centre for Excellence in HIV/AIDS	New strategy to use highly active antiretroviral therapy to reduce disease transmission rates and prevent HIV
California Institute for Regenerative Medicine	"Turning stem cells into cures"
Faster Cures/The Center for Accelerating Medical Solutions	Accelerating medical research process to find new treatments for deadly and debilitating diseases
Global Water Challenge	Network of nongovernmental NGO partners, government officials, and community stakeholders to develop sustainable water and sanitation projects
Greater Kansas City Community Foundation	A strategy for higher education in Kansas City
Hawaii Department of Health	Statewide health improvement initiative funded by tobacco litigation settlement
Lancet Global Mental Health Group	Call for global health community, donors, multilateral agencies, and other mental health stakeholders to scale up coverage of services for mental health disorders, especially in low- and middle-income countries
Lumina Foundation for Education	An $88 million experiment to raise transfer and graduate rates of community colleges
Pathways Mapping Initiative	A resource for assembling and disseminating actionable intelligence about "what works" in community-based interventions for children and families
Public Education Leadership Project	A coherent framework for creating successful strategies and organizations to manage urban school districts

There are some real-world examples of noncorporate networks from which we can begin to extrapolate useful models for the nonprofit sector. I will consider their teachings in later chapters; for now, Exhibit 2.13 provides a summary of several such cross-boundary initiatives.

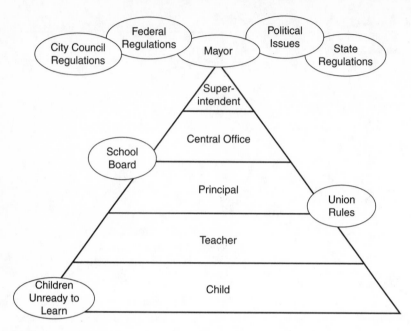

Exhibit 2.14   Educational Decision Makers Face Challenges on Different Levels
Source: Robert Waldron, Jumpstart presentation, A Gathering of Leaders, New Profit Inc., Mohonk
Mountain House, 15 Feb. 2006.

Let me wrap up this discussion about the severity and scope of the
problems we face by offering one useful depiction of a network response
to the challenges facing public education. At the 2005 Gathering of
Leaders convened by New Profit, Inc., Rob Waldron, former chief executive of Jumpstart ("Working toward the day every child in America
enters school prepared to succeed"), presented "an integrated approach
for NGO's [nongovernmental organizations] to lead systemic change."[77]
He observed first that "educational decision makers face challenges on
different levels," which he mapped as shown in Exhibit 2.14.

He then saw that "social entrepreneurs have already created programs
to address isolated issues" relating to those challenges (see Exhibit 2.15)
and concluded that we need to "combine these programs to form a
comprehensive support system for children," as depicted in Exhibit 2.16.

There are signs that more integrated approaches to stubborn problems are beginning to take hold. For example, the New Commission
on the Skills of the American Workforce has proposed a realignment

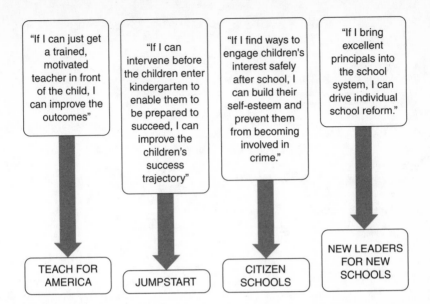

Exhibit 2.15 Social Entrepreneurs Have Already Created Programs to Address Isolated Issues
Source: Robert Waldron, Jumpstart presentation, A Gathering of Leaders, New Profit Inc., Mohonk Mountain House, 15 Feb. 2006.

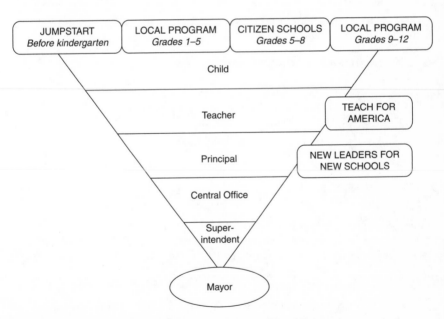

Exhibit 2.16 A Comprehensive Support System for Children
Source: Robert Waldron, Jumpstart presentation, A Gathering of Leaders, New Profit Inc., Mohonk Mountain House, 15 Feb. 2006.

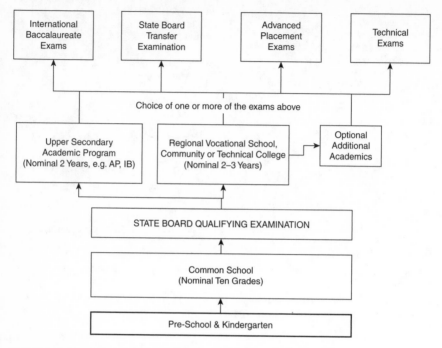

Exhibit 2.17   Schema for Student Progression through the System

Source: New Commission on the Skills of the American Workforce, "Tough Choices or Tough Times," National Center on Education and the Economy (2007), p. 11, www.skillscommission.org/pdf/exec_sum/ToughChoices_EXECSUM.pdf.

of public school components (see Exhibit 2.17) that includes preschool programs, which would represent a valuable extension of the standard K–12 template. The expanded system also might benefit, however, from other complementary social sector offerings, such as after-school, family support, college access, and workforce development programs like those offered by Citizen Schools, BELL, College Summit, Raising a Reader, and YearUp.

The difficulty of coordination is exacerbated by the fact, as Katherine Fulton and Andrew Blau of the Monitor Group presciently observe, that "philanthropy itself is not a system":

Individual institutions and givers in philanthropy are not in any sense reliant on one another; they exist independently and can act without much reference to what others do. Thus, there is no system where actors must respond to one another, adapt to one another, or learn from one another. This is not to say that donors and foundations don't relate or learn from one another at all. They do, but only to the extent that they choose to. And they also compete with one another—for ideas, reputation, and credit, which can discourage the free exchange of ideas and lead to fragmentation of effort and isolation.[78]

The Wallace Foundation offers an inspiring counterexample. Starting in 2003, the foundation adopted "a novel approach to creating better OST [out-of-school-time] opportunities for more children" in which it selected five cities "to develop and test a city-wide approach that brought to the table top leaders from government, schools and the OST provider community to plan well-coordinated ways of providing high-quality OST to more young people, especially those with the highest needs." Exhibit 2.18 maps the elements, interactions, and outcomes of their design.

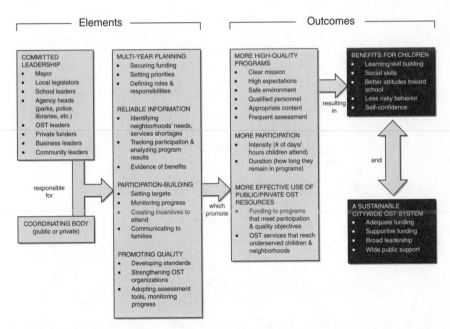

Exhibit 2.18 Citywide Approach to Building Sustainable, High-Quality Out-of-School-Time Opportunities

Source: The Wallace Foundation, "A Place to Grow and Learn: A Citywide Approach to Building and Sustaining Out-of-School Time Learning Opportunities," February 2008, www.wallacefoundation.org/SiteCollectionDocuments/WF/Knowledge%20Center/Attachments/PDF/APlacetoGrowandLearn.pdf.

Assuming that I've made a convincing case that the United States can't allow these kinds of problems to persist, and assuming further that Waldron and others have it right (which I believe they do) about what it will take to meaningfully address those problems, the next question becomes: "Why can't we deliver those solutions now?" Let us turn to that important question.

Notes

1. Henry Rogers Seager, *Social Insurance: A Program of Social Reform* (New York: Macmillan, 1910).

2. Shirley Sagawa, "Fulfilling the Promise: Social Entrepreneurs and Action Tanking in a New Era of Entrepreneurship," prereading materials, Gathering of Leaders, 15–17 Feb. 2006, www.sagawajospin.com/Fulfilling%20the%20Promise_Sagawa_February%202006.pdf.

3. James Truslow Adams, *The Epic of America* (Buchbeschreibung: International Collectors Library 1931), p. 404.

4. Joanna Schneider Zangrando and Robert L. Zangrando, "Black Protest: A Rejection of the American Dream," *Journal of Black Studies* 1, no. 2 (December 1970): 141–159.

5. William Safire, *New Political Dictionary* (New York: Random House, 1993).

6. Tennessee Valley Authority, "From the New Deal to a New Century," 4 Oct. 2007, www.tva.gov/abouttva/history.htm.

7. Tennessee Valley Authority, "The Great Experiment," 15 Apr. 2008, www.tva.gov/heritage/experiment/index.htm.

8. Tennessee Valley Authority, "From the New Deal to a New Century."

9. United States Social Security Agency, The Social Security Act (Act of August 14, 1935) [H. R. 7260], Social Security Online, www.ssa.gov/history/35actpre.html.

10. Edward Humes, "Nixon and Kennedy, Bonnie and Clyde: The G.I. Bill and the Arts," *Over Here: How the G.I. Bill Transformed the American Dream* (Orlando, FL: Harcourt, 2006). CaliforniaAuthors.com. 4 Oct. 2007, www.californiaauthors.com/excerpt-humes-3.shtml.

11. Bill Gates Sr. and Chuck Collins, "A GI Bill for the Next Generation," Chuck Collins Online, www.chuckcollinsonline.com/estate-taxation-and-tax-fairne.

12. Humes, "Nixon and Kennedy, Bonnie and Clyde."

13. Beth Sokol, "Fear of Polio in the 1950s," *The Beat Begins: America in the 1950s*, www.honors.umd.edu/HONR269J/projects/sokol.html.

14. "Polio," *Morbidity and Mortality Weekly Report* 42, no. 53 (1994): 83–88; 50, no. 53 (2003): 119.

15. United States Congress, Subcommittee on Highways, Transit, and Pipelines of the Committee on Transportation and Infrastructure, "Celebrating 50 Years: The Eisenhower Interstate Highway System," House of Representatives, 109th Congress, 2nd Sess. (Washington, DC: GPO, 2006), pp. 26–27, http://worldcat.org/oclc/122257134.

16. Wendell Cox and Jean Love, "40 Years of the U.S. Interstate Highway System: An Analysis of the Best Investment a Nation Ever Made," *The Public Purpose* (June 1996). American Highway Users Alliance, www.publicpurpose.com/freeway1.htm.

17. Tobacco.org, "1st Surgeon General Report: Smoking and Health" (1964), www.tobacco.org/resources/history/1964_01_11_1st_sgr.html.

18. Gene Borio, "Tobacco Timeline: The Twentieth Century 1950–1999—The Battle Is Joined," Tobacco.org, 2003, www.tobacco.org/resources/history/Tobacco_History20-2.html.

19. James Panero, "Brought to You by the Letter S," *New York Times Book Review*, 26 Dec. 2008, www.nytimes.com/2008/12/28/books/review/Panero-t.html?_r=1&scp=5&sq=sesame%20street%20book%20review&st=cse.

20. "Head Start," Wikipedia, en.wikipedia.org/wiki/Head_Start.

21. National Commission on Excellence in Education and U.S. Dept. of Education, "A Nation at Risk: The Imperative for Education Reform," 3 Aug. 2007, www.ed.gov/pubs/NatAtRisk/index.html.

22. Teach For America, "Teach For America Benefit Raises $860,000," 3 Aug. 2007, www.teachforamerica.org/assets/documents/2003_benefit.pdf.

23. Paul Tough, "What It Takes to Make a Student," *New York Times Magazine*, 26 Nov. 2006, accessed 3 Aug. 2007, www.nytimes.com/2006/11/26/magazine/26tough.html?ex=1186200000&en=934b24d030fcfb11&ei=5070.

24. Janny Scott and David Leonhardt, "Shadowy Lines That Still Divide," *New York Times*, 15 May 2005, www.nytimes.com/2005/05/15/national/class/OVERVIEW-FINAL.html?ex=1186286400&en=af046ea306570594&ei=5070.

25. Ben Bernanke, Remarks, Greater Omaha Chamber of Commerce, CQ Transcripts Wire, 6 Feb. 2007, WashingtonPost.com, www.washingtonpost.com/wp-dyn/content/article/2007/02/06/AR2007020600882.html.

26. Katherine Bradbury and Jane Katz, Federal Reserve Bank of Boston, "Are Lifetime Incomes Growing More Unequal? Looking at New Evidence on Family Income Mobility," *Regional Review*, 3 Aug. 2007, www.bos.frb.org/economic/nerr/rr2002/q4/issues.pdf.

27. Isabel Sawhill and John E. Morton, "Is the American Dream Alive and Well?" (Washington, DC: Economic Mobility Project, The Pew Charitable

Trusts, 2007), p. 5, www.economicmobility.org/assets/pdfs/EMP%20American %20Dream%20Report.pdf.

28. Eric Schwarz, "Realizing the American Dream: Historical Scorecard, Current Challenges, Future Opportunities," pre-reading, A Gathering of Leaders: Social Entrepreneurs and Scale in the 21st Century, 15–18 Feb. 2005, accessed 4 Aug. 2007, www.uwmb.org/livingthedream/Realizing-the-American-Dream .pdf.

29. Gopal K. Singh and Mohammad Siahpush. "Widening Socioeconomic Inequalities in U.S. Life Expectancy, 1980–2000," *International Journal of Epidemiology* 35, no. 4 (2006): 969–979, http://ije.oxfordjournals.org/cgi/ content/full/35/4/969.

30. Gary Fields, "Murders of Black Teens Are Up 39% Since 2000-01," *Wall Street Journal*, 29 Dec. 2008, http://online.wsj.com/article/SB1230501 24581438021.html?mod=googlenews_wsj.

31. Donald K. Stern and Nancy Gertner, "A Balanced Approach to Fighting Violence," *Boston Globe*, 21 April 2007, www.boston.com/news/globe/editorial_ opinion/oped/articles/2007/04/21/a_balanced_approach_to_fighting_ violence.

32. Bill Cosby and Alvin F. Poussaint, M.D., *Come on People: On the Path from Victims to Victors* (Nashville, TN: Thomas Nelson, 2007), p. 27.

33. Ibid., pp. 8–9.

34. Eric Wanner, "Foreword," in Kathryn Neckerman, ed., *Social Inequality*, pp. xii–xv (New York: Russell Sage Foundation, 2004).

35. Crispin Tickell, "Human Effects of Climate Change: Excerpts from a Lecture Given to the Society on 26 March 1990," *Geographical Journal* 156, no. 3 (November 1990): 325–329.

36. Julian Cribb, "Predicting the Future: It's Becoming a Science," *Cosmos*, 20 Sept. 2006, accessed 15 Apr. 2008, www.cosmosmagazine.com/node/672.

37. Bob Herbert, "When Is Enough Enough?" Editorial, *New York Times*, 30 June 2007, http://select.nytimes.com/2007/06/30/opinion/30herbert.html? _r=1&hp&oref=slogin.

38. Orlando Patterson, "Jena, O. J. and the Jailing of Black America," Editorial, *New York Times*, 30 Sept. 2007, www.nytimes.com/2007/09/30/opinion/30 patterson.html?n=Top%2fOpinion%2fEditorials%20and%20Op%2dEd%2fOp %2dEd%2fContributors%2fOrlando%20Patterson.

39. Jeff Howard, "Still at Risk: The Causes and Costs of Failure to Educate Poor and Minority Children for the Twenty-First Century," in David T. Gordon, ed., *A Nation Reformed? American Education Twenty Years After "A Nation at Risk"* (Cambridge, MA: Harvard Education Press, 2003), pp. 81–97.

40. Scott and Leonhardt, "Shadowy Lines That Still Divide."

41. David Brooks, "Reviving the Hamilton Agenda," editorial, *New York Times,* 8 June 2007, http://select.nytimes.com/search/restricted/article?res=F20F1FFA34540C7B8CDDAF0894DF404482.

42. Ben Stein, "Out of the Clubhouse and Into the Classroom," editorial, *New York Times*, 10 Dec. 2006, accessed 4 Aug. 2007, http://select.nytimes.com/search/restricted/article?res=F50E11F93C550C738DDDAB0994DE404482.

43. Ben Stein, "The Hedge Fund Class and the French Revolution," editorial, *New York Time*, 29 July 2007, accessed 4 Aug. 2007, www.nytimes.com/2007/07/29/business/yourmoney/29every.html.

44. Pew Charitable Trusts, press release, "Two-thirds of American Families Earn More than Their Parents—Yet the Ability to Climb the Economic Ladder Depends on Parents' Income," www.economicmobility.org/newsroom/pressreleases?id=0005.

45. Howard, "Still at Risk."

46. Anthony Ramirez, "Angry Exchanges, To and Fro, at Rally," *New York Times*, June 4, 2006.

47. Susan Kinzie, "Colleges See Flare in Racial Incidents," *Washington Post*, 26 Sept. 2007, www.washingtonpost.com/wp-dyn/content/article/2007/09/25/AR2007092502353.html; Nicole Johnson, "Teens Say They're Victims of Gang Violence at School," Live5news.com, 8 Oct. 2007, www.live5news.com/home/10324567.html.

48. Strong American Schools, "Get The Facts About America's Schools," 2008, www.edin08.com/uploadedFiles/get-the-facts.pdf.

49. Bill Clinton, "How We Ended Welfare, Together," editorial, *New York Times*, 22 Aug. 2006, www.nytimes.com/2006/08/22/opinion/22clinton.html?ex=1313899200&en=fc65ae4741105227&ei=5088&partner=rssnyt&emc=rss.

50. Celia W. Dugger, "Overfarming African Land Is Worsening Hunger Crisis," *New York Times*, 31, March 2006, www.nytimes.com/2006/03/31/world/africa/31soil.html?ei=5088&en=a95f9eb19c751f1f&ex=1301461200&partner=rssnyt&emc=rss&pagewanted=print.

51. "About the Alliance for a Green Revolution in Africa," www.agra-alliance.org.

52. Stephen Goldsmith and William D. Eggers, *Governing by Network: The New Shape of the Public Sector* (Washington, DC: The Brookings Institution 2004), p. 8.

53. Hendrik Hertzberg, "Ghostbusters," editorial, *New Yorker*, 1 Oct. 2007, www.newyorker.com/talk/comment/2007/10/01/071001taco_talk_hertzberg.

54. Thomas E. Mann, "Congress as 'The Broken Branch,'" interview with Charles Babington, *Washington Post*, 11 Oct. 2006, www.washingtonpost.com/wp-dyn/content/article/2006/10/10/AR2006101001155_pf.html.

55. United States Congress, Congressional Budget Office, "The Retirement Prospects of the Baby Boomers: Economic and Budget Issue Brief" (Washington, DC: CBO, 2004), accessed 15 Apr. 2008, www.cbo.gov/doc.cfm?index =5195&type=0.

56. Robert J. Samuelson, "Paying for Aging Baby Boomers," *Newsweek*, 6 Aug. 2007, www.msnbc.msn.com/id/20010728/site/newsweek/page/0/print/1/ displaymode/1098.

57. John J. Havens and Paul G. Schervish, *A Golden Age of Philanthropy?* (Boston: The Boston Foundation, 2006), Boston College Center on Wealth and Philanthropy, www.bc.edu/research/cwp/features/goldenage.html.

58. Jon Hurdle, "Philadelphia Blacks Campaign to Cut Murder Rate," Reuters, 21 Oct. 2007, www.reuters.com/article/domesticNews/idUSN21361866200 71021?sp=true.

59. Jon Hurdle, "Six-Figure Bonuses Retain U.S. Commandos," Reuters, 21 Oct. 2007, www.reuters.com/article/domesticNews/idUSN21361866200 71021?sp=true.

60. David Zion and Amit Varshney, "You Dropped a Bomb on Me, GASB," equity research, Credit Suisse, 2007, http://online.wsj.com/public/resources/ documents/DroppedB.pdf.

61. National Center on Education and the Economy, "Tough Choices or Tough Times" (Washington, DC: New Commission on the Skills of the American Workforce, 2007), accessed 15 Apr. 2008, www.skillscommission.org/pdf/ exec_sum/ToughChoices_EXECSUM.pdf.

62. William L. Watts, "Deficit Forecast's Trimmed on Higher Tax Receipts," MarketWatch, 23 Aug. 2007, www.marketwatch.com/news/story/cbo-trims-federal-budget-deficit/story.aspx?guid=%7BF7216CD7-A769-4CFA-BF4D-2ADFC9E2ED1F%7D.

63. Kirsten A. Gronbjerg and Lester M. Salamon, "Devolution, Marketization, and the Changing Shape of Government-Nonprofit Relations," in Lester M. Salamon, ed., *The State of Nonprofit America* (Washington, DC: Brookings Institution Press, 2002), pp. 447–470.

64. John McQuaid, "The Can't-Do Nation: Is America Losing Its Knack for Getting Big Things Done?" editorial, *Washington Post*, 5 Aug. 2007, www. washingtonpost.com/wp-dyn/content/article/2007/08/02/AR20070802017 52.html.

65. Jeffrey L. Bradach, Thomas J. Tierney, and Nan Stone, "Delivering on the Promise of Nonprofits," *Harvard Business Review* (December 2008), http:// harvardbusinessonline.hbsp.harvard.edu/b01/en/common/item_detail.jhtml? id=R0812G.

66. Michael E. Porter and Mark R. Kramer, "Philanthropy's New Agenda: Creating Value," *Harvard Business Review* (November–December 1999): 122.

67. Cynthia Gibson and Ruth McCambridge, "Why Every Foundation Should Fund Infrastructure," *Nonprofit Quarterly* 12, Special Issue, Infrastructure (2004): 12.

68. William J. Clinton Foundation Annual Report 2006–2007, www.clinton foundation.org/pdf/annual-report-2006.pdf.

69. Peter Karnoff, "Generosity and Sacred Search: Motivation," in Karnoff and Jane Maddox, *The World We Want* (Lanham, MD: Rowman/Littlefield, 2007), p. 225.

70. John P. Kotter, "Leading Change: Why Transformation Efforts Fail," *Harvard Business Review* (March-April 1995), harvardbusinessonline.hbsp.harvard.edu/b01/en/common/item_detail.jhtml?id=4231.

71. Jay W. Forrester, "Counterintuitive Behavior of Social Systems," *Technology Review* 73, no. 3 (January 1971): 52–68. Constitution Society, www .constitution.org/ps/cbss.htm.

72. Ibid., pp. 1, 19.

73. Robert S. Kaplan and David P. Norton, *Alignment: Using the Balanced Scorecard to Create Corporate Synergies* (Boston: Harvard Business School Press, 2006), p. 6.

74. Goldsmith and Eggers, *Governing by Network*, p. 77.

75. Kaplan and Norton, *Alignment*, p. 256.

76. Rosabeth Moss Kanter, "Collaborative Advantage: The Art of Successful Alliances," *Harvard Business Review* (July–August 1994).

77. Robert Waldron, Jumpstart presentation, A Gathering of Leaders, New Profit Inc., Mohonk Mountain House, 15 Feb. 2006.

78. Katherine Fulton and Andrew Blau, "Cultivating Change in Philanthropy," Monitor Group, 2005, p. 7.

Chapter 3

Fragmentation

To give away money is an easy matter and in any man's power.
But to decide to whom to give it, and how large, and when, and
for what purpose and how, is neither in every man's power nor
an easy matter.

—*Aristotle*

W eneed to understand the causes of underperforming philanthropy so that we might discover what kinds of
corrective measures could help improve things. I've already
asserted that the lack of social progress in recent decades is attributable in
large measure to the way we fund nonprofit organizations. The problem,
as I see it, isn't a lack of money per se. In the aggregate, the social sector
has more money than ever before and the future looks bright on that score
for decades to come. The problem—or at least one of the most serious
ones—is that the money isn't matched up with its best potential uses.

The disconnection originates from the fact that it's extremely difficult
to measure nonprofit performance or impacts. As a result, funding simply
isn't based on performance, but on relationships nonprofits cultivate with
funders and the inspiring stories and anecdotes nonprofits tell about their
admirable missions, dedicated teams, and strenuous efforts, all in lieu of
rigorous information about what they've actually accomplished. This
makes it quite difficult for social investors to direct their donations to
nonprofits that produce the most impact.

Since it's so difficult for funders to determine in a rigorous way whether their donations achieved their objectives, they tend to be overly cautious in the ways they make funding decisions. Foundations, for example, try to reduce their risks by making lots of small, short grants with lots of strings attached. That way, the chances of spectacular failures are reduced, but, alas, so are the chances of spectacular successes, at least in terms of producing significant and enduring benefit for large segments of the populations in need.

Essentially, these philanthropists "overdiversify" their investments because it's so difficult to differentiate among them in terms of performance. Absent any reliable means of maximizing the social return of their portfolios, they err on the side of minimizing the risk of putting too many eggs in too few baskets, or, to revive my earlier analogy, too many drops in too few buckets.

I refer to this multifaceted problem of funders overhedging their bets as "fragmentation." I'll show why fragmented funding can't produce transformative social impact and argue that we need more robust nonprofit capital market institutions to address the fragmentation problem.

Excessive fragmentation is fundamentally a problem of *distribution*: trying to divide a given amount of money among too many recipients for too short a time with too many restrictions on its use. Assuming there's enough money available in the system as a whole to produce much more social benefit than is currently achieved—which I believe there is—the solution requires us to find a way to bring about a more optimal distribution, one that is better informed and therefore capable of allocating funds in a way that increases the social impact produced. My hypothesis is that there are identifiable ways to improve the workings of the nonprofit capital market to achieve a more effective distribution of philanthropic dollars that can accomplish so much more.

Financial versus Nonprofit Capital Markets

The private sector has made enormous advances in the art and science of managing money to maximize financial returns. Indeed, the driving purpose of private capital markets is to optimize the deployment of invested assets. In the financial world, "smart money"—funding guided by professionals who offer sophisticated investors sound advice on a range of investment opportunities informed by rigorous knowledge of the factors contributing to the achievement of identified objectives—is always on the lookout for the best companies to fund. Smart money doesn't wait for invitations to wine-and-cheese parties.

Once it lands, smart money keeps a close eye on its investments, ever vigilant to insure that it is funding companies with the best prospects for achieving their performance objectives. The capital markets are designed to guide money where it can be used most effectively, helping the best companies to grow, create the most jobs, and produce the best products at the lowest prices:

> [I]n the past few decades there has been a revolution in finance that has allowed a much deeper understanding of risk and generated more efficient ways of managing it. This has resulted, overall, in a massive increase in the productivity of capital, the lifeblood of capitalism, and has benefit most of us, by driving faster economic growth, as well as handsomely rewarding its most capable practitioners.[1]

The market economy doesn't work perfectly, of course, but at least it's designed to maximize the results that its participants desire. (The financial debacle that began in 2008 resulted from skilled miscreants, abetted by insouciant regulators, who prevented the market from sending authentic price signals. As Rutgers economist Michael D. Bordo reminds us, "No financial market can function normally when basic information about the solvency of market participants is lacking."[2])

In the for-profit sector, capital-seeking companies produce standardized data that independent analysts use to publish research reports about corporate performance. Investors and their advisors use that information to guide their investment decisions. As a result, the market rewards superior performance and nurtures the growth of more effective companies (see Exhibit 3.1).

Regrettably, the same cannot be said for the social sector. Unlike the private sector, the social sector is almost entirely lacking in anything that could be called "smart money." As Harvard's Michael Porter put it, "Philanthropy is decades behind business in applying rigorous thinking to the use of money."[3] While financial markets encourage

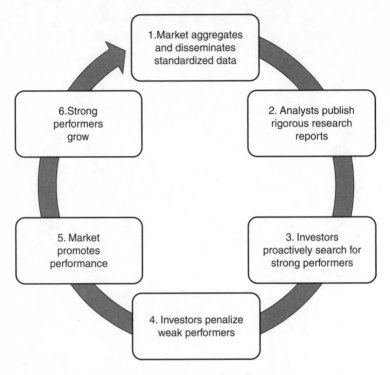

Exhibit 3.1   Financial Markets Reward Performance

and reward performance, social capital markets encourage and reward fundraising.

Of course, unlike the private sector, the social sector faces the fundamental challenge that noneconomic performance is difficult to measure, a problem exacerbated by the fact that most nonprofits have few resources for such esoteric endeavors. Virtually all nonprofits, irrespective of the results they achieve, devote far too much time to building relationships and telling compelling stories to entice donations. "Social funding decisions are often based on limited information, personal interest and emotion rather than as part of a strategic approach."[4] Prudent philanthropists, lacking information about the performance track records of the many donation choices they confront, overhedge their bets and dole out smaller amounts to more seemingly worthy recipients. Thus, the nonprofit capital market is built around fundraising, not the maximization of social impact (see Exhibit 3.2).

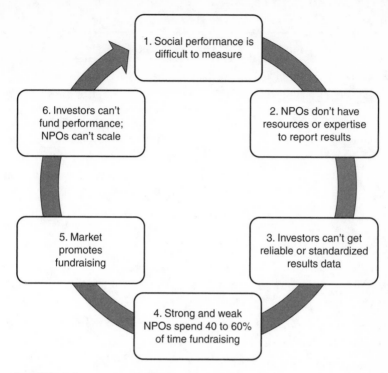

Exhibit 3.2 Nonprofit Markets Reward Fundraising

However, there is cause for encouragement. This is a time in which philanthropic associations and thought leaders are moving mountains to devise ways of improving the effectiveness of charitable funding. For example, Foundation Source, an advisor to hundreds of family foundations, has developed a taxonomy of five different approaches to strategic philanthropy (see Exhibit 3.3).

Something good is bound to grow from such fertile soil. What we lack is a coherent framework by which to harmonize and extend these divergent approaches in the areas of greatest potential benefit.

For reasons I'll explain in this chapter, nonprofits can't possibly raise enough money to achieve transformative social impact within the constraints of the existing fundraising system. I submit that significant social progress cannot be achieved without what I'm going to call "third-stage funding," that is, funding that doesn't suffer from disabling fragmentation. The existing nonprofit capital market is not capable of

Exhibit 3.3   Taxonomy of Five Different Approaches to Strategic Philanthropy.

Approach	Purpose	For Donors Who...
Checkbook Philanthropy	Providing immediate crucial support to the nonprofit sector	• Want to give back to the organizations or causes that have been important in their lives • Fund causes and participate in events as part of a social network of contributors • Seek to spread their money around to many organizations • Want to provide general support to organizations rather than targeting their dollars to specific programs
Responsive Philanthropy	Supporting needs and priorities	• Develop deep philanthropic expertise in a few focused areas • Fund specific programs, as opposed to supporting organizational overhead • Place some conditions on the acceptance of grants, such as requirements for matching funds or reporting back results • Maintain an arm's-length relationship with grantees rather than engage in active management or hands-on assistance
Venture Philanthropy	Building capacity for growth and sustainability	• Prefer long-term partnerships with a handful of organizations doing good work • Desire heavy involvement in the day-to-day affairs of the organizations they fund • Want to apply their business/management practices to their philanthropy • Want to fund small-scale projects that can grow into larger initiatives

Results-Based Philanthropy	Solving social problems by addressing root causes	• Have a particular social problem in mind that they want to address/solve • Want to have a significant role in "setting the agenda" for change • Are willing and able to devote significant resources to their philanthropy • Are not afraid of controversy
Collaborative Philanthropy	Sharing solutions and building knowledge	• Want to assume a "big picture" approach in solving community needs • Are willing to give up some control over specifics in exchange for greater influence for the group as a whole • Want to be part of a network of like-minded, hands-on givers who feel similarly committed and are passionate about the same issues

Source: Page Snow and Sharon Schneider, "Strategic Philanthropy: Five Approaches for Making a Difference," (Foundation Source Press, 2007), http://www.foundationsource.com/scripts/view.asp?t= cmsbrochure&i=31.

providing third-stage funding. Such funding can arise only when investors are sufficiently well informed to make big bets at understandable and manageable levels of risk. Existing nonprofit capital markets neither provide investors with the kinds of information needed—actionable information about nonprofit performance—nor provide the kinds of intermediation—active oversight by knowledgeable professionals—needed to mitigate risk. Absent third-stage funding, nonprofit capital will remain irreducibly fragmented, preventing the marshaling of resources that nonprofit organizations need to make meaningful and enduring progress against $100 million problems.

Our challenge is to create the conditions under which "smart philanthropy" looks for the most promising opportunities to make donations that will maximize social impact. The development of a third-stage nonprofit capital market that channels funds to grantees on the basis of performance is an essential step on the path to a reinvigorated American Dream and the demise of an underclass that discredits a great nation.

Organic Growth Isn't Enough

There is so much to celebrate in the social sector, from the unprecedented increase in giving to the tremendous innovation social entrepreneurs bring to the resolution of long-standing problems of first-order difficulty and consequence. At the same time, stubborn institutional and structural challenges make it difficult to convert available funds into real social progress for millions of people denied the basic tools for achieving self-sufficiency in disadvantaged communities.

How can nonprofits achieve the kinds of exponential growth required to make serious headway against the overwhelming universe of need? Why doesn't increased philanthropy directly produce systemic change and transformative impact? Why is the second half of the glass so hard to fill?

To answer that question, let's look back to one of the great social enterprises mentioned earlier, Jumpstart, which is headquartered in Boston. School-readiness is a serious problem for disadvantaged families, with more than one-third of American kindergartners arriving at school unprepared to learn and half of all low-income children starting first grade up to two years behind in preschool skills, such as vocabulary and social engagement. Jumpstart "is working toward the day every child in America enters school prepared to succeed," and it has compiled an impressive record since its inception in 1993:

- 13,000 poor and low-income kids served annually in 20 states by 3,500 trained adult volunteers from more than 70 colleges.
- 20% annual growth since 2002 (see Exhibit 3.4).
- An impressive array of national sponsors, including American Eagle Outfitters, AmeriCorps, Pearson, Sodexho, and Starbucks.
- Most important, externally administered evaluations show that children who participate in Jumpstart programs consistently build skill levels at a greater and statistically more significant rate than nonparticipating children.[5]

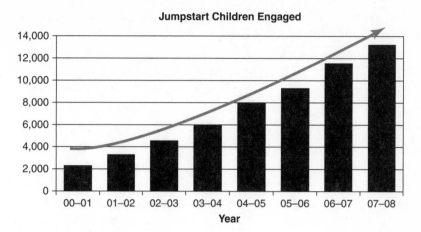

Jumpstart Children Engaged

Exhibit 3.4 Jumpstart Growth
Source: Jumpstart, "Our Impact," 11 Sept. 2007, www.jstart.org/index.php?submenu=about us&src=gendocs&link=Our Impact&category=Main.

However, Jumpstart's 13,000 children comprise just 0.4% of the 3.3 million who need their help. If Jumpstart grew by 250%, it would reach 1% of the total. At a 20% annual growth rate, that would take 12.5 years.

The most successful social enterprise, Teach For America, helps 425,000 of the 13 million children facing "educational inequity," which represents 3.3% of the total need. At the 16% annual growth rate it achieved from 2000 through 2005, it would reach 5.3% of the need in ten years.

None of this constitutes criticism of Jumpstart, Teach For America, or similar organizations. To the contrary, these are the preeminent organizations that are poised to transform educational and economic opportunity in this country.

But incremental, organic growth is not going to solve massive social problems, no matter how good the programs are, how dedicated the staff, or how dazzling the fundraising team. Money is by no means the only limiting factor, but it's the first one. When it comes to growing non-profit organizations by orders of magnitude, there's no chicken-and-egg problem: lots more money has to come before anything else can happen.

Over the last couple of years, there's been a lot of innovation in nonprofit fundraising. Many smart, hardworking, and creative people are making tremendous progress in extracting more money and in-kind services from people and organizations that have both. If we lump all of these innovations into a huge new amorphous category—let's call it Fundraising 2.0—it's an impressive achievement. They're squeezing every last bit of horsepower out of the old fundraising engine the way that computer designers used to add on inefficient "kluges" to extend the lives of their tired old machines. But it's going to take an entirely new engine if we want to move the needle on social progress.

Please don't get me wrong. The old fundraising engines aren't going away, nor should they. For most nonprofits, fundraising is a difficult but manageable fact of life most of the time. There's plenty of life left in the enormous variety of methods and sources for raising philanthropic dollars. Also, charitable giving is a vital social nexus to civic engagement. But the hard truth is that the existing set of fundraising tools and practices is not going to transform a great nonprofit that helps 5,000 kids each year into one that serves 500,000, much less the 5 million who need it, within a time horizon that we would consider acceptable.

This is the reality facing the social sector: for some set of vitally important and massively pervasive social problems, there does not exist any system for making available the kinds of capital needed to meet 5, 10, or 20% of the need. We owe it to ourselves to be very clear about this point: with almost $300 billion going into the U.S. social sector every year, enough money *exists* to make a real difference, but it's just not *available* in the amounts or on the terms needed to produce significant social impact. I'm hardly the first person to see things this way. Consider these words of Randall Ottinger:

> I observed that for many people, philanthropy is quite random. They connect with a cause because someone asks them to be on the board, or invites them to a fundraiser, or takes them to visit a nonprofit organization. Rarely do they think strategically about how to invest in social causes. I began to worry that the transfer of baby boomers' wealth might not only fall short of its potential, but also further fragment the nonprofit sector. If history is a guide, the influx of trillions of dollars is likely to lead to the creation of many more nonprofits. With so many new nonprofits from which to choose, donors are likely to make even less focused, less strategic social investments.[6]

Limits of Innovation

Social sector innovation, as we have seen, is central to our conception of a renewed and extended American Dream. When you look at the most exciting nonprofit organizations, the ones that make you think they really might change the world for the better, you inevitably find tremendous innovation. Whether it's preparing kids to enter public schools ready to learn, reducing truancy and increasing high school graduation and college-attendance rates, reducing violence and drug use, increasing employment skills, or improving health practices, today's best social entrepreneurs have arrived at some important insight that has enabled them to start to overcome the obstacles that led to past failures in dealing with intransigent problems. Then they've built and grown resourceful and adaptable organizations that can deliver those innovations to more and more people in more and more places over longer periods of time.

In *The Innovator's Solution,* Harvard's Clay Christensen distinguishes two broad categories of business innovation that are relevant to our discussion: "sustaining" and "disruptive."[7] Sustaining innovations come from established competitors making better products for their existing customers at higher profit margins. Disruptive innovations are the province of new-market entrants that fly under the radar to introduce alternatives to customers that can't afford or don't need premium products. There are "low-end disruptions," which "address overserved customers with a lower-cost business model," and "new-market disruptions," which "compete against nonconsumption," that is, people who aren't buying existing products.

New-market disruptions have particular salience to social sector innovation:

> We say that new-market disruptions compete with "nonconsumption" because new-market disruptive products are so much more affordable to own and simpler to use that they enable a whole new population of people to begin owning and using the product, and to do so in a more convenient setting....New-market disruptors' challenge is to create a new value network, where it is nonconsumption, not the incumbent, that must be overcome.[8]

Christensen offers community colleges as an example of his model:

In some states, up to 80 percent of the graduates of reputable four-year
state universities take some or all of their required general education
courses at much less expensive community colleges, and then transfer
those credits to the university—which (unconsciously) is becoming a
provider of upper-division courses. Some community colleges have
begun offering four-year degrees. Their enrollment is booming, often
with nontraditional students who otherwise would not have taken these
courses.[9]

Disruptive innovation is exactly where social entrepreneurs excel.
Consider these examples from the 2008 Fast Company Social Capitalist
Awards:[10]

- Civic Ventures is engaging millions of Baby Boomers as a vital workforce for social change by establishing the "encore career," work that
  matters in the second half of life.
- DonorsChoose engages citizens in an online marketplace where
  teachers describe specific educational projects and individuals choose
  which projects to fund.
- Heifer International provides livestock to poor families in developing
  nations to use for farming, food production, and fertilization.
- PATH invented a syringe simple enough for village health workers
  to use that prevents the spread of infectious diseases. PATH licensed
  the rights to a syringe manufacturer, which produces large quantities
  for public sector buyers at affordable prices.
- Reach Out and Read trains doctors and nurses to provide literacy
  advice and free developmentally appropriate books at each well-child
  visit between the ages of six months and five years.

Indeed, Christensen joined with a number of nonprofit colleagues
to extend the disruptive innovation model to the social sector, recasting
them as "catalytic innovations" in recognition of their "potential as a
means to overcome persistent social problems."[11]

However, innovation is a necessary but not sufficient condition
for breakthrough growth. As Christensen puts it, "disruption does not

guarantee success: It just helps with an important element in the total formula."[12] The nonprofit sector abounds with innovation that has the *potential* of disrupting underperforming social institutions that are failing to meet the needs of the underclass—that is, folks who are effectively "nonconsumers" of America's bounty. But the formidable challenges of *delivering* those opportunities to a substantial portion of those who need them remain. Just because a social entrepreneur has figured out how to teach disadvantaged kids to succeed in school or single mothers-to-be to practice healthy prenatal habits, that does not mean those innovations will be adopted widely anytime soon.

Social entrepreneurship has developed a growth model (see Exhibit 3.5) that begins with an entrepreneurial insight brought to life in a young organization that is similar in many respects to a business start-up. The most promising of these fledgling firms attract financial and managerial support within the portfolios of venture philanthropists, which introduce performance-measurement systems, strategic planning, and management discipline to produce truly catalytic innovations. There follows a period of organic growth in which the organization crosses

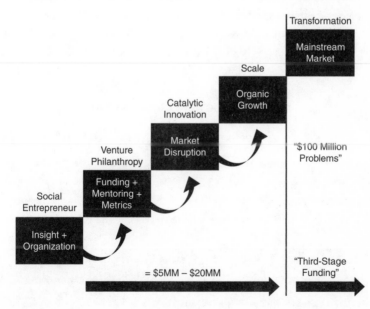

Exhibit 3.5 From Social Entrepreneurship to Transformative Impact

some undefined threshold of size often referred to as "scale," but generally falls well short of either systemic change or transformative social impact.

The boundary between what the best social entrepreneurs have accomplished in the last decade or so and what still remains beyond their grasp is the frontier I've referred to as $100 million problems. Different social problems will require different approaches to solving them, but it is likely that similar growth strategies will have to be put in place before we can hope to cross the line.

First, I believe that achieving systemic change will require alignment among complementary nonprofits and cross-sector initiatives with business and government. As such efforts generally will be unfamiliar to all participants, they will need to develop large-scale pilot projects to test out coordinated efforts of significantly greater scope than the social sector normally undertakes.

Second, transformative social impact will arrive only when disruptive innovations that have achieved some level of scale are ready to be adopted by "mainstream" markets. That is, society will not be changed until today's innovations become tomorrow's orthodoxy. (I'll discuss how that can happen in the next section.)

A similar version of this growth model (see Exhibit 3.6) has been developed by the Growth Philanthropy Network (GPN), ably led by

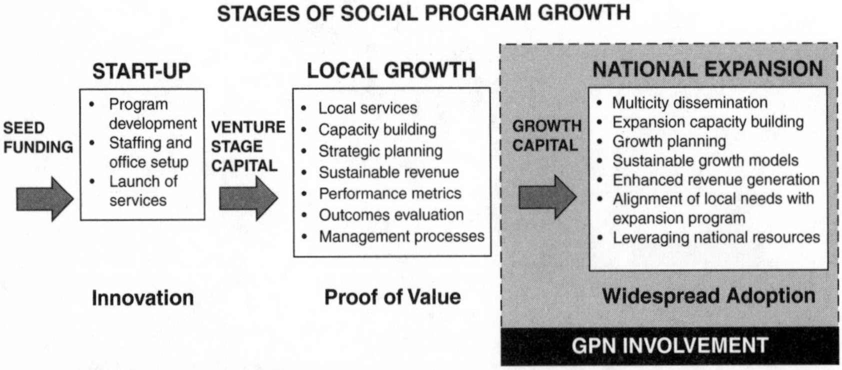

Exhibit 3.6 Growth Philanthropy Network
Source: Growth Philanthropy Network, "Positioning and Model," 16 Apr. 2008, http://209.123.244.17/abt_positioning.cfm.

Alex Rossides, whose mission is to "exponentially increase the positive social impact of best-in-class programs that improve the lives of children and families." At each of three stages growth, the model considers the interplay of two variables, funding and market penetration:

- During the *start-up phase*, social programs use *seed funding* to introduce their *innovation*
- As the program pursues *local growth*, it relies on *venture-stage capital* to *prove the value* of its innovative approach
- National expansion requires *growth capital* to fund *widespread adoption*

Both factors—money and market penetration—are important to solving the fragmentation problem. I discuss the money dimension at the end of this chapter, but first let's consider the subject of market adoption, which I believe has not been sufficiently explored by social sector thinkers and practitioners.

Market Adoption

Just as Clay Christensen taught us how innovative ideas become disruptive strategies, Geoffrey Moore, author of *Crossing the Chasm*, deconstructed "how and why high-technology markets develop for *discontinuous innovations*, and why these markets evolve as they do."[13] Discontinuous innovation refers to "the implementation of new technologies, products or business models that represent a dramatic departure from the current state of the art in the industry." Moore added a number of important insights to the now-familiar formulation of the "diffusion of innovations" devised in 1962 by Everett M. Rogers and depicted in his famous bell curve (see Exhibit 3.7) in which customers are divided into successive segments based on their readiness to adopt new innovations as they come to market.

Rogers's model works well for progressive enhancements in which the essential nature of an established product remains intact, but some features or functions are improved. For example, when personal computers first became available, the keyboard and the central process unit,

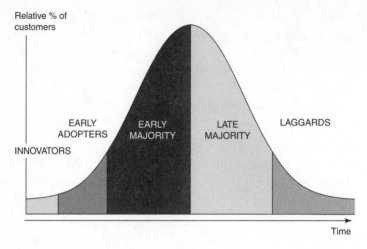

Exhibit 3.7 Diffusion of Innovation
Source: Everett M. Rogers, *Diffusion of Innovations*, 5th ed. (New York: Free Press, 2003).

or the keyboard and the monitor, were usually attached to one another, a design inherited from mainframe terminals. The adoption of a detached keyboard connected by a cable was a nice ergonomic convenience, but it didn't change the computer itself. As many such continuous improvements were added, personal computer sales grew steadily.

Moore discovered that Rogers's model did not fit so well to disruptive technologies that materially changed the core product. Disruptive or discontinuous innovations offered significant new benefits but also imposed new burdens on customers who were used to and reasonably satisfied with the established product. An example would be the portable computers introduced in 1982. Despite their obvious advantages, they were expensive with tiny keyboards and screens, susceptible to theft, and, early on, quite heavy. Some models, nicknamed "luggables," weighed as much as 30 pounds.

Moore focused on how those disadvantages would affect customers' willingness to adopt the new version of the product and, hence, the prospects that it would succeed in the marketplace. Chief among his contributions was his recognition that, unlike in Rogers's model, the progression of new technology products through customer segments is often sudden and tumultuous rather than smooth and incremental. Moore accepted Rogers's five-part segmentation, but he saw "cracks"

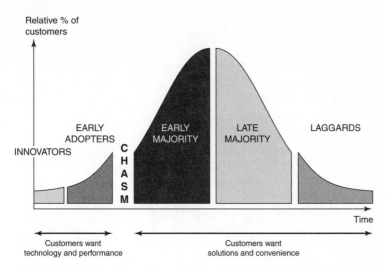

Exhibit 3.8   The Revised Technology Adoption Life Cycle
Source: Geoffrey A. Moore, *Crossing the Chasm: Marketing and Selling Disruptive Products
to Mainstream Customers*, rev. ed. (New York: Collins Business Essentials, 2006).

between each of them, one of which, between the early adopters and
the early majority, was so wide and perilous he called it "the chasm" (see
Exhibit 3.8.)

   Second, Moore warned that such discontinuities were particularly
dangerous once producers of innovation had won over the adventurous "enthusiasts" and "early adopters" but not the more pragmatic
"early majority." The inability to navigate and traverse this chasm would
inevitably bring about the early demise of what had once seemed like
promising young companies. Moore modified Rogers's bell curve—
which Moore called the "revised technology adoption life cycle"—to
better explain the terrain facing intrepid purveyors of innovation.

   Social entrepreneurs and their funders have yet to see the close analogy between the innovative work they do and the introduction of new
technology products in terms of the circumstances that enable exponential growth. It is not difficult, though, to situate the social entrepreneur
growth model onto Moore's technology adoption life cycle (see Exhibit
3.9). I believe there are compelling comparisons between the growth
trajectories of business and social innovators that offer important insights
into what it will take to solve $100 million social problems.

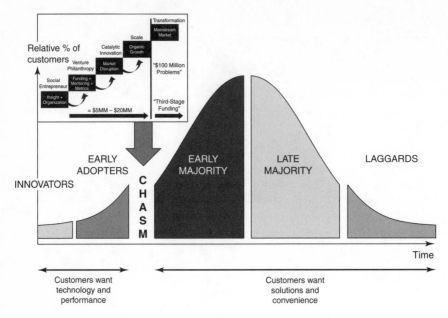

Exhibit 3.9   Social Entrepreneurs Confront Moore's Chasm

Social entrepreneurs begin life as unproven start-ups trying to interest seed funders in their as-yet undeveloped ideas to solve challenging social problems. Their initial objectives, just like their private-sector counterparts, are to develop a promising innovation and find risk-tolerant partners who see its promise. At this earliest stage, they target "customers" who are themselves "innovators," pioneers who are interested in innovation for its potential, not for what it can do today. Such customers have a high tolerance for risk, they are comfortable with trial and error in the pursuit of new solutions that might someday prove useful, and they are willing to work with entrepreneurs to develop their innovations.

In order to advance to the next customer segment, social entrepreneurs must enhance their innovations to enable some new and compelling real-world application. They need risk-tolerant partners—"early adopters"—who want to help build out the new application. These visionary customers want to find out if the innovations can be disruptive (or catalytic) and they are looking for practical opportunities for implementation. They understand that high reward involves high risk, and they are willing to work with social innovators to develop customized solutions that can be tested in the field. Customer examples include venture philanthropies and adventurous foundations such as Edna McConnell Clark and William and Flora Hewlett.

Now comes the chasm, an interregnum of indeterminate duration in which incremental growth continues but breakout growth has not yet begun. The crucial fact of life for social entrepreneurs overlooking this precipice is that the mainstream market customers on the other side of the chasm are different in kind (not just in degree) from the early-market customers they've already won over. Unlike the risk-tolerant codevelopers who supported them in the early market, mainstream customers—*who are the only source of potential growth sufficient to produce transformative social impact*—are fundamentally pragmatic.

The early majority of mainstream customers are interested in just one thing: innovative business solutions that work. They are willing to consider adopting a new paradigm if, but only if, they have a high level of confidence that the new approach works and adds significant value. But they have little tolerance for risk, customization, codevelopment, or learning curves. Their sole objective in working with social entrepreneurs is finding opportunities to convert innovations into mainstream solutions, and their "buying" decision is governed entirely by their ability to confirm that the new approach works as promised. Customer examples include large public foundations and government agencies that require a lot of convincing and protracted grantmaking cycles.

Implications of Moore's Model

Let's pause here to absorb what the application of Moore's growth model teaches us about the pathway from social innovation to transformative social impact.

First, it is vital to recognize that there is, in fact, a broad and deep chasm between what the most effective social sector organizations have already accomplished and what they hope to accomplish: that "one day" they will reach "all children." What the chasm tells us is that going from helping, say, 50,000 to 500,000 or 5,000,000 kids is not a gradual or continuous growth process, because mainstream market customers are not simply an accumulation of more and more early-market customers. At some point, there aren't enough risk takers to carry social entrepreneurs to the next level of market penetration. The early market can support the adoption of innovative solutions in the small tail on the left side of the customer adoption curve, but the numbers of potential customers just don't exist to produce anything that could reasonably be considered "systemic change" unless and until some of the skeptical and cautious pragmatists in the mainstream markets are convinced to try them out.

The genesis of the chasm lies in the fundamentally different mind sets of the decision makers in each market. In many respects, early-market customers are the opposite of their mainstream market counterparts (see Exhibit 3.10).

As one social sector illustration, think about the ways that different foundations make grant decisions. A few are quite comfortable with "institution and field building," that is, breaking new ground for the nonprofit sector as a whole and funding ideas that may or may not produce discernible social benefit in the near term. Those funders are receptive to challenging ideas that might "move the needle" or advance the "start of the art," and they're used to working with social innovators

Exhibit 3.10 Psychographic Profiles of Visionaries versus Pragmatists.

Visionaries	Pragmatists
Intuitive	Analytic
Seek revolutionary advances	Seek evolutionary advances
Contrarian	Conformist
Self-referencing	Reference others perceived as similar
Avoid the herd	Stay with the herd
Risk taking	Risk averse
Motivated by future opportunities	Motivated by current problems
Seek what is possible	Pursue what is probable
Seek best technology	Seek best solution or vendor

Source: Paul Wiefels, *The Chasm Companion* (New York: HarperBusiness, 2002), p. 3.

who are still experimenting with new and unproven, but highly promising approaches. Such foundations often have been created for the very purpose of fueling social innovation, and their endowments and governing structures are conducive to taking chances on unpredictable, but potentially game-changing initiatives.

But a far larger group of foundations are better suited to supporting well-established nonprofits providing reliable services with direct and predictable benefits. They see their role as funding known entities with demonstrated track records and proven capabilities and capacities. These are the funders who restrict themselves to funding "programs" and eschew "overhead." It is not surprising that this much more risk-averse group would structure their grantmaking processes around very different factors than the smaller set of risk-tolerant, early-adopter foundations.

Second, once we accept that there is a chasm between early and mainstream markets, we have to discover how to cross the chasm, that is, how to attract and satisfy those mainstream customers. When we say that they're looking for "innovative business solutions that work," what exactly does that entail for social change organizations? We know that mainstream customer solutions are not merely a magnification of what social entrepreneurs already offer their risk-taking early-market customers. What were differences in degree in early markets become differences in kind at the chasm.

This is the sweet spot of Moore's model. He divides the early majority into two subsegments and prescribes "market development" strategies to penetrate each one. (I hope that social sector readers will not be put off by the use of such crass business terminology, which simply refers to methods for understanding and responding to the quite-different needs of mainstream customers.) In Moore's model, the mainstream market subsegments have the unfelicitous but somewhat instructive names of "the bowling alley" and "the tornado."

As we delve into each, please keep in mind that the bowling alley and the tornado comprise sequential subsegments of the early majority of mainstream market customers that reside just on the other side of the chasm. Each subsegment features identifiable customer characteristics and examples, as well as practicable objectives for reaching those customers (see Exhibit 3.11).

Exhibit 3.11 Reaching Mainstream Market Customers.

	Bowling Alley	Tornado
Customer Characteristics	• "Bowling alley" refers to knocking down one "pin" (customer group) at a time, in sequence • Specific customer groups looking to solve specific problems • Existing paradigm doesn't work well enough • Needs reliable and predictable performance based on evidence • Key is to identify best mainstream customer targets	• The "tornado" refers to the sudden increase in adoption velocity once mainstream customers are satisfied that the innovation has become a pragmatic and reliable choice • Hypergrowth customers ready to make the innovation into the new paradigm • Innovation is now accepted as safe and effective choice
Customer Examples	• Managers and officials with large, difficult, and critical mandates and no workable solutions	• Mainstream officials and managers who can justify a disruptive change based on successful bowling alley customers
Objectives to Reach Customers	• Identify most receptive customer prospects • Develop a complete and reliable "whole-product" solution for them • Support customer during the adoption process to insure success • Repeat with other targeted bowling alley customers	• Develop a "whole product" that provides a general solution for the entire early majority • Build capacity to support broad adoption • Expand marketing effort

Source: Adapted from Geoffrey A. Moore, *Crossing the Chasm: Marketing and Selling Disruptive Products to Mainstream Customers*, rev. ed. (New York: Collins Business Essentials, 2006).

Another way to think about the chasm is as a discontinuity in the level of *pain* that a customer will accept for any given level of *gain*. In the early market, innovators and early adopters accept a lot of risk, so they know it's entirely possible they'll see little or no benefit, at least in the

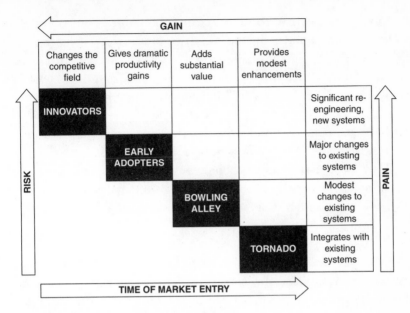

Exhibit 3.12   Discontinuity Analysis Tool
Source: Wiefels, *The Chasm Companion*, p. 105.

short term. This notion is anathema to mainstream markets, which take basically the opposite view: pragmatists won't adopt any new approach unless they feel quite confident that they will derive significant benefits from the innovation (see Exhibit 3.12).

The main differentiator between the two subsegments of mainstream market customers is the extent to which they're willing to endure some pain: bowling alley customers will accept some pain for a lot of gain, whereas tornado customers aren't interested in pain. For them, every buying decision has to be safe and sound, so they will adopt innovations only after the bowling alley customers assure them there's no risk in doing so.

Why Does Transformative Impact Cost So Much?

Moore's model helps us understand how to go about answering the important question at hand: Why do successful nonprofits need much greater funding than the existing capital market can produce in order to solve $100 million problems and produce transformative social impact?

Moore teaches that, to move beyond the limited demand of early-market customers and cross the chasm in order to reach the far larger segments of customers in mainstream markets, innovators first have to identify and then meet the needs of bowling alley customers who have these general characteristics and decision-making criteria:

- They are managers and officials with large, difficult, and critical mandates and no workable solutions.
- They need complete, reliable, and predictable performance that addresses their specific problem set based on evidence.
- They need active support during the adoption process to insure success.

Identifying and meeting these needs can be far more difficult than it first appears. Consider a successful after-school program that has a good track record of serving, say, 10,000 high school kids in three cities for five years. The management team, education sector leaders, and community groups all believe their solution is poised for significant geographic expansion. As a step in that direction, there have been extensive discussions with several large urban and metropolitan school districts about the potential for forming one or more partnerships with the goal of providing after-school activities for more than 100,000 K–12 students in hundreds of school facilities. Assuming that the after-school program sees this as an important strategic opportunity to promote system-wide improvements in student performance, what would it take to knock down this first big pin in the bowling alley?

The challenge is to convince the first bowling alley customer that you have a complete and reliable solution to their specific problem set. In the case of the large school district, the school leadership presumably agrees that comprehensive after-school services can fill many of the gaps that prevent their students from achieving educational success. They suspect that the programs they offer during school hours and within school walls will be for nought without significant after-school support. Everyone agrees that the after-school program's core solution—the curriculum, support activities, teaching model, mentoring approach, volunteers, and so on—is sound. But that's a long way from a viable system to bring that solution to a much larger playing field in a way that is reliable and maintains quality. The school district is concerned that the after-school program won't be able to pull off a tenfold expansion, and it's nervous about asking foundations and government funders for the required financial commitments.

Moore describes the challenge this way:

> Chasm-crossing and bowling alley market development efforts hinge on creating effective whole products. Whole product development during these phases focuses on removing *adoption complexity*. Your success is directly correlated to your ability to field complete product solutions for customer segments laboring under broken processes that you can fix. By working through all the elements, thereby demonstrating your understanding of the segment(s) in question, you overcome the natural reluctance of pragmatists to adopting applications that still contain a degree of complexity and risk.[14]

A whole product "comprises the minimum set of products and services needed to fulfill the target customer's compelling reason to buy." It doesn't have to be perfect, but it has to respond in a credible way to every important dimension of the customer's complex problem set. If it does not, "the compelling reason to buy is not addressed satisfactorily and the market does not emerge."[15]

This is why crossing the chasm is so treacherous: mainstream customers need to be convinced to a high level of confidence that the entrepreneur's solution is sufficiently comprehensive and solid that they should go through all the trouble and uncertainty of adopting a significantly different approach to solving one or more of their critical problems. The customer's mind set is "Why take a chance?" Perhaps it would be better off with the status quo, however imperfect it might be. Convincing such a customer to make a different decision takes a long time and requires a lot of "consultative selling" to understand and address the prospective customer's concerns.

Moore advises entrepreneurs to think of their discontinuous innovations as the core of the whole product solution, around which they must place "all the other complementary products and services needed to fulfill the promised value proposition." He offers a generic depiction of such an integrated product set for a high-technology product trying to penetrate mainstream markets (see Exhibit 3.13).

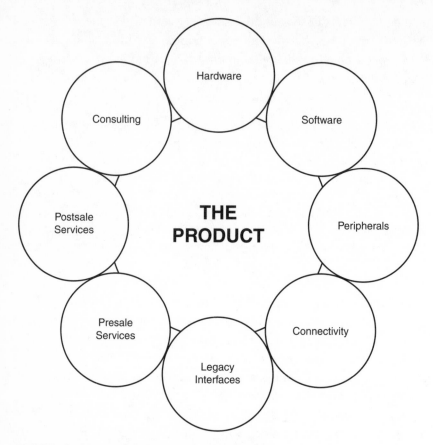

Exhibit 3.13 Simplified Whole Product Model
Source: Geoffrey A. Moore, *Crossing the Chasm: Marketing and Selling Disruptive Products to Mainstream Customers*, rev. ed. (New York: Collins Business Essentials, 2006).

A comparable whole product for our hypothetical after-school program in a large urban school district might contain the elements depicted in Exhibit 3.14. Most of these additional elements either were not required or were very much smaller when the program served only early-market customers. But without a critical mass of all the necessary pieces in place, school district decision makers and institutional funders would be unlikely to assume such formidable risks.

Consider another example of workforce development. The Finance Project has developed a framework of broad "service domains and categories" to guide its research of federal funding sources for workforce development (see Exhibit 3.15).

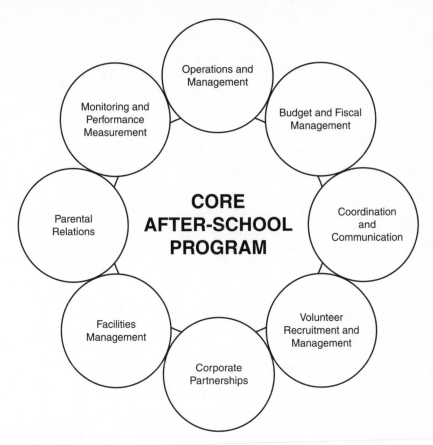

Exhibit 3.14   After-School Whole-Product Solution

Of course, not every mainstream workforce development solution will require all of the listed elements, but there is likely to be some combination without which the bowling alley customer's minimum requirements would not be satisfied. And although the Finance Project does not explicitly situate its framework within Moore's whole product model, they seem to be thinking along similar lines:

This framework reflects the major types of programmatic activities and elements that workforce development initiatives tend to support such as employment services, job retention and advancement, and education and training. The framework contains supportive services that promote

Exhibit 3.15 Workforce Development.

Employment, Retention, and Advancement	Education and Training	Youth Workforce Development	Supportive Services	Infrastructure
Job readiness	Adult basic education, literacy, GED Attainment	Basic education, literacy	Child care	Technology
Job search and placement	Vocational education and training	Secondary school diploma, GED attainment	Transportation	Facilities
Work experience	Postsecondary education	Vocation education and training	Health-care	Technical assistance and training
Job creation	Job-specific training	Postsecondary education	Nutrition assistance	Case management
Job retention, follow-up services	Skill upgrade training	Work experience	Housing	Research and evaluation
Career counseling and planning	Entrepreneurial, microenterprise training	Follow-up services	Wage supplements	Labor market information, data
		Leadership development	Mental health, substance abuse	System building
		Mentoring	Domestic violence prevention	Planning, coordination, and collaboration

Source: Adapted from Nannette Relave, "Finding Funding: A Guide to Federal Sources for Workforce Development Initiatives" (New York: The Finance Project, 2005), accessed 16 Apr. 2008, http://76.12.61.196/publications/workforcefunding.pdf.

employment and job retention, and infrastructure activities that help
workforce initiatives provide services. . . . The service domains and categories described in the framework are interrelated and many funding
sources identified in the catalog can support more than one set of
activities.

In fact, each of the ten cross-boundary initiatives listed in Exhibit
2.13 can be mapped out in much the same way as Moore's whole product
model. It should be self-evident that it would cost considerably more to
bring all these complementary elements together at the same time and
manage them to work effectively in alignment.

We can now understand why the fragmented nonprofit capital market cannot bring about systemic change or transformative social impact.
The path from early markets to mainstream markets progresses from serving a large number of small niche customers that are willing to assume
considerable risk to serving a small number of large establishment customers that are not. Niche customers do not require whole product
solutions or extensive support during the adoption process; mainstream
customers do. Generally speaking, early-market customers can make
their own way; mainstream customers must navigate complex networks
of interlocking partnerships needed to support a whole product ecosystem. While creative and entrepreneurial nonprofits with limited amounts
of unpredictable capital can accomplish a lot in the early markets, they
cannot meet the challenges of crossing the chasm into the mainstream
markets with short-lived, strings-attached, drop-in-the-bucket funding.

Nor can nonprofits cross the chasm by accumulating many more
such ephemeral drops in many more buckets. To the contrary, for large
mainstream customers, the overabundance of choices of fundable innovators without helpful information to decide which ones are the most
effective merely exacerbates the problem by increasing the chances of
guessing wrong. Fragmentation happens.

Moving toward Third-Stage Funding

The financial sector has evolved a kind of step function for funding
technology companies from their earliest, untested days right through

to their entry into the Fortune 500. Without this well-developed system of sequenced and tiered funding sources, the technology boom that began in the 1970s and fueled the unprecedented economic growth of the last decades (and the resulting surge in philanthropy) would not have been possible. As technological innovation created opportunities for producing significant new business value, financial professionals devised mechanisms to meet the initial capital needs of those emerging businesses and, equally important, support them along their entire life cycle as they grew to become mature companies, moving from the periphery of the market to the mainstream.

In the *Venture Management Handbook,* Cliff Conneighton describes the relationship between organizational development and capital sourcing before companies go public (see Exhibit 3.16).

The concept of multistage funding is well established in the business sector but poorly understood on the nonprofit side. Different terms might be used to name the various stages, but the basic idea is that the sources of business funding and the amounts of funding provided evolve over the entire development cycle of new businesses. The risk-return profile of the funding opportunity changes as the business moves from idea to start-up to product launch and beyond, and so does the sophistication and risk profile of participating investors:

- At the earliest stage, untested business ideas seek start-up funding from "friends and family" based on their personal connections to the entrepreneurs. Sometimes "angel" investors inject five-figure amounts of cash where a new technological or other innovation seems particularly alluring.
- After some level of demonstrated success in product development, venture capitalists come into the picture and conduct rigorous "due diligence" to select promising investment opportunities. It is at the Venture Capital (VC) stage where the investors first condition their money upon giving advice to the start-up about key hires, strategy, and organizational development.
- The VC round is often continued through multiple iterations as earlier VCs are replaced (i.e., bought out) by later VCs with fresh time horizons and risk/return profiles that better match the funding needs of adolescent companies.

Exhibit 3.16   Company Stages and Investment Rounds.

Stage	Business Status	Investment Round
Pre-seed	• Research has proved principle of technology. • Intellectual property protection has been established.	
Seed	• Company consists of one or more founders with a rough business plan or concept. Management team is incomplete. • Product is in the prototype or raw design and/or development stage.	• A seed round is an initial round invested at a very early stage of development, typically with the founders and chief technologist on board but without a complete management team in place. It is used to prove the concept.
Start-up	• Initial business plan is complete. Most key management team members are in view. • Product is in or near customer testing stage.	
First	• Management team is essentially complete. • Product is shipping. • Customer revenue is flowing in. • Capital is used primarily for market acceleration.	• First round, second round, etc.: This ordinal nomenclature is used to describe most venture rounds. • The stock issues may be called series A preferred, series B preferred, etc., and sometimes the round is also named A, B, etc.
Second or mezzanine	• Management team, product, and business plan are well tuned and accelerating; exit options are in view.	• Mezzanine is the last venture round prior to an initial public offering.

Source: Cliff Conneighton. *Venture Management Handbook* (Hollis, NH: Venturebooks, 2003). Adapted from Figure 6, Company Stages, and Figure 13, Nomenclature for Rounds of Investment.

A rule of thumb common among VCs is that, on average, only two out of ten investments will hit their return targets. Those that do are picked up by investment banks for passage into the big leagues, generally through initial public offerings of stock or acquisitions by or mergers with public companies.

Each stage of the new company's progress is matched with a category of investor deemed appropriate to the size of the opportunity and risk assumed. In addition, investors exercise control and guidance over the companies in their portfolios commensurate with the stakes associated with increasingly larger financial bets. Early-stage investors pass their charges along to more sophisticated investors, who continue the Darwinian process of survival of the fittest before handing their charges off to the next stage of investment.

In this way, the markets nurture new entrants and ratchet the levels of financial and nonfinancial support to meet the ever-increasing challenges facing the business organization. Virtually all of the Internet household names—Amazon, Yahoo, eBay, and Google—and high-tech mainstays—such as HP, Apple, and Dell—were born and raised through this kind of process until they reached the point where they could reliably serve tens of millions of customers.

A similar but embryonic version of tiered-funding has migrated over to the nonprofit sector with the arrival of venture philanthropy. With an average of 115 new nonprofit organizations being formed every day in the United States, the great mass of them join the "long tail" of small-cap organizations that never grow beyond $100,000 or so in funds raised from friends and family in the local community. A few develop real innovations that attract small grants to hire full-time staff and establish a stable foothold and a local brand that garners wider funding and some measure of staying power. In time, the most promising start-ups attract the attention of small foundations that sponsor fellowships and grants to sustain innovative leaders and programs. This round of fits-and-starts "first-stage funding" helps nonprofits growing through their infancy

"Second-stage funding" begins when, after additional years of demonstrated endurance and capacity building, the best of these non-profit toddlers seek admission into the portfolios of one or more venture philanthropists, such as New Profit, Venture Philanthropy Partners, and

NewSchools Venture Fund, where they endure an excruciatingly long and rigorous due diligence process. Those few that make the cut receive their first seven-figure infusions of cash over a period of three to five years or so, together with high-caliber management support from first-tier consulting firms, such as the Monitor Group and Bridgespan.

I want to pause for a moment to avoid any impression that second-stage funding is not a significant development. To the contrary, I believe that venture philanthropy is itself a transformative innovation in American social progress. The model has matured considerably over the last decade to the point that its efficacy has been firmly established, yet less than 1% of all charitable funding is deployed this way. So venture philanthropy has tremendous growth potential and represents the most dependable instrument for nurturing fledgling social entrepreneurial organizations that could not otherwise build the kind of organizational muscle needed for significant increases in impact. The fact that the value of venture philanthropy seems so self-evident now should neither diminish the signal importance of the innovations depicted in Exhibit 3.17, nor slow their propagation to as many qualified nonprofits as possible.

This is the path that most of the organizations in Exhibit 1.5 have taken to scramble to their present peaks. But this is also where the analogy to private capital markets begins to break down. According to Heiner Baumann, former chief knowledge and learning officer at New Profit, Inc.:

> Dollars aside, the other piece that's missing is the next step up from New Profit. While New Profit typically helps social enterprises grow to approximately $10 million over four or five years, no issue-agnostic, nationally oriented, next-stage funder exists that can support these organizations' expansion from $10 million in revenue to $20 million or $30 million.[16]

The problem with such an anemic system is that, with everyone looking to help build the first floor, there's no way to build the second, third, or higher floors. If there were a nonprofit version of the game Monopoly, the board would be covered with lots of undeveloped properties, a few with little houses, but none with hotels.

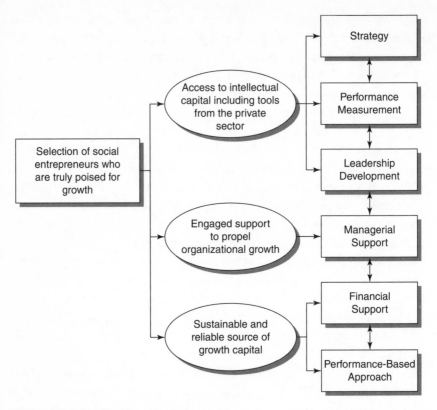

Exhibit 3.17 The New Profit Approach
Source: "Performance-Based Philanthropy," New Profit, Inc., p. 19, August 10, 2006.

In many ways, this is an entirely understandable state of affairs. Although their motivations are quite different, nonprofit funders care about financial risk as much as for-profit funders do. The bigger the bet, the more risk there is. Leaving aside the supernova brand-name NPOs such as the Red Cross and the United Way, the nonprofit sector has painfully little experience in developing successful social change organizations with budgets higher than $10 million. Above six or seven figures is severe nose-bleed territory for many funders and recipients of donated funds. The demands of managing, say, up to $5 million are different in kind from managing beyond that threshold in terms of people, facilities, systems, operations, and all the rest.

Keep in mind that most successful NPOs started out with a small group of intrepid founders who kept at it and learned painful but unavoidable lessons through trial and error. When they start to take in substantial amounts of funding, at some point they stretch the limits of their managerial and organizational capacities. Most NPOs were not designed to manage hundreds, much less thousands, of employees, with corresponding numbers of buildings, sites, programs, and participants.

The Not-So-Little Capital Market That Can't

The term "capital markets" refers to the collection of financial institutions, instruments, and processes by and through which funds flow to support the development, operation, and growth of organizations. As we've seen, the most noteworthy characteristic of nonprofit capital markets is how underdeveloped they are relative to the private sector. To be sure, there has been a good deal of progress and innovation in nonprofit funding mechanisms in recent years. Still, the social sector finds itself facing significant practical, historical, and structural shortcomings on the financial front, including fragmentation and undercapitalization, unrealistic time horizons and funding restrictions, burdensome application and reporting requirements, excessive transaction costs, and chronic shortages of working and growth capital.

The problem of ineffective capital markets manifests itself in two primary ways. We've looked at (and will return to) the fragmentation problem, in which well-intentioned philanthropy is dispersed too widely and spread too thin to do much good. But there is also the "burden" problem: fundraising is much too hard, expensive, and time-consuming.

Of course, both aspects of capital-market immaturity are related. In large part, fundraising is such a burden because social sector funding is so fragmented. Nonprofit leaders are forced to constantly look for support in many places, each of which fails to provide sufficient funds to meet the need.

As one crude illustration of the labor-intensivity and inefficiency of modern-day fundraising, take a look at the breakdown of job postings on the *Chronicle of Philanthropy* Web site on a typical day (see Exhibit 3.18). The most striking figure is the percentage of all jobs categorized as fundraising: 55%.

Exhibit 3.18   Philanthropy Job Listings.

Category	Number of Jobs	Percentage
Fundraising	552	55%
Executive	148	15%
Program	166	17%
Administrative	132	13%
TOTAL	998	100%

Source: "Philanthropy Careers," *Chronicle of Philanthropy*, 16 Apr. 2008, www.philanthropy.com/jobs.

Call me crazy, but I think the fact that more than half of the nonprofit job openings at any given time are for fundraising tells us two things. First, there must be an awful lot of turnover in those positions, which, it turns out, there is. Second, no wonder nonprofits can't produce as much impact as we'd all like: as much as half of their people spend all their time looking for money. These figures surely understate the extent of the problem since virtually all nonprofit executives devote significant time to fundraising. Any way you look at it, far too much staff time relates to chasing dollars.

The *Chronicle* breaks those 552 funding jobs into 14 categories: alumni affairs; annual fund; capital campaigns; corporate and foundation relations; direct marketing; donor relations; fundraising administration; grant seeking; major gifts; membership; planned giving; prospect research; special events; and other fundraising. No wonder, then, that funding job titles proliferate. On that same date, virtually all of the nonprofit jobs listed in Massachusetts involved some variation on "fundraising" argot:

> Vice President of Development; Gift Planning Officer; Leadership Annual Giving Officer; Major Gifts Officer; Director of Development and Director of Communications for Development; Foundation and Corporate Relations Officer; Director of Foundation Development; Associate Director of Development; Chief Development Officer; Gift Planning Officer; Director, Corporate and Foundation Relations; Director of Development; Director of Donor Relations; Foundation and Corporation Relations Officer; Development Officer for Institutional Support; Director of Development; Planned Giving Officer; Associate Director of Development for Annual Giving and Donor

Acquisition; Senior Annual Funds and Special Gifts Officer; Director of Institutional Support and Development Operations; Director of Planned Giving, Legacy and Endowments; and Associate Director, Grants.

As a touchstone of user-friendliness, Bridgestar, a leading online listing of nonprofit jobs, has a checkbox to "Exclude Fundraising Positions," which makes for lean pickings on some days.

Just as the corporate sector spent too much time and effort managing people, money, data, and business relationships before information technology became ubiquitous, so, too, does the nonprofit spend too much time and effort on fundraising that could be used more productively on mission-related activities.

The burden problem is understood by and familiar to virtually every nonprofit professional. Fundraising is the activity that everyone detests and considers their number-one problem, a leading source of burnout and turnover. Even though finding the money to sustain and grow organizations and programs is vital, its accomplishment doesn't directly advance the mission. Fundraising produces funding, not results. It is just a means to an end, but it dominates everything else.

Not only is there an insatiable demand for funds, but nonprofits now face a metacrisis in hiring fundraisers that has been described as a "fundraising frenzy," a "raging national crisis," and a "predatory environment."[17] Large-cap nonprofits such as the Nature Conservancy and the University of Michigan employ one or more in-house recruiters just to hire in-house fundraisers. One might be forgiven for asking how to stop the madness. Once again, we can see how the fragmented capital market drives nonprofits to focus on the wrong things.

As we look ahead, however, it is encouraging to see there are important developments pointing toward a more rational capital allocation system: new financial intermediaries such as nonprofit private placement agents; professional advisory services and consultants; dedicated growth funders; mass market funds; and a plethora of online donation marketplaces.

The arrival of SeaChange Capital Partners in New York and NFF Capital Partners in Boston is a particularly significant development that heralds the advent of sophisticated financial intermediaries founded by high-caliber financial professionals dedicated to managing major funding transactions for investors in nonprofit organizations. The appearance on the scene of such Wall Street veterans as Chuck Harris (formerly of Goldman Sachs) and George Overholser (formerly of Capital One) signals the formation of a robust nonprofit capital market capable of handling the hundreds of billions of dollars that come into the sector every year. Such third-party intermediaries may be better equipped than many foundations and other traditional nonprofit funders to assume the greater risks associated with making significantly larger and longer-term investments in organizations that appear capable of transforming society.

We call such new-generation funders "financial intermediaries" because they add value by standing between investors and nonprofits capable of bringing about systemic change. As SeaChange puts it on its Web site, "We intend to identify nonprofits with records of measurable success and to present opportunities for supporting them to a network of potential donors, including wealthy individuals, foundations, and others." And SeaChange will add value in much the same way that private placement agents do in the business world, with the notable difference of focusing on maximizing social impact rather than financial return:

> We will do for many donors what they lack the resources and know-how to do for themselves: we will identify, vet, and monitor our grantees; and we will bring to nonprofit organizations sophistication in accounting for performance. SeaChange will also engage donors in ways that go beyond the financial and offer them the chance to accomplish through a network what few of them could accomplish individually.
>
> SeaChange will help outstanding tax-exempt organizations raise growth capital. There will be no financial return on capital donated. By focusing on performance, measured in social returns and in milestones of progress toward them, we will help make the contributions of donors more effective.[18]

These are audacious experiments by serious people who intend to change the way tax-deductible donations are raised and distributed. It will take a few years, no doubt, before we can say whether these new institutions have proved themselves out and serious money begins to flow through them in a sustained and growing way.

But even the advent of private placement agents is not likely to provide all the horsepower needed for deploying such large amounts of nonprofit capital. It is not difficult to imagine a social sector initiative—such as a national network of coordinated preschool and out-of-school time programs serving millions of urban poor families, or a consortium of nongovernmental organizations dedicated to building a rudimentary transportation infrastructure across vast stretches of the African continent—that would require not merely tens, but hundreds of millions or even billions of donated dollars that would exceed the capacity of any privately sponsored fund that could be reasonably imagined.

We need to understand what the essential elements of a nonprofit capital market are that would be capable of identifying favorable investment opportunities, attracting experienced executives to shepherd start-ups through sustained growth, assessing the relative performance of portfolio companies, collaborating with competitors to pool risk, and engineering mergers and acquisitions to achieve scale. In the next chapter, we'll consider what additional mechanisms need to be developed to generate third-stage funding.

Notes

1. Matthew Bishop and Michael Green, *Philanthrocapitalism: How the Rich Can Save the World* (London: Bloomsbury Press, 2008), pp. 77–78.

2. Michael D. Bordo, "An Historical Perspective on the Crisis of 2007–2008," remarks prepared for the *Central Bank of Chile Twelfth Annual Conference on Financial Stability, Monetary Policy and Central Banking*, Santiago, Chile, 6–7 Nov. 2008, p. 15, http://michael.bordo.googlepages.com/An_Historical_perspective.pdf.

3. Matthew Bishop, "The Business of Giving," *The Economist*, 25 Feb. 2006, reprinted in Venture Philanthropy Partners, "The Business of Giving: A Survey of Wealth and Philanthropy," http://venturephilanthropypartners.org/globals/press/Economist_Survey_March2006.pdf.

4. Arthur Wood and Maximilian Martin, "Market-Based Solutions for Financing Philanthropy," 6 Apr. 2006, www.ashoka.org/files/Market-Based-Solutions-UBS_Ashoka.pdf.

5. Jumpstart, "Our Impact," 11 Sept. 2007, www.jstart.org/index.php?submenu =about_us&src=gendocs&link=Our_Impact&category=Main.

6. Randall Ottinger, "Portfolio Philanthropy: How Philanthropists Can Apply Portfolio Theory to Make Wiser Social Investments," *Stanford Social Innovation Review* (Fall 2007), www.ssireview.org/articles/entry/portfolio_philanthropy.

7. Clayton M. Christensen, *The Innovator's Solution: Creating and Sustaining Successful Growth* (Boston: Harvard Business School Press, 2003), p. 45.

8. Ibid.

9. Ibid., p. 58, Table 2-2.

10. "45 Social Entrepreneurs Who Are Changing the World," *Fast Company* (December–January 2008); Monitor Group, "The 2008 Social Capitalist Awards," 16 Apr. 2008, www.fastcompany.com/social/2008/index.html.

11. Clayton M. Christensen et al., "Disruptive Innovation for Social Change," *Harvard Business Review* (December 2006), accessed 16 Apr. 2008, http:// harvardbusinessonline.hbsp.harvard.edu/b01/en/common / item_detail.jhtml? id=R0612E&referral=2340.

12. Christensen, *The Innovator's Solution,* p. 55.

13. Geoffrey Moore, *Marketing and Selling Disruptive Products to Mainstream Customers* (New York: Harper Business, 1991); Paul Wiefels, *The Chasm Companion* (New York: HarperBusiness, 2002), p. 3.

14. Wiefels, *The Chasm Companion,* p. 131.

15. Ibid., p. 112.

16. Heiner Baumann, "The Growth Capital Market in the U.S.," *Alliance* 10, no. 1 (March 2005): 38, www.newprofit.org/documents/HBAlliance ArticleMar05.pdf.

17. Holly Hall, "Fund-Raising Frenzy," *Chronicle of Philanthropy*, 9 Aug. 2007, http://philanthropy.com/premium/articles/v19/i20/20001901.htm.

18. SeaChange Capital Partners, "FAQS, " 16 Apr. 2008, http://seachangecap.org/ faqs.html.

Chapter 4

Intermediation

The economic problem of society is . . . the utilization of knowledge which is not given to anyone in its totality.
—*Freidrich Hayek, The Use of Knowledge in Society*

We've seen that the United States is at a point where the tools for becoming economically and socially self-sufficient are systematically unavailable to tens of millions of Americans. As a result, a marginalized underclass is growing larger and becoming more entrenched. At the same time, the public sector has become much less effective at cushioning the vagaries of the economy, and factors such as demography, debt, globalization, and hyperpartisanship are likely to erode government performance further.

Yet the social sector has much more money than ever, and a new wave of entrepreneurial organizations has unlocked creative approaches to many of the most difficult problems that block access to the American Dream. But with a nonprofit capital market that fragments philanthropy into amounts that are too small to fund meaningful growth of the most promising nonprofits, these increases in philanthropy and social innovation do not translate into significant or sustained social progress. Unless more consolidated funding can find its way to the places where it can do the most good, the situation is unlikely to change.

How can we improve the allocation of philanthropic capital to overcome fragmentation for superior mid-cap nonprofits working on $100 million problems? On what basis should funding be reallocated? What do we mean by "improve the allocation" of nonprofit funding? Is it hopelessly presumptuous to suggest that there are "better" ways to distribute charitable donations, given that those funds are donated voluntarily by millions of people making free choices about the causes and organizations they want to support?

"Better" Philanthropic Choices

The idea of reallocating philanthropy has nothing to do with mandating a different set of funding decisions than donors want to make on their own. Rather, reallocation addresses the extent to which donors have the tools to make *informed* choices about their giving and the *effectiveness* of those choices.

For the most part, the nonprofit market does a good job of informing participants about which organizations are working on which kinds of problems. If you want to support nonprofits based on the kinds of people they help, the problems they address, where they work, or how they provide help, there are any number of ways to do so; but if you want your money to go to places where it can have the most impact, that's not so easy. The market is almost a complete failure when it comes to differentiating among nonprofits based on performance, results, or impact.

Given what we've seen about the erosion of the American Dream, increasing inequality, and decreasing social and economic mobility over the past 30 years, it's hard to argue that the nonprofit capital market optimizes capital flows. Under the circumstances, it would seem indefensible to leave the underperforming status quo in place if we have the power to do better.

The notion of "improving" the distribution of charitable funding depends on what we want to maximize. If we want simply to increase to the greatest extent possible the range of choices to whom we give money and how we get it to them, it would be hard to improve on the current do-it-yourself fundraising system that has spawned nearly 2 million nonprofits and all manner of ways to give. The barriers to entry are low, with a growing army of inspired volunteers and an IRS code that imposes minimal eligibility requirements for tax-advantaged status. There is a growing spirit of civic engagement, recently exemplified by California's creation of the nation's first cabinet-level office on "service and volunteering"[1] and the presidential candidate forum on national service. The distributional wonders of the Internet are as available to nonprofit organizations and philanthropists as they are to producers and consumers of every other good, service, and interaction offered online, and the social sector is migrating there with imagination and verve.

So increasing the quantity or variety of choice is not a driving imperative for an improved nonprofit capital market. If that's all we want, things are fine as they are.

But the quality of choice is another matter. For those who want to maximize the impact of their giving, that is, the extent to which the grantees accomplish the objectives that motivated the giving—whatever those objectives might be—there is considerable room for "improving" the allocation of philanthropy.

An Economic Approach to Reducing Fragmentation

Performance-driven philanthropy presents us with a quintessentially economic problem: matching supply and demand to maximize overall satisfaction. If I'm a philanthropist motivated by maximizing impact, then my charitable reserves represent a potential "demand" for social impact. My challenge is to figure out how to "buy" the most impact for my donations. If I'm a nonprofit that produces a "supply" of social impact by helping people overcome difficult obstacles, my challenge is to find donors to whom I can "sell" that impact, and I want to make sure I get "paid" for all the impact I produce. If philanthropic buyers are getting the most impact per dollar donated, at the same time that nonprofit sellers are collecting the most dollars per impact produced, then we've achieved the optimal allocation of nonprofit capital to maximize the performance of the social sector.

That is what Jim Collins, author of *Good to Great*, would call our "big hairy audacious goal":[2] to match the demand for and supply of nonprofit impact at the highest possible level of social betterment. We want to avoid a situation in which, for a given amount of philanthropy, we produce less impact than if we shifted funding to other nonprofits. Until charitable funding is going to places where it can do the most good, the social sector in general, and the nonprofit capital market in particular, will be underperforming.

An ideal system would be one in which every single charitable dollar was donated based on perfect knowledge of the precise impact of all potential giving opportunities. Obviously, that ideal cannot be achieved. But the system we have now is one in which virtually every tax-deductible dollar is allocated with essentially no information about impact. Between the unattainable ideal and the uninformed reality, there is a lot of room to do better.

Of course, we're never going to achieve perfection in our search for maximizing nonprofit impact, just as financial investments don't always go to the companies that produce the most profit. The enduring strength of our economy since World War II, however, shows that markets gravitate toward more productive enterprises and away from less productive ones. If that happened in the nonprofit sector, surely we'd increase the overall level of social benefit produced.

Extracting Information about Nonprofit Impact

The reason that doesn't happen now is that the nonprofit sector produces little useful or reliable information about nonprofit impact. If we can't assess and compare the potential impacts of alternative donations, we can't optimize the allocation of philanthropic capital. Andrew Wolk and Colette Stanzler of Root Cause/Social Impact Research (for which I did some work) have cogently explained this "nonprofit information gap":

> Social impact investors want rigorous and reliable information about nonprofit performance to make sound investment choices. Unfortunately, they face two major information challenges:
>
> **Measurement Challenges**
>
> Quality information about nonprofit performance is scarce. The data available are often fragmentary and unsystematic and lack standardized

outcome measures. . . . Even within a social problem "subsector," or an approach to a social issue, few accepted standards of what to measure exist. As a result, organizations cannot be compared or evaluated by using the same parameters or applying the same standards.

Access Challenges

Social impact investors encounter tremendous difficulty accessing useful information about social issues and organizations working on those issues. Performance-based information is hard to find, understand, and use.[3]

The nonprofit information gap results from the elusive nature of social impact data. Attributing and measuring the impact of nonprofit organizations is an inherently ambiguous undertaking that is unavoidably subject to interpretation. It has quantitative and qualitative dimensions, both of which are multivariate. Under such circumstances, the pursuit of some kind of mathematically definitive way of measuring and comparing nonprofit performance is, I believe, a fool's errand.

If we don't allow the perfect to become the enemy of the good, we can improve philanthropic productivity by reducing the information gap, even if we can't eliminate it. We should strive to create capital market mechanisms that can increase "signals" and reduce "noise" of nonprofit effectiveness in a dynamic and continuous search for "better" philanthropic investment opportunities.

Such an approach is more "scientific" than might at first appear. We tend to think of the nonprofit sector as inherently less efficient than the for-profit sector because we indulge in the false assumption that business results are quantitative and therefore susceptible to fairly precise and transparent calculation. There's some validity to that, of course, but this is a difference in degree rather than in kind.

Contrary to common belief, prices and profits are not perfect measurements of business performance. Though they certainly are "harder" than nonprofit results, they do have "softer" aspects, such as customer loyalty and satisfaction, that bear some similarities to nonprofit outcomes. Even with respect to quantitative information, "company data, even though it is audited, also requires interpolation and interpretation." Legions of stock analysts—many of whom disagree with one another—"make estimates of a company's revenue and earnings, determine its value, and compare its value with its price."[4]

Even if for-profit data is, say, 80% hard and 20% soft, and nonprofit data is, say, 30% hard and 70% soft, it's possible that the mechanisms the private sector uses to optimize the balance of supply and demand to approach maximum return on investment could be adapted to improve the allocation of nonprofit capital to increase the social return on investment to a meaningful extent.

The core problem is quite similar in both sectors. Friedrich Hayek, who shared the 1974 Nobel Prize for Economics with Gunnar Myrdal "for their penetrating analysis of the interdependence of economic, social, and institutional phenomena,"[5] chided economists who disregarded "the unavoidable imperfection of man's knowledge and the consequent need for a process by which knowledge is constantly communicated and acquired." Hayek explained that "the price system" of private enterprise was not some idealized measure of objective value, but simply "a mechanism for communicating information":

> The most significant fact about this system is the economy of knowledge with which it operates, or how little the individual participants need to know in order to be able to take the right action. In abbreviated form, by a kind of symbol, only the most essential information is passed on and passed on only to those concerned. It is more than a metaphor to describe the price system as a kind of machinery for registering change, or a system of telecommunications which enables individual producers to watch merely the movement of a few pointers, as an engineer might watch the hands of a few dials, in order to adjust their activities to changes of which they may never know more than is reflected in the price movement.[6]

Price, in other words, is shorthand for an unknowably large amount of uncertain information that enables myriad economic actors to (as Hayek put it) "move in the right direction" when conditions change in a material way. But information about prices is never perfect and never complete:

> The peculiar character of the problem of a rational economic order is determined precisely by the fact that the knowledge of the

circumstances of which we must make use never exists in concentrated or integrated form but solely as the dispersed bits of incomplete and frequently contradictory knowledge which all the separate individuals possess. The economic problem of society is . . . a problem of how to secure the best use of resources known to any of the members of society, for ends whose relative importance only these individuals know. Or, to put it briefly, it is a problem of the utilization of knowledge which is not given to anyone in its totality.[7]

This is not so different from the nonprofit sector. Millions of people have varying degrees of knowledge about various aspects of nonprofit organizations, whether as donors, employees, students, citizens, media consumers, or recipients of telephone and direct mail solicitations. No one knows everything about nonprofit performance, but many of us know something that sheds some light, however great or small, however general or specific, however apparent or obscure, about which organizations are more effective than others.

The essential problem of comparing nonprofits based on performance and impact is not that there is nothing equivalent to prices or profits in most of the social sector. Nor is the problem the absence of impact data as such. Rather, the problem is that the social sector hasn't developed a sufficiently robust "mechanism for communicating [the] information" we do have. As they used to say on *The X Files,* "The truth is out there," but it's so widely dispersed that we haven't yet found a way to retrieve it. Consolidating information about nonprofit performance is the sine qua non of developing third-stage capital capable of producing greater social impact.

In order to defragment nonprofit capital to provide more effective funding that can enhance social impact, we need to defragment the universe of information about nonprofit performance. But we don't have to invent some magical new currency by which we can precisely quantify the impact that every nonprofit produces and compare that impact on an apples-to-apples basis to the impact of every other nonprofit.

Any significant movement in the direction of increasing the signal and reducing the noise about nonprofit effectiveness could spark a correspondingly significant improvement in the deployment of philanthropic capital. Chris Anderson, editor in chief of *Wired* magazine and author of *The Long Tail: Why the Future of Business Is Selling Less of More*,[8] has mapped out a pathway for us to explore.

"Long-Tail" Economics

From his perch atop the masthead of "the first word on how technology is changing the world," Anderson noticed that the business model that had dominated the American entertainment industry since the end of World War II—the production and distribution of blockbuster movies, hit TV shows, and bestselling books and music albums—was "starting to tatter at the edges." Hits were still the most important source of profit for the humongous entertainment industry, but they had become noticeably less dominant than they once were:

> In short, although we still obsess over hits, they are not quite the economic force they once were. Where are those fickle consumers going instead? No single place. They are scattered to the winds as markets fragment into countless niches. The one big growth area is the Web, but it is an uncategorizable sea of a million destinations, each defying in its own way the conventional logic of media and marketing.[9]

When Anderson set out to learn why the most popular hits accounted for a smaller share of industry revenue than they had for decades, he discovered that digitization was changing "the economics of scarcity"—selling vast quantities of a few bestselling products—into "the economics of abundance"—selling small quantities of a huge variety of niche products: "The onesies and twosies were still only selling in small numbers, but there were so, so *many* of them that in the aggregate they added up to a big business."[10] Anderson saw that "new efficiencies in [online] distribution, manufacturing, and marketing were changing the definition of what was commercially viable across the board" once "the bottlenecks that stand between supply and demand in our culture start to disappear and everything becomes available to everyone."[11]

When Anderson compared the popularity (measured by sales) of different products (books, movies, Web sites, etc.) and the number of different products that produce those sales, over and over again he got a curve with a short, narrow head and a long, flat tail (see Exhibit 4.1). His

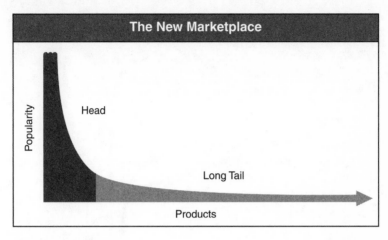

Exhibit 4.1   Long Tail
Source: Adapted from Chris Anderson, "About Me," *The Long Tail,* 16 Apr. 2008, www
.longtail.com/about.html.

big insight was that although the relatively small number of products in
the head accounted for half the cumulative revenue for all products sold,
so did the relatively large number of products in the tail. Even though
content publishers still focused on hit records and films and bestselling
books, digital publishers like Amazon.com and NetFlix proved there was
a lot of money to be made in the tail, where many niche products sold
just a few copies each.

A similar distribution dynamic operates in the nonprofit sector, as
shown in Exhibit 4.2. In fact, there are two significant long-tail curves,
one for the amount of revenue and one for the number of nonprofits.
For both of the long-tail curves, the *x*-axis is the same, which divides
nonprofits into eight revenue brackets: starting from the left, they are

1. Greater than $100 million
2. Between $10 million and $100 million
3. Between $5 million and $10 million
4. Between $1 million and $5 million
5. Between $500,000 and $1 million
6. Between $250,000 and $500,000
7. Between $100,000 and $250,000
8. Less than $100,000

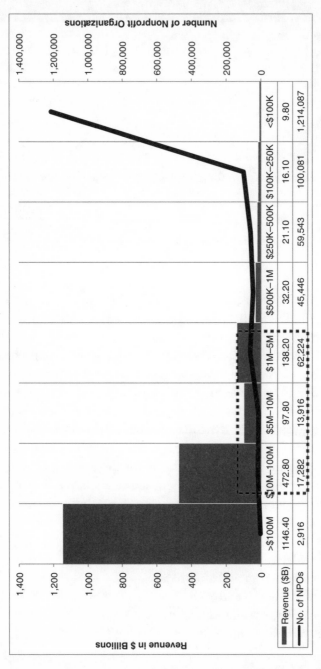

	>$100M	$10M–100M	$5M–10M	$1M–5M	$500K–1M	$250K–500K	$100K–250K	<$100K
Revenue ($B)	1146.40	472.80	97.80	138.20	32.20	21.10	16.10	9.80
No. of NPOs	2,916	17,282	13,916	62,224	45,446	59,543	100,081	1,214,087

Exhibit 4.2 Long Tail of Nonprofit Funding

The categories along the x-axis are taken from data published by the IRS and the Urban Institute.[12] They don't align perfectly with my analysis, but they're fine for purposes of illustration. Recall that I have previously described mid-cap nonprofits as having between approximately $5 million and $20 million, which includes all of category (3) but only parts of (2) and (4). The dashed box on Exhibit 4.2 shows very roughly how my working definition of mid-caps overlaps with the IRS/Urban Institute categories. Of course, there's nothing sacred about my $5 million to $20 million range, as there undoubtedly are nonprofits with less than $5 million in revenue that are effectively mid-caps in terms of my analysis, and there are nonprofits with more than $20 million for which the same could be said. The dashed box should provide useful boundaries for the discussion to follow: large caps are to the left of the dashed box, and small caps are to the right.

On the left side of both curves we find a few thousand large-cap nonprofits that have been around a very long time and have acquired high levels of brand recognition, such as Goodwill Industries and major universities and hospitals. They raise billions of dollars that represent a large percentage of aggregate donations. The Bridgespan Group found that only 144—less than 1%—of the more than 200,000 U.S. nonprofits established since 1970 achieved $50 million in annual funding by 2003.[13] At the right half of the curves, nearly 1.5 million small nonprofits each receive low levels of donations, but cumulatively, they receive a substantial percentage of all charitable giving.

Now, before we get too carried away with the obvious parallels between the long tails of retail sales and Web site traffic, on one hand, and the comparable long tail of the nonprofit sector, on the other, let's be sure to understand that Anderson focused on the *virtues* of the long tail: ubiquitous and low-cost production and distribution of digital content make it possible for otherwise unprofitable niche products to survive and even thrive. The same virtues are found in the nonprofit world: the Internet and social networking have exponentially increased the opportunity and exponentially decreased the cost of starting new social-purpose organizations, and the resulting explosion in the growth of nonprofit organizations has unquestionably enriched community life in this country. By all means, let 2 million flowers bloom.

Yet the accelerated formation of new nonprofits has greatly exacerbated the problem of capital fragmentation. With 2 million nonprofits competing for donations, press coverage, site visits, revenue streams, volunteers, and all the rest, it is much more difficult for the most effective nonprofits to distinguish themselves from the ever-increasing crowd of mid-cap wannabes and unproven newcomers. Philanthropists confront an intimidating landscape comprising a "vast range of social needs, seemingly infinite ways of addressing them, and large numbers of undifferentiated organizations doing so."[14] Since almost all nonprofits, including the most productive social enterprises, are chronically underfunded, the proliferation of "niche" nonprofits comes at the expense of the greater aggregate social impact the capital market could otherwise fund.

Not so long ago, the nonprofit sector exemplified the economics of scarcity, with philanthropy concentrated disproportionately among wealthy donors and large-cap fundraisers, just as television was dominated by big-name advertisers working symbiotically with a few powerful broadcast networks. Now the economics of abundance are galvanizing a seismic shift toward millions of small donations solicited and distributed online that find their way to a burgeoning number of mission-driven start-ups that no longer face prohibitive costs of entering the social marketplace.

In most respects, the democratization of philanthropy is a beneficial development. For example, GlobalGiving, the world's largest online donation marketplace, has distributed more than $14 million in donations to over 1,300 projects from more than 41,500 unique donors since 2002.[15] Collectively, those metrics represent an average donation of over $10,000 per project, which is quite a sizable investment for the kinds of small-cap organizations that are listed on the site, especially since the average donation is just $337. This is powerful intermediation at work.

Meanwhile, mid-cap social entrepreneurs encounter the economics of neither abundance nor scarcity but what I would call "abundant scarcity." They have grown beyond being mere blips on the radar screen, but they have not yet become household names that transcend the unforgiving limitations of labor- and time-intensive bilateral fundraising. Their engines have enough horsepower to produce significant impact and the potential to accomplish much more, yet their consumption of fuel outstrips the availability of supply as increasing numbers of larger and smaller producers on either side of the curve compete for the same pool of expanding but finite resources.

Are there ways to increase the share of fundraising proceeds that go to mid-caps? Could the nonprofit capital market bulk up the body of Anderson's curve? I think it can.

Between the Short Head and the Long Tail

Even though Anderson concerned himself primarily with the shrinking of the head (fewer bestsellers) and the lengthening of the tail (more niche products), his analysis also explains the dynamics in the middle, or body, of the curve. He identifies three forces of long-tail economics:

1. Democratizing the tools of production, so that the availability of "more stuff" offers more choices and lengthens the tail
2. Democratizing the tools of distribution, so that greater access to more niches increases sales and fattens the tail
3. Connecting supply and demand, which drives business down the tail from hits to niches[16]

Resource allocation is the beating heart of private sector economics, of which demand, supply, and their connective tissue are the stuff of life. Anderson's three forces each concern a radical process of *disintermediation* incited by new technologies of production, distribution, and communication. By decreasing the influence and control wielded by traditional sources of economic power, both producers and consumers become far less dependent on middlemen to decide the three great questions of distribution: (1) What's available? (2) Who wants it? and (3) How can they get it? The answers, Anderson explains, are moving in the direction of (1) whatever you want, (2) everyone, and (3) any way they want.

Each of these forces is at work in the evolving nonprofit sector. The United States now has about 1.2 million young nonprofits with annual budgets of less than $100,000 that do noble work enriching people's lives in thousands of local communities across the country. Another nearly 200,000 operate with revenues between $100,000 and $1 million. Together, they comprise a little over 94% of all nonprofit organizations.

Low production and distribution costs have enabled the proliferation of so many niche players of such modest financial means, and digital communication tools (such as free and low-cost e-mail marketing and fundraising utilities) have allowed the founders and supporters of these highly specialized organizations to find and sustain each other. As the U.K.'s Stephen Dawson has observed, "[T]here are zero barriers to entry in philanthropy, and it is easy to make mistakes."[17] As a result, "an individual looking to participate in the philanthropic sector is faced with a bewildering array of players."[18]

When Anderson uses the term "democratize" in his three forces of long-tail economics, he's referring to a process of decentralization: the transfer of economic power from the corporate few to the grassroots many. The long-tail nonprofit market works much the same way. It disaggregates the supply of nonprofit production in response to widely distributed demand for civic engagement through an organically developed smorgasbord of social organizations. It also facilitates connections between the two by reducing the cost and increasing the availability of virtually frictionless communication.

Of course, democratization is also the process behind fragmentation, including the fragmentation of nonprofit capital. As we have seen, while fragmentation is relatively benign for large- and small-cap nonprofits, it severely limits the ability of mid-caps with limited fundraising resources to grow large enough to produce systemic change or transformative impact. For the more than 75,000 mid-cap nonprofits in the $1 million to $50 million range, long-tail economics means abundant scarcity, a twilit state of chronic underfunding, constrained growth, and unrealized impact. To provide mid-cap nonprofits with the financial horsepower to take on $100 million problems as the next step in reinvigorating the American Dream, we have to find ways to consolidate and channel nonprofit funding, rather than increase its dispersion through democratization.

I am not suggesting that we make it harder to start new nonprofits or interfere with people's charitable choices. Nor am I asserting, when it comes to organizations working to bring about social change, that bigger is always better. I do maintain, for the reasons I've given earlier, that bigger is sometimes better, and that, in far too many cases, the existing fundraising system is structurally incapable of helping proven, innovative nonprofits that produce the most impact to become big enough to make significant and sustained progress against social problems that have become intolerable for a great nation and show no sign of abating.

But make no mistake: the approach I'm advocating is essentially the opposite of Anderson's process of democratization. If we want the mid-cap segment of the nonprofit sector to foster vastly greater social progress than we have seen for some three decades, we need to offset the virtually infinite variety that defines the long tail and drains precious financial resources. In its place, we need institutions and tools that foster selectivity, sound judgment, and even wisdom. Instead of being remorselessly indifferent to the distribution of philanthropic capital, we need to be able to differentiate intelligently among the bounty of too many choices based on attributes about which we know very little: performance and results.

As things stand now, the nonprofit sector has plenty of democratization, but not enough horsepower where it counts. If we're serious about making much better use of billions of donated dollars, we're going to need a new kind of adult supervision to complement the long tail of democratization. We'll need to nurture three things: (1) informed investors who are committed to finding more effective nonprofits, (2) more capable social enterprises that are demonstrably prepared to meet the challenges of hypergrowth, and (3) more vigilant and purposeful oversight to make the latter accountable to the former.

Intermediation

In Anderson's "new marketplace" of the long tail, the creation, marketing, distribution, and sale of niche products is largely self-organizing. eBay, for example, began as a purely digital marketplace with low transaction costs, sophisticated search tools, and facilitated auctions, and buyers and sellers did the rest spontaneously. But after the initial Internet euphoria wore off, customer confidence was shaken by widespread fraud, nonpayment, nondelivery, identify theft, and the like. Bidding on a $10 vintage Bart Simpson Talking Pez Dispenser didn't pose much of a risk, but who in the world would put up $2,800 for a Gibson CS-356 semi-hollow body electric guitar if there was a fair chance the "seller" was a fake and the instrument didn't exist?

eBay recognized that it had to introduce some adult supervision if its otherwise wide-open marketplace was going to grow. And so it developed robust administrative features that helped it become a multibillion-dollar online powerhouse:

- E-mail confirmation of buyers, sellers, listings, and transaction
- Dispute resolution
- Marketplace research
- Buyer protection
- Warranty services
- Certified providers

Wikipedia, the collaboratively written Web encyclopedia, matured and grew in similar fashion. In addition to what Wikipedia calls "community level controls"—that is, users and contributors keeping a watchful eye out for malicious editing and vandalism—the publisher introduced editorial panels and software-facilitated controls to protect the integrity of the content on the site. Anyone who wants to can become an "editorial administrator," provided they gain enough peer approval "to ensure a high level of experience, trust, and familiarity across a broad front of projects within Wikipedia."[19]

These kinds of "intermediation" arose in response to perceived gaps that inhibited adoption of products and services offered by unfamiliar long-tail producers. Virtually every successful example of long-tail economics, including Internet dating, social networking, online gaming, affinity groups (such as diet support groups and collectors of arcane trinkets), Web-based e-mail, shopping, and contextual advertising, have incorporated confidence-inspiring intermediation tools and processes as a necessary prerequisite to unconstrained growth. Just as the establishment of conspicuous and reliable transaction-processing security was an essential predicate to the widespread acceptance of online commerce, muscular but benevolent intermediation has become a vital, if underappreciated, differentiating factor of life online.

Intermediation is also integral to the formation of Geoffrey Moore's "whole products" that innovative producers must develop to "cross the chasm" from small early markets to large mainstream markets. Just as e-commerce couldn't take off without secure credit card transaction processing, so, too, must mid-cap nonprofits provide a complete and integrated set of product and service offerings to convince social impact investors to provide third-stage capital. New forms of growth capital will not emerge until mid-caps sufficiently reduce what funders perceive as significant adoption risk. In particular, social sector intermediaries must address two prerequisites to mid-market growth: organizational capacity and risk management.

Organizational Capacity

Conventional wisdom holds that expenses for nonprofit capacity detract from the amount of program services that social enterprises provide to populations-in-need. One recent survey reported that "sixty-two percent [of respondents] believe the typical nonprofit spends more than what is reasonable on overhead expenses such as fundraising and administration."[20] This kind of thinking is reinforced by charity rating organizations that emphasize easily reportable measures of charity "efficiency" such as the percentage of total expenses that pay for direct program services rather than operations. According to this view, the less a nonprofit spends on nonprogrammatic expenses, the better.

The operative assumption is that nonprofit funding is a zero-sum game in which every dollar spent on organizational capacity is a dollar diverted from helping people. There exists, of course, a kernel of wisdom here: "excessive" overhead expenses, however that might be defined, are bad. But lurid stories about lavish headquarters and six-figure executive salaries have assumed mythic proportions, obscuring the fact that such excesses are far more the exception than the rule. There isn't a lot of nuance to most discussions about nonprofit "efficiency": more often than not, the baby of organizational capacity gets thrown out with the bath water of too much concern for a kind of unappeasable cost-cutting that is ultimately self-defeating.

The asserted dichotomy of funding organizations versus funding programs, and the supposed trade-off between the two, is manifestly false. This was driven home in a 2004 report of the Nonprofit Overhead Cost Project entitled "Getting What We Pay For: Low Overhead Limits Nonprofit Effectiveness."[21] The authors defined "organizational infrastructure" as "accounting, fundraising, information technology, human resources, physical plant, and other common organizational elements that undergird a nonprofit's mission and programs." They made two important findings. First, "inadequate infrastructure compromises organizational effectiveness." Second, "restricted funding and small size lead to inadequate infrastructure":

> Absent good, comparative information about program or mission effectiveness, donors and charity watchdogs often place excessive reliance on financial indicators. Of particular concern to us is the use of overhead cost and fundraising cost ratios as stand-ins for measures of program effectiveness. No organization in our study was an extravagant spender on fundraising or administration. Yet contrary to the popular idea that spending less in these areas is a virtue, our cases suggest that nonprofits that spend too little on infrastructure have more limited effectiveness than those that spend more reasonably.[22]

The kinds of infrastructure weaknesses that the report identified included insufficient and inexperienced administrative staff, noncompetitive salaries, lack of accounting, budgeting, and fundraising expertise and software, inadequate cash reserves, and dilapidated facilities. Notably, the study found that infrastructure challenges were particularly pervasive and acute among the organizations I've called the small caps: "nonprofits with less than $1 million in annual expenditures."

The more physical assets a business needs to serve its customers, the more sales it needs to pay for those assets. When Chris Anderson looked at retail sellers, he saw three different categories based on their relative mix of physical and digital assets (see Exhibit 4.3):

1. "Physical retailers" have traditional stores with limited shelf space and expensive inventory. Tower Records couldn't afford to carry or display that many different titles, so it relied primarily on sales of hit records.
2. "Pure digital retailers" like iTunes or Rhapsody (the music service of Real Networks) have no shelves and their "inventory" of downloadable songs doesn't cost anything to store, so they can carry many more titles, even ones that sell very few copies, and still be profitable.

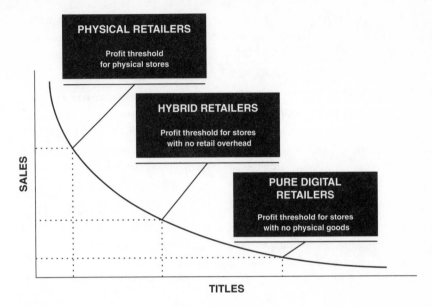

Exhibit 4.3 Three Steps to Infinite Variety
Source: Arik Johnson, "The Long Tail." Competitive Intelligence, Aurora WDC, 16 Apr. 2008, www.aurorawdc.com/ci/000340.html. Chart adapted from Anderson, *op. cit.,* p. 92.

3. "Hybrid retailers" such as Amazon.com, whose sales aren't limited by shelf space but that do own expensive warehouses full of costly inventory to meet customer demands for quick delivery, offer more choice than physical bookstores but still rely on bestsellers to reach profit targets.[23]

It's easy to forget that Amazon once faced a world of criticism for the enormous cost of its warehousing investments. A November 1999 *Business Week* article recalling the controversy asked, "What's With All the Warehouses?" and answered, "E-tailers see they'll need bricks and mortar, too":

> Once upon a time in the ancient World Wide Web, about two years ago, there lived a virtual retailer called Amazon.com Inc. (AMZN) Freed by the magical Internet from the need to build physical stores, Amazon focused on building a cool Web site and attracting millions of customers. No clerks, no big warehouses—just sheer opportunity as far as the eye could see.

It was a nice fairy tale. And it was dead wrong. Now, over the squawks of investors who had hoped for a quicker path to profits, Amazon is spending $300 million to outfit more than 3 million square feet of warehouse space to store its books, CDs, and other products . . . .

What gives? Mostly, it's one cold fact: The Net is not yet the frictionless marketplace that people like me keep insisting it will become. E-tailers that depend on hundreds of distributors and manufacturers to handle inventory and delivery face all sorts of problems. Products run short, they're delivered late, and multiple items from one order arrive days apart, making them costly for consumers to return if need be . . . .

But any merchant serious about building a lasting business online can't farm out such critical tasks for long. Savvy e-tailers know that if they want the kind of bulletproof customer experience that will keep buyers coming back, they must build and stock warehouses, pack the boxes themselves, and hire enough staff to handle customer calls and returns.[24]

The "administrative-overhead-is-bad" argument it too simplistic because it doesn't fit all segments of the nonprofit market equally. Large caps that raise and spend billions are going to have administrative costs that rival private companies of similar size. Small caps can and do get by with borrowed furniture and a battered personal computer running QuickBooks.

But mid-cap social entrepreneurs typically employ aggressive business models that require complex combinations of "whole products" and far-flung infrastructure (see Exhibit 4.4). The infrastructure needs and fundraising resources match for large caps and small caps, but they don't for mid-caps (see Exhibit 4.5). Large-cap nonprofits need to maintain high levels of infrastructure and growth, but they have fundraising resources to meet their needs. Small caps don't need to grow very much (since they target local community needs that increase only gradually), so their lack of fundraising resources isn't a strategic obstacle.

Mid-caps need to achieve dramatic growth if they're going to make real headway against $100 million problems, but they don't have the resources to raise five or ten times as much money as they do now. With both limited "shelf space" (infrastructure) and large amounts of expensive "inventory" (clients, staff, volunteers), they're caught between a rock

Exhibit 4.4 Examples of Mid-Cap Nonprofit Infrastructure.

Social Enterprise	Whole Product	Infrastructure
BELL (Building Educated Leaders for Life)	Tutoring, mentoring, experiential learning, parental support	8,000 scholars in 40 public school sites in 4 cities; more than 1,000 teachers and tutors
Citizen Schools	Citizen teachers; apprenticeships; curricula; community explorations; school partnerships; culture of achievement	37 locations, 6 states, 3,800 students, 2,800 volunteers
Jumpstart	School success; family involvement; future teachers; older adult corps; service learning; curriculum pilot; full classroom model pilot	3,500 college students, 13,000 children, 20 states, 70 communities
Teach For America	Teaching as leadership; instructional planning and development; classroom management and culture; diversity, community, and achievement; learning theory; literacy development; alumni network	5,000 corps members teaching in over 1,000 schools in 26 regions; by 2010, TFA plans to support 800 alumni as school leaders, 100 as elected officials and 12 as social entrepreneurs
YearUp	Marketable job skills; stipends; apprenticeships; college credit; behavior management system; multiple levels of support	Over 200 students in 4 cities; over 60 corporate partners, 100 community partners and 300 volunteers

Source: Data collected from Web sites of organizations listed.

and a hard place: they can't take on substantially more clients (move to the right) because they can't raise substantially more revenue to fund organizational development (move up the curve).

In Anderson's new marketplace, digital production, marketing, and distribution lengthened the tail by moving sales down the curve, shifting customers away from traditional market leaders burdened with costly inventory and limited shelf space and toward Internet start-ups with

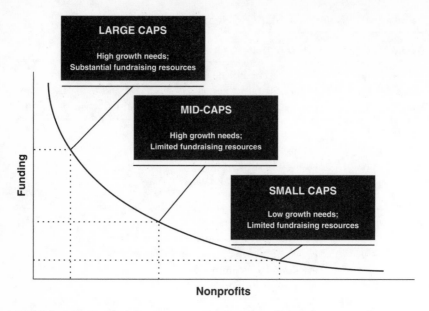

Exhibit 4.5   Fundraising Resources versus Growth Needs

low-cost virtual inventory and access to an unlimited product catalog. In the nonprofit sector, the same phenomena shift donors away from traditional charities with costly overhead toward more than a million Web-based organizations that get by on tiny amounts of funding.

Anderson's three forces of long-tail economics teach us how we can "reverse engineer" the excessive fragmentation of the evolving nonprofit market. The elimination of production and distribution "bottlenecks" grew the long tail. But those "bottlenecks" comprised the infrastructure that supported the old entertainment industry when it was based on selling large volumes of a few hit products: studios, film and recording equipment, production and distribution facilities, movie theaters, and so on.

During the height of Internet mania, "bricks and mortar" was a derisive term used to describe traditional companies weighed down by business models that relied on inelastic and expensive physical plant and retail locations. Start-ups with virtual "storefronts" that focused on attracting "eyeballs" and "traffic" to gain a "first mover advantage" and "get big fast" were called "pure plays," meaning they were 100% digital. Contrary to predictions that real stores would fade away, the market instead matured so that many once-pure Internet retailers added an intermediating layer of infrastructure to become "bricks and clicks" producers. At the same time, traditional retailers added online channels to take advantage of low-cost marketing and distribution opportunities.

To build the capacity required to respond to the unmet needs of millions of disadvantaged American families, mid-cap nonprofits need adequate infrastructure:

> Investing in the people and systems that make products and services better is well established in the for-profit sector. Consider the millions spent on staff and warehouse facilities before Amazon.com ever went on line. Similarly, the three business leaders who founded Venture Philanthropy Partners with 27 other investors have been involved in substantial capacity building investments in the business world for years. They asked why organizations created to eradicate poverty and solve the complex social problems of our society are often not financed in a way that allows them to develop or maintain their infrastructure. . . .

> For the nonprofit sector as a whole to achieve a greater social impact, more organizations must address their gaps in organizational capacity. Having honed their model or their program, they need to invest the necessary time and effort in building their organizational capacity to deliver that program more effectively and efficiently or to replicate their success in other locations. Unless they do, they will never be capable of fulfilling their promise.[25]

Managing Risk

Getting more funding to mid-caps that understand the importance of developing organizational infrastructure to increase impact is essential to advancing social progress in this country. But increasing funding to build long-term capacity entails risk. Without prudent risk management, funders will be skeptical about making substantial investments in ambitious projects whose benefits won't be immediately obvious.

There are two principal forms of nonprofit capital risk. The first is the risk that a social investor will pick the "wrong" grantees: that is, choose one or more nonprofits that are less likely to achieve the results that motivate the investor than other nonprofits to which the investor could have made donations instead. This "selection error" reflects the opportunity cost of uninformed philanthropy. Mitigating selection errors requires intermediaries to collect and analyze information about performance and results to inform the selection of grantees.

The second type of nonprofit capital risk is the potential inability of selected social entrepreneurs to execute their growth plans successfully. Mitigation of "execution risk" requires intermediaries to help social entrepreneurs deploy growth funding effectively.

These are the kinds of prudent risk taking that fortified capital markets would be designed to encourage. Highly-engaged social investors who care about funding transformative social impacts understand that systemic change is much more difficult to achieve and that a lower success rate is an inevitable by-product of "swinging for the fences." The role of nonprofit capital market intermediaries is to reduce these risks by sponsoring more rigorous search processes to identify the most promising nonprofits and provide financial and nonfinancial support, both at the time of initial investment and as circumstances change, just as financial intermediaries do for their portfolio investments.

George Overholser, founder and managing director of NFF Capital Partners, describes his model this way:

> NFF Capital Partners is not in the business of raising money. Rather, we are in the business of helping our nonprofit clients to raise money, and our funder clients to deploy money in powerful ways. . . .
>
> Typically, our assignments involve capital campaigns of $5 million to $30 million. As a trusted intermediary, our role is to perform financial due diligence in anticipation of funder questions, to assist the organization in preparing an investment prospectus, to design [growth capital] accounting treatment that will be used to monitor investment flows, to draft a provisional investment term sheet that promotes equity-like behaviors, and, after the money has been raised, to provide several years of investment monitoring and reporting services on behalf of all investment parties.[26]

"Nonprofit Finance Agents"

Long-tail customers with highly specialized preferences go online to find far-flung niche producers ready to satisfy them. For example, eBay disintermediates demand, supply, and exchange for buyers and sellers of Star Wars collectibles, Tibetan singing bowls, and other special-interest items in over 50,000 categories.

In the nonprofit sector, "nonprofit finance agents" (sometimes called "private placement intermediaries") essentially reverse the same three forces to stimulate social enterprise growth. SeaChange Capital Partners and NFF Capital Partners find those organizations for their exclusive clientele by devoting resources to conducting due diligence that donors at large cannot perform themselves. Rather than encourage the proliferation of new and untested organizations that would further dilute the impact of giving, they selectively screen for sophisticated social impact investors and robust nonprofits with viable growth plans, and then closely monitor the expenditure of large funding pools that would give nosebleeds to most foundations. SeaChange cofounder Chuck Harris explains their model of nonprofit intermediation this way:

> The fundamental piece of the mechanism is to seek to fund the business plans of these nonprofits rather than fund a piece of their program. We plan to do that by going out to high-net-worth individuals and family foundations with a well-crafted story and growth possibilities, with detailed modeling of future possibilities for the organization and lots of disclosure about what they've done in the past. We plan to conduct the financing much like a private placement in the business sector, with the goal of raising $5 million, $10 million, $15 million for organizations on the threshold of a growth phase. As I say, what we hope to do is most closely analogous to an equity private placement where you do a document, you take the management on the road, you meet with philanthropists, either individually or in groups, and you ask for significant contributions to fund the business model.[27]

As we've seen, the same forces that produce "infinite variety" in the private sector produce capital fragmentation in the nonprofit sector. Private funding agents like SeaChange hope to increase impact by decreasing fragmentation.

If these early experiments prove successful, we will see a small but elite group of mid-cap nonprofits with the organizational equivalent of six-pack abs. Although tens of thousands of mid-cap nonprofits could not all take advantage of the same strategies that SeaChange and others

Exhibit 4.6 Disintermediation versus Two Types of Intermediation.

Economic Forces	Long-Tail Disintermediation (Business and Nonprofit)	Private Nonprofit Intermediation	Mid-Cap Nonprofit Intermediation
Objective	Increase the number and variety of niche products and nonprofits	Increase the impact of selected social enterprises	Increase the impact of high-growth mid-caps
Approach	Come one, come all	By invitation only	Performance screening
Demand	Reduce barriers that limit the numbers and kinds of producers and donors	Select sophisticated social impact investors	Consolidate funding streams of social impact investors
Supply	Reduce barriers that restrict distribution channels and media, including fundraising	Perform due diligence to find the best social enterprises	Collect and report impact data to screen for successful social enterprises
Exchange	Expand supply and demand connections (including fundraising) via online access	Help chosen grantees deploy funds and report progress on growth plans	Develop performance indices to connect funding and impact

have developed, the same dynamic forces must be addressed before intermediation can occur.

Exhibit 4.6 summarizes the key attributes of long-tail disintermediation and private intermediation. Conditions seem ripe for a third way.

The objective of long-tail disintermediation in both the for-profit and nonprofit sectors is to increase the quantity of consumer choice to the greatest extent possible. In a long-tail world, everyone wants to find whatever they want as conveniently as possible, whether they're looking for goods and services or worthy causes. A "come one, come all" approach reduces barriers to forming new businesses and nonprofits. But ubiquitous supply and ubiquitous demand won't accomplish anything unless there are many more distribution and funding connections among them. So disintermediation depends on "Web 2.0" communications media and transaction platforms to support frictionless exchanges that are largely independent of time and place. As a result, both participation and interactions among participants are made as wide open as possible

Private nonprofit intermediation has the opposite objective: to maximize the quality of participating nonprofits in terms of their capacity to produce social impact and to grow. This requires a strict invitation-only approach. Intermediaries apply stringent selection criteria to offer investment opportunities in carefully crafted nonprofit portfolios comprised exclusively of organizations that can execute bold growth plans. The intermediaries also develop a limited number of robust connections between sophisticated philanthropists and sturdy social enterprises that involve careful money management and progress reporting. Thus, participation is narrowed and interactions are managed, but the quality of both are enhanced.

Public intermediation for mid-cap nonprofits would occupy a middle ground of quantity and quality. Participation by funders and grantees, as well as connections among them, would be broad but not unlimited, requiring the development and application of some level of screening criteria. Investors would need ways to inform and monitor their investments, and grantees would bear the burden of accounting for their performance. But since the resources don't exist for strict exclusivity or intensive oversight of thousands of mid-caps, structural mechanisms would have to be developed to facilitate participation, selection, and performance measurement. The resulting mid-cap market segment would be less democratic (to use Anderson's description) than the long tail and more democratic than the short head.

Closed versus Open Intermediation

In financial markets, "private placement" deals are limited to sophisticated investors for a very simple reason: unlike members of the general public who might invest in the stock market through a 401(k), mutual funds, or other strictly regulated investments, private placements fund investments that are not ready for primetime. The financial returns are higher because the risks are greater, both in the sense that the companies are less well established and that there is less reliable information available about them. Sophisticated investors understand those risks and purchase high-wire stocks with their eyes open. But before a company can sell stock to the general public, it is legally required to make far more extensive disclosures about its prospects and the attendant risks.

In the social sector, multiyear grants of $5 million to $30 million are many times larger than most foundations or individual philanthropists typically make. Intermediaries like SeaChange Capital and NFF Capital represent to their experienced clients that their vetted and bundled investment opportunities offer potentially greater social returns and correspondingly greater risks that those returns won't be achieved. These guys aren't going to place bigger bets for ordinary social investors who don't fully understand both the upside and the downside, and they're not going to recommend funding any but the best social enterprises.

Part of the value that boutique intermediaries bring to their investor clients is undertaking careful due diligence to find the cream of social entrepreneurs. Consider SeaChange's "General Criteria for Future Grantees":

1. Operating revenue of between $5 million and $50 million;
2. A clearly articulated mission and related goals;
3. A proven leadership team;
4. An engaged Board of Directors and other committed stakeholders;
5. A track record of five-years or more;
6. A dynamic organization committed to learning and developing the people who work there;
7. A defined set of sought-after social benefits, systems for measuring progress toward these outcomes, and a body of evidence indicating success at an attractive cost;
8. A well-developed plan for self-sustaining growth, either in breadth or depth, toward a strategic goal.[28]

Innovative intermediaries like SeaChange are acutely aware of the primitive state of the nonprofit capital market. That's why they offer one-stop shopping: recruiting investors who understand the opportunities and risks; recruiting nonprofits that are capable of executing ambitious growth plans; and managing the application, accounting, and reporting of the funding. It's also the reason this is not a one-size-fits-all model for donors and grantees of all sizes and risk profiles.

As these new financing agents represent the first bricks in the foundation of a performance-driven social sector, conducting invitation-only field experiments makes perfect sense. "Walk before you run" is good advice. But it is not too early to start laying the groundwork for "Nonprofit Intermediation 2.0." There is much to figure out and many other experiments to design, fund, and conduct, all of which will take some number of years. Our long-term goal should be to extend the work of emerging private placement models to support the further development of performance-driven philanthropy in which larger segments of the public could participate.

Social Factor

Even though private placement intermediaries are exclusive, that does not mean they are elitist. Their choice of clients is not motivated by a desire to place themselves above ordinary folks, but to improve the chances that they will succeed at something that has proved to be maddeningly difficult. By imposing stringent criteria for the selection of investors and grant recipients, they hope to maximize the impact of the specialized philanthropic funds they raise and materially improve the lives of more people to a far greater extent than traditional funding has allowed.

If their early efforts work, they presumably will be replicated, but probably without significantly lowering their high standards concerning donor sophistication and grantee capabilities. In that event, there will be more private placements, but high selectivity will remain an essential ingredient of the model and its successful application.

At the same time, the proliferation of private placements will not change the fundamental problem that is the concern of this book, namely the inability of the overall nonprofit capital market to channel funds to their most effective uses. By setting up professionally managed funding pools for best-in-class social enterprises, private placements sensibly insulate their efforts from the deficiencies of the capital market at large. They don't try to correct those deficiencies, nor should they. That simply is not the purpose of boutique private placements, and it is not a valid crit-icism to say such funding isn't available to everyone. As the old software joke goes, "That's not a bug, it's a feature."

However, with regard to the rest of the nonprofit capital market, enhancing broad social participation is essential to our effort to advance performance-based philanthropy. Private placements have good reason to exclude the general public, but broad-based donor communities seeking to overcome long-standing barriers to basic opportunity don't. Under-standing the social dimension of charitable giving provides insight into both the dynamics of the nonprofit market and the prospects for improv-ing how it allocates funds.

Let's start with the fact that nonprofit revenues are not distributed among nonprofits according to the familiar "bell curve." If they were, we would expect to see a few organizations with a lot of money, a few organizations with just a little money, and most organizations in the middle ranges of revenue. In the so-called *normal distribution* represented by the bell curve, the largest number of organizations (the median) would have close to the average (the mean) amount of revenue (see Exhibit 4.7).

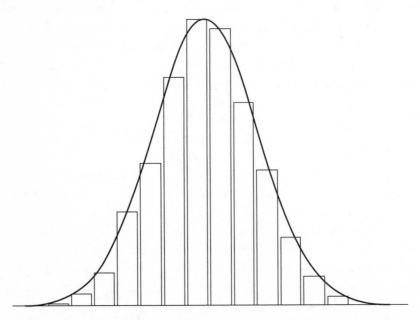

Exhibit 4.7   Normal Distribution

Exhibit 4.8 Distribution with Independent Probabilities

Normal distributions develop in response to natural laws of probability. When balls drop through the sequential series of evenly distributed pegs illustrated in Exhibit 4.8, the probabilities of the ball falling either to the left or to the right in any given row are the same, so the balls accumulate at the bottom in a bell curve. Most of the balls fall toward the middle and fewer balls fall toward the sides in a symmetrical pattern. This is the kind of pattern we would expect to see if every nonprofit had the same chance of being selected by each donor as any other.

But as we've seen, that's not how the distribution of nonprofit funding looks. Instead, as shown in Exhibit 4.2, there are (1) a relatively small number of large caps (primarily major universities, leading culture and

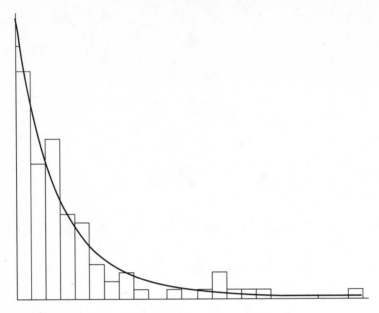

Exhibit 4.9   Power Law Curve

arts centers like museums and orchestras, health-care institutions, and household-name charities like the Red Cross) with enormous endowments and revenue streams well above $100 million, (2) more than a million small caps with less than $1 million each, and (3) a relatively small group of mid-caps between the two in terms of revenue. A few organizations have revenues well above average, and most organizations have below-average revenue.

The shape of this curve (see Exhibit 4.9) is a familiar one to mathematicians and it is one that is very common among social systems. It is generally referred to as a "power law," with "power" being used in its exponential sense. The defining characteristic of a power law, observes Clay Shirky, is that "most elements in a power law system are below average, because the curve is so heavily weighted towards the top performers." On his economics and culture blog, he explains how power laws develop in social settings:

> In systems where many people are free to choose between many
> options, a small subset of the whole will get a disproportionate amount

of traffic (or attention, or income), even if no members of the system actively work towards such an outcome. This has nothing to do with moral weakness, selling out, or any other psychological explanation. The very act of choosing, spread widely enough and freely enough, creates a power law distribution.[29]

Shirky goes on to explain that "diversity plus freedom of choice creates inequality, and the greater the diversity, the more extreme the inequality." Why is this so?

The answer lies in the social relations among people and how this affects their preferences. If people's choices had no effect on the choices made by other people, then each option would have an equal probability of being selected based only on each person's own preferences. If those autonomous choices were made and then totaled, a few people would make unusual (or low-probability) choices, but most people would make choices in the middle range, resulting in a typical bell curve.

But, of course, our choices *are* affected by other people's choices. David Brooks summarized "a tide of research in many fields" showing that "our decision-making is powerfully influenced by social context—by the frames, biases, and filters that are shared subconsciously by those around."[30] If someone you know liked a certain movie, you're more likely to see it. Most people are more likely to read books after they've become bestsellers. Positive feedback among social groups tends to skew bell curves so they behave according to power laws. The rise of "preferential attachments" magnifies success, so the vertical "head" of the power law curve goes higher and becomes skinnier, while the horizontal "tail" grows longer and flatter.

Suppose we magnetized the balls dropping from the funnel in Exhibit 4.8. The path of one ball would affect the path of the next ball, and the path of that ball would affect the path of the next one, and so on. The distribution of balls at the bottom would become skewed in the direction of the balls that dropped earlier, as shown in Exhibit 4.10. As the preferential-attachment effect increases, the curve would skew farther to the left.

The bell curve is called a "normal distribution" because it conforms to the "norm" of probability laws in their simplest form, when every choice is made independently. But when social norms affect probability,

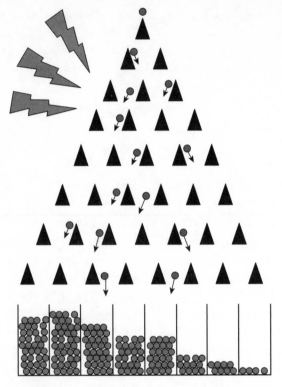

Exhibit 4.10   Distribution with Preferential Attachment

power laws are the natural result. Philanthropy is allocated according to
long-tail economic forces precisely because the nonprofit capital market
is a social institution. REDF's Cynthia Gair says that "money attracts
money, and philanthropists are best positioned to expand donor pools
because people like to put their money into pots that have already been
'vetted' by others."[31] Leaders of the Bronfman Philanthropies make a
similar observation: "It is much easier to engage outside funding and
partners when your work is visible to the public."[32]

Right now, preferential attachment in philanthropy is both too strong
(tall, skinny head) and too weak (long, flat tail) to maximize social impact.
In between, innovative mid-caps bump up against a low ceiling of arrested
development. To help more innovative mid-caps achieve their full potential, we need more of the attachment impulse to be "just right," that

is, based on organizational performance and impact. That means more intermediation, more information about results, and more attention to organizational capacity, which is the nonprofit equivalent of "shelf space."

Private placements intermediate the allocation of money among a select group of donors and nonprofits. But the nonprofit capital market allocates money among *all* donors and *all* nonprofits. If we want to improve the market's performance in terms of the social impact it produces, we have to find ways to intermediate the muddled social sector in all its chaotic glory.

Notes

1. Arnold Schwarzeneger, "Governor Arnold Schwarzenegger Announces First-in-the-Nation Cabinet Position for Service and Volunteering," California State Northridge, 26 Feb. 2008, Office of the Governor, State of California, 16 Apr. 2008, http://gov.ca.gov/speech/8880.

2. Jim Collins, *Good to Great: Why Some Companies Make the Leap . . . and Others Don't* (New York: Collins, 2001), p. 190.

3. Social Impact Research, "Need & Opportunity," Root Cause, 16 Apr. 2008 (interior citations omitted), www.socialimpactresearch.org/need_and_opportunity.

4. Joel Kurtzman, *How the Markets Really Work* (New York: Crown Business 2002), p. 131.

5. "The Sveriges Riksbank Prize in Economic Sciences in Memory of Alfred Nobel 1974," Nobelprize.org, 16 Apr. 2008, http://nobelprize.org/nobel_prizes/economics/laureates/1974.

6. Friedrich Hayek, "The Use of Knowledge in Society," *American Economic Review* 35, no. 4 (September 1945): 519–530. Brad Cox, ed., Virtual School, 16 Apr. 2008, www.virtualschool.edu/mon/Economics/HayekUseOfKnowledge.html.

7. Hayek, "The Use of Knowledge in Society."

8. Chris Anderson, *The Long Tail: Why the Future of Business Is Selling Less of More* (New York: Hyperion, 2006).

9. Ibid., p. 2.

10. Ibid., p. 9.

11. Ibid., p. 11.

12. Internal Revenue Service, Exempt Organizations Business Master File, October 2008; The Urban Institute, National Center for Charitable Statistics,

"Registered Nonprofit Organizations by Level of Total Revenue," http://nccsdataweb.urban.org/NCCS/Public/index.php.

13. William Foster and Gail Fine, "How Nonprofits Get Really Big," *Stanford Social Innovation Review* (Spring 2007), www.ssireview.org/articles/entry/how_nonprofits_get_really_big.

14. Paul G. Schervish, John J. Havens, and Mary A. O'Herlihy, "Charitable Giving: How Much, by Whom, to What, and Why," in Walter W. Powell and Richard Steinberg (eds.), *The Nonprofit Sector: A Research Handbook,* 2nd ed. (New Haven, CT: Yale University Press, 2006), www.bc.edu/research/cwp/meta-elements/pdf/charitablechapter.pdf.

15. GlobalGiving Fact Sheet, www.globalgiving.com/aboutus/media/backgrounder.html.

16. Anderson, *The Long Tail,* pp. 54–56.

17. Matthew Bishop and Michael Green, *Philanthrocapitalism: How the Rich Can Save the World* (London: Bloomsbury Press, 2008), p. 93.

18. Arthur Wood and Maximilian Martin, "Market-Based Solutions for Financing Philanthropy," *Viewpoints,* 6 Apr. 2006, pp. 58–63. Available at SSRN: http://ssrn.com/abstract=980097.

19. "Researching with Wikipedia," Wikipedia, 16 Apr. 2008, en.wikipedia.org/wiki/Wikipedia:Researching_with_Wikipedia#Editorial_administration.2C_oversight_and_management.

20. Ellison Research, "Americans' Perceptions of the Financial Efficiency of Nonprofit Organizations," February 2008, p. 8, www.ellisonresearch.com/releases/0208_ERWhitePaper.pdf.

21. Nonprofit Overhead Cost Project, "Getting What We Pay For: Low Overhead Limits Nonprofit Effectiveness," Indianapolis: National Center for Charitable Statistics, 2004. "Fundraising and Administrative Costs," Center on Philanthropy at Indiana University and Center on Nonprofits and Philanthropy at the Urban Institute, 16 Apr. 2008, http://nccsdataweb.urban.org/kbfiles/311/brief%203.pdf.

22. Ibid.

23. Anderson, *The Long Tail,* pp. 89–91.

24. Robert D. Hof, "What's with All the Warehouses?" *Business Week,* 1 Nov. 1999, accessed 16 Apr. 2008, www.businessweek.com/1999/99_44/b3653046.htm.

25. McKinsey & Company, "Effective Capacity Building in Nonprofit Organizations," 2001, Venture Philanthropy Partners, 16 Apr. 2008, p. 29, www.vppartners.org/learning/reports/capacity/elements.pdf.

26. Nonprofit Finance Fund, "About NFF Capital Partners," 16 Apr. 2008, www.nonprofitfinancefund.org/details.asp?autoId=119.

27. Charles Harris, "Q&A with Chuck Harris," interview with Mitch Nauffts, *Philanthropy News Digest* 28 (September 2007), SeaChange Capital Partners, accessed 16 Apr. 2008, http://seachangecap.org/news/seachange-pnd-092807.pdf.

28. SeaChange Capital Partners, "General Criteria for Future Grantees," accessed 16 Apr. 2008 http://seachangecap.org/news/seachange-grantees-criteria.pdf.

29. Clay Shirky, "Power Laws, Weblogs, and Inequality," Clay Shirky's Writings about the Internet, accessed 16 Apr. 2008, http://shirky.com/writings/powerlaw_weblog.html.

30. David Brooks, "The Social Animal," *New York Times*, 12 Sept. 2008, p. A23, www.nytimes.com/2008/09/12/opinion/12brooks.html.

31. Cynthia Gair, "Roadmap #1: Strategic Co-Funding," Out of Philanthropy's Funding Maze, REDF, p. 10, www.redf.org/user/login?destination=node/548.

32. Charles Bronfman and Jeffrey Solomon, "Pull the Right Levers for Maximum Effect," *Financial Times*, 12 July 2008, www.ft.com/cms/s/0/67b9151e-4faa-11dd-b050-000077b07658.html?nclick_check=1.

Chapter 5

Growth Capital

The wheel is still turning but the gerbil is on its last legs.
—Edward Skloot, Slot Machines, Boat-Building and the
Future of Philanthropy

We don't have time for incremental growth.
—Leslie R. Crutchfield and Heather McLeod Grant,
Forces for Good: The Six Practices of High-Impact Nonprofits

To this point, our discussion of "the disheartening problem of 'scale'" introduced in Chapter 1 has focused on macroeconomic quandaries: the decades-long inability of governmental and social programs to help a large and growing underclass move toward self-sufficiency. This lack of systemic progress is unlikely to change until successful mid-cap nonprofits develop enough capacity to move the needle of opportunity.

This brings us to the microeconomic dimension of these structural and institutional problems. Even if highly engaged philanthropists were willing to provide third-stage funding, and even if sophisticated intermediaries arrived to channel and oversee those large infusions of capital, most mid-caps wouldn't qualify for such funding. Nor could they make effective use of geometrically larger, longer, and more flexible grants to achieve the kind of exponential growth needed to make headway against $100 million problems. Both problems—the ineligibility for and the inability to use third-stage funding—arise from the fact that most nonprofit organizations don't engage in the basic financial management practices that are indispensable to the creation and deployment of growth capital.

Unless this changes, third-stage funding is unlikely to materialize. Macroeconomic improvements to the allocation of nonprofit capital cannot take root without the commensurate advancement of financial management at the microeconomic level, that is, within mid-cap non-profit organizations themselves. The advent of nonprofit growth capital depends not only on the availability of "risk funding" that only interme-diaries can engineer but also on a plentiful supply of qualified nonprofits that those same intermediaries deem capable of putting large injections of capital to productive use. Both are necessary; neither alone will be sufficient.

The combination of third-stage funders (guided by robust inter-mediaries) and "growth-ready" mid-caps can create the conditions for a nonprofit growth-capital market capable of producing transformative social impact. In the next chapter, we shall consider alternative mech-anisms for connecting both sides of this new market. For now, let's understand what's different about growth capital and what mid-caps must do to become eligible to receive it.

Revenue versus Capital

Operating a sustainable business (or a nonprofit) and growing it are two quite different things. To run a business, the organization needs to bring in enough money to cover its ongoing expenses. If its expenses exceed its available cash for any appreciable length of time, it won't be able to pay its bills, including its payroll, rent, and supplies. Unless it can raise more cash to keep its employees coming to work, buy needed materials and supplies, and keep the doors open and the lights on, at some point it will have to shut down.

If operating cash falls short of operating expenses, the organization runs a deficit that eventually will lead to its demise. Thus, running a viable business requires, at a minimum, that income and expenses "break even." The income that organizations use to fund ongoing business operations is called "revenue."

By contrast, growing a business or nonprofit requires a reliable source of funds that exceeds expenses. If the organization has just enough cash to break even, it will incur deficits if it diverts some of that revenue to grow the business. For example, if a company operating at break-even hired new employees or bought new equipment to develop new products or enter new markets, it wouldn't be able to meet its existing payroll or pay its current vendors, and its basic operations would fail. (Obviously, I'm not taking loans or working capital from other sources into account.) So a "going concern" must generate enough revenue to sustain current operations indefinitely, but a growing business must generate a steady stream of additional funding in excess of break-even requirements. This additional funding is called "growth capital."

Organizations that don't understand and respect the essential difference between revenue and growth capital straddle the knife-edge between failing to grow and failing altogether. That knife-edge is where many mid-caps live.

Inasmuch as growth capital is a separate and distinct kind of funding (see Exhibit 5.1), its acquisition requires different behaviors and practices, not just more of what organizations are already doing. Few nonprofits, including few mid-caps, either understand or do what growth funders expect before they'd consider forking over significant grants to help the organization multiply its capacity by a factor of two or three. Far fewer understand how to make the case for the kind of tenfold growth needed to solve $100 million problems.

Growth capital offers the possibility of reversing the traditional fundraising paradigm by creating, as I stated in Chapter 1, "a system that

Exhibit 5.1 Revenue versus Capital.

	Revenue	Growth Capital
Fragmentation?	Yes	No
Donors	Many; assorted	Few; sophisticated
Intermediation?	No	Yes
Grantees	All nonprofits	Mid-caps and large caps
Uses	Fund operations	Expand organizational capacity
Growth	Gradual	Steep

helps highly engaged social impact investors find and fund the best mid-cap nonprofits, instead of having those nonprofits spend all their time looking for growth capital." Let's take a closer look at how this happens.

Investor Confidence

Question: What would it take to convince the new generation of highly engaged philanthropists who want to maximize social impact to contribute, say, $100,000 to a single social enterprise instead of giving $10,000 to each of ten different nonprofits? Answer: A really convincing case of substantially greater impact. Or, as the authors of the foundational article on venture philanthropy put it, "Some observers of philanthropy have argued that better capacity and performance may make donors more confident and therefore more willing to make more or bigger grants."[1]

These new-age donors consider philanthropy an important and purposeful avocation into which they put an unusual amount of thought. Paul G. Schervish, Mary A. O'Herlihy, and John J. Havens of the Boston College Social Welfare Research Institute found that "[n]ever before . . . have so many wealth holders, with such an entrepreneurial experience, at such a young age, with such great wealth, and with so much future time, and in so many arenas been this consciously intercessional, and purposefully self-reflective about their philanthropy. . . ."

> We found that as a group, they are explicitly and consistently *agent-animated philanthropists*. That is, they tend to expect and encourage nonprofits to pursue, as a path to achieve their service goals, the business goals of efficiency, strategic thinking, innovation, risk-taking, good management, accountability, measurable goals, and growth in scale. They have confidence in being able to seek out, attack, and alleviate social and organizational problems. They are universally imbued with an optimistic, energetic, and problem-solving mentality. They generally believe that education and development of human capital provide the best solutions to society's problems.[2]

This entrepreneurial mind set should make this new wave of enlightened wealth holders uniquely receptive to the notion that, under the right circumstances, consolidated giving can accomplish far more, dollar for dollar, than fragmented giving can. To be sure, it is always more difficult to make the case for a major gift than a minor one. But the fact that highly engaged donors tend to be "consciously intercessional and purposefully self-reflective" is conducive to giving third-stage funding a try as a promising response to decades of disappointment in extending the reach of the American Dream.

Of course, the motivations of potential growth capital funders are not uniform. But if, as the Boston College professors found, "wealth holders are thinking about how to be wise and generous about the allocation of their wealth," how can capital market leaders help them acquire the confidence to experiment with third-stage funding?

Crossing the Funding Chasm

Exhibit 5.2 compares the four kinds of nonprofit funding considered in this book, one of which (third-stage funding) I am proposing as a necessary innovation to advance social progress. To recap briefly, first-

Exhibit 5.2   Comparison of Nonprofit Funding Stages.

	1st-Stage Funding	2nd-Stage Funding	Private Placement	3rd-Stage Funding
Funding Source	Local	Sophisticated investors	Sophisticated partners	Social impact investors
Intermediation	None	Venture philanthropy	Financial management agents	Unknown
Fragmentation	Extensive	Some	Minimal	Reduced
Impact Information	Little to none (primarily relationships and storytelling)	Due diligence: organizational capacity; output metrics	Growth plan; private placement memorandum	Growth readiness
Transparency	Limited	Considerable	Extensive but private	Unknown
Capacity Development	Limited	Considerable	Extensive	Substantial

stage funding is the name I use for the vast majority of traditional "bilateral" or one-to-one fundraising, in which nonprofits of every size and description reach out to potential donors primarily through affinity relationships and sympathetic appeals for financial support, rather than results achieved or impact produced. No intermediaries stand between donors and recipients, and transparency about operations and results is essentially limited to minimal legal requirements, such as establishing that the organization is a bona fide 501(c)(3).

When most nonprofits are forced to compete for the finite attention and generosity of casual philanthropists using just traditional fundraising tools, the inevitable results are dissipating fragmentation, stunted organizational development, and constrained impact.

In second-stage funding, the select group of adolescent nonprofits that secure one of the few coveted spots in venture philanthropy portfolios achieve much higher levels of organizational capacity and effectiveness. The sophisticated investors participating in the venture fund have longer time horizons than casual donors, the due diligence process for admission is rigorous, and knowledgeable mentors provide skilled intermediation across the full range of financial, human resources, performance measurement, and business development challenges. Measuring and reporting performance against established metrics increase accountability and transparency. Some foundations provide capacity-building grants that work much the same way.

"Nonprofit finance agents," the most recent innovation that is still in its infancy, offers the highest potential for achieving the McKinsey ideal of organizational capacity (see Chapter 2). Here, intermediaries having the highest levels of financial acumen partner with the most sophisticated social impact investors. Before making aggregated investments of millions of dollars on behalf of the syndicate, the agents help prepare investment prospectuses similar to those used to move billions of private equity dollars in the business world. As a result, within the closed confines of the funding syndicate, transparency about grant recipients is at its maximum. Developers of this new model envision that such a select and carefully nurtured group of social enterprises will produce the biggest bang-per-buck.

The path from first-stage to second-stage to nonprofit funding agents marks a progression of increasing organizational prowess and corresponding social benefit. At the microeconomic level, it also represents a progression of increasing scale, with more than 90% of first-stage grantees stuck below $1 million in revenue, venture-backed nonprofits reaching up to the $10 million to $20 million range, and privately placed grantees aiming for substantially higher capitalizations. But as we saw in the long-tail discussion in Chapter 4, the number of nonprofits in each funding segment runs in the other direction: most nonprofits remain stuck for all time in stage 1, a few find their way to stage 2, and fewer still find their way to financing intermediaries.

It remains to be seen whether the disproportionate results achieved by the smaller number of turbocharged organizations will produce transformative social impact. By definition, both venture philanthropy and private placements are highly selective and therefore limited to very small numbers of exceptional nonprofits. Could the nonprofit capital market produce significantly greater social output by bringing growth capital to a significantly larger share of organizations than existing intermediaries with highly selective portfolios can support?

Geoffrey Moore's "crossing the chasm" model can help answer that important question. Under Moore's formulation, venture philanthropies and private placement agents resemble the "innovators" and "early adopters," respectively, of the new capital market. They represent essential but small-scale experiments under tightly controlled conditions that have proved out daring new business models and theories of change without which broad-spectrum growth capital would be inconceivable. The question becomes, then, whether we can devise a value proposition for the much larger segment of the nonprofit capital market that corresponds to Moore's "early majority pragmatists" to stimulate growth capital for the thousands upon thousands of mid-cap nonprofits that are not among the fortunate few adopted by the likes of SeaChange Capital Partners, NFF Capital Partners, and the Edna McConnell Clark Foundation.

Moore instructs that the bridge across the chasm requires a "whole product solution" that removes "adoption risk" and satisfies "the target customer's compelling reason to buy." In our case, that means a compelling reason why social impact investors should be willing to incur higher investment risk by concentrating larger amounts of philanthropy among fewer recipients for longer periods of time on more flexible terms.

Can we discover ways to "overcome the natural reluctance of pragma-tists to adopting applications that still contain a degree of complexity and risk,"[3] in this case mid-cap growth capital, without as much handholding as venture philanthropists and private placement intermediaries provide to their exclusive clientele?

Making the Nonprofit World Safe for Growth Capital

It turns out there is an excellent case to be made for making the kinds of riskier bets that nonprofit growth capital represents. Building on the work of "a small but growing number of organizations . . . involved in providing growth capital," William Foster of the Bridgespan Group has distilled the basic recipe by which "donors can learn how to scout out and grow the best nonprofits . . . [and] certain nonprofits can . . . learn how to attract cash for expansion":

1. The organization addresses a critical need.
2. The organization has strong leadership.
3. The organization has strategic clarity.
4. The organization's programs are demonstrated successes.
5. The organization's programs are cost-effective.
6. The organization has grown successfully.
7. The organization has a sustainable funding model.[4]

A mid-cap social enterprise that meets these requirements should be able to make a compelling case that it represents a reasonable invest-ment risk for the kind of funding that has the potential to make serious headway against $100 million social problems. Indeed, such a show-ing should be both necessary and sufficient to rally high-engagement donors to the cause of defragmented capital: a mid-cap that does not satisfy these requirements should not be entrusted with much larger amounts of longer-term and less-restricted funding, but social impact investors should embrace consolidated funding for exceptional social entrepreneurs that are evidently prepared to build and grow new insti-tutions capable of providing opportunity for all.

Planning for Sustainable Growth

One of the key differentiators among mid-cap nonprofits is their pre-paredness for future growth. To become an NFF Capital Partners client, for example, it is not enough that nonprofit "boards are already strong, their management teams are already complete, [and] their programs are mostly proven." They must also "already have strong strategic plans."[5] Likewise, when considering potential grantees, SeaChange Capital Part-ners looks for "[a] well-developed plan for self-sustaining growth, either in breadth or depth, toward a strategic goal." This is what Foster means when he refers to "strategic clarity" as one of the requirements for growth capital.

Aspirations for breakout growth are coded into the DNA of social entrepreneurs. Bridgespan reports that virtually all of its clients want to grow. Arrayed against the core impulse to grow, however, is a rueful acknowledgment that this shared aspiration has not yet been realized. Lisbeth B. Schorr, lecturer in Social Medicine at Harvard University, has observed that "[w]e have learned to create the small exceptions that can change the lives of hundreds. But we have not learned how to make the exceptions to the rule to change the lives of millions."[6] Larry Cuban, an emeritus professor at Stanford University, recently said that "Teach for America and these other new entrepreneurs are on to something, but they're not near to changing classroom teaching nationwide."[7]

Professor Thomas Kane of the Harvard Graduate School of Educa-tion told Bob Herbert of the *New York Times* that "We've got a bunch of little things that we think are moving in the right direction, but we haven't stepped back and thought, 'O.K., how big an improvement are we really talking about?'"[8] In 2001, the president of Compumentor (now TechSoup) told Edward Skloot, then the executive director of the Surdna Foundation, that "funders that have invested in what they believe to be a macro solution are disappointed by tiny incremental gains."[9] Bridgespan found that only 144 of the more than 200,000 U.S. nonprofits started since 1970 have reached annual revenue of $50 million.[10]

The gap between the wish to grow and its fulfillment has spurred encouraging innovation in both the theory and practice of nonprofit growth strategy. For example, Professor J. Gregory Dees and his colleague Beth Battle Anderson of the Center for the Advancement of Social

Entrepreneurship (CASE), based at Duke University's Fuqua School of Business, have published excellent foundational work on the important topic of "Scaling for Social Impact: Exploring Strategies for Spreading Social Innovations." Among the many contributions of their approach is a comprehensive matrix of "options for scaling an innovation," which matches three kinds of "local distribution channels" with six "mechanisms for spreading impact." In each case, they offer detailed guidance for choosing the best approach based on such considerations as the nature of the organization and its innovation, and the "Five R's" of Receptivity, Readiness, Resources, Risks, and Returns.[11]

Duke University's Fuqua School of Business is the source of another important contribution, this time by Professors Paul N. Bloom and Aaron K. Chatterji, entitled "Scaling Social Entrepreneurial Impact."[12] The authors present an instructive model using the acronym "SCALERS" to identify seven "organizational capabilities or strategic levers that matter most for scaling social impact"—staffing, communicating, alliance-building, lobbying, earnings-generation, replicating, and stimulating market forces—and seven "situational contingencies [that] can intensify or diminish the importance" of the SCALERS—labor needs, public support, potential allies, supportive public policy, start-up capital, dispersion of beneficiaries, and strength of economic incentives.[13]

On the practitioner front, leading social enterprises (often working with management consultancies) have demonstrated the capacity to develop strategic growth plans of impressive scope and rigor. For example, Citizen Schools, one of the leaders in the after-school movement (ably led by Eric Schwarz, author of the American Dream Scorecard, discussed in Chapter 2), developed a plan called "Growth Capital for Financial Sustainability" that helped Citizen Schools become one of only three flagship grantees participating in the Edna McConnell Clark Foundation's $120 million Growth Capital Aggregation Pilot. Andrew Wolk and Kelley Kreitz of Root Cause have published "Business Planning for Enduring Social Impact: A Social-Entrepreneurial Approach to Solving Social Problems" that directly connects the demand for and supply of growth capital:

> Imagine a day when organizations whose primary mission is social impact—nonprofits, government agencies, and for-profit enterprises

alike—use business plans as their road maps to facilitate the rapid generation of successful and lasting solutions to a wide variety of social
problems, including poverty, domestic violence, unequal access to
healthcare, and the achievement gap in education.

Imagine a day when funders use these business plans to make investment decisions, track progress, and inform further decisions about
reinvestment—ultimately directing capital logically and predictably to
the organizations that demonstrate the best performance and impact.[14]

When potential growth-capital funders face the chicken-and-egg
problem of making bigger financial bets under conditions of extreme
uncertainty, they need not hesitate over concerns about mid-cap planning capabilities. Our best mid-cap leaders are plenty smart enough,
with the help of enlightened researchers who have applied themselves to
addressing this critical success factor, to develop strategic growth plans
worthy of third-stage funding. There is, however, a more challenging
organizational deficiency which most mid-cap nonprofits are neither
aware of nor equipped to handle.

Accounting for Growth

The migration from loyalty-based to merit-based philanthropy will entail
a shift in the workload between nonprofits and their funders. With traditional philanthropy, nonprofits devote a disproportionate level of effort to
labor-intensive forms of outreach: fundraising events, direct mail solicitations, online appeals, and so on. As explained earlier, the excessive
amount of time diverted to fundraising is one of the primary reasons
social sector accomplishments are so modest relative to the problems
they address.

But if social enterprises hope to attract larger investments more
efficiently, they should expect to provide prospective donors with a corresponding increase in financial transparency so that investors can readily
make informed decisions. Sophisticated investors are unlikely to fund
even well-developed growth plans if the underlying financial assumptions are obscure. Third-stage funders won't accept such plans at face
value; they must be backed up with verifiable financial data.

The kinds of social impact investors that are most likely to comprise the "early majority pragmatists" of the new nonprofit capital market will know first-hand how private companies raise and spend growth capital. Later-stage investments involve difficult judgments about what it will take to provide a new kind or expanded scale of business activity, as well as how long and how much funding it will take. There are risks those judgments will be wrong, that the plan isn't feasible, that it won't be executed successfully, and that it will fail to attract new customers to the extent forecast.

Also, money used to fund growth must be managed with a long-term perspective and without immediate results. If a company runs out of capital when the plan is, say, 60% complete, it doesn't get 60% of the benefit, it gets no benefit. As the money was essentially wasted, the investors are going to be very unhappy and it will be much more difficult for the company to raise investment capital in the future because of its inability to execute the growth plan. Such a company does not grow because the market exacts a penalty for poor performance.

It follows that financial growth capital investors tend to be extremely careful before making such potentially lucrative but plainly riskier bets. And once they've decided to open their checkbooks, they are vigilant about monitoring the company's performance and looking for signs of misplaced assumptions and unexpected surprises.

Nonprofits seeking growth capital must expect and prepare for similar levels of up-front and ongoing scrutiny. But few nonprofits understand what kinds of financial information growth capital investors require. Nor are their books set up to provide it. Until a fundamental shift in nonprofit accounting practices takes place, the conditions necessary for the creation of third-stage funding will not exist. I'm no accountant, but even I can understand that growth funders will not provide large amounts of unrestricted and long-term investments for organizational development and strategic growth unless they are confident that prospective grantees can answer four simple questions over the entire lifespan of the grant:

1. Do you know how to use the money to achieve strategic growth?
2. Are you in fact using the money the way you said you would?
3. Are you making the progress along the way you expected to make?
4. If not, do you know how to correct the situation?

Simply put, "the purpose of financial analysis is to detect signs of failing fiscal health and to highlight the appropriate corrective action."[15] It is entirely reasonable that investors expect such baseline information as a prerequisite to considering third-stage funding.

It is far more the rule than the exception that even when the best mid-cap nonprofits can answer "yes" to the first question, their answers to the other three questions are usually "no." This is a correctible accounting problem that serious-minded nonprofit leaders looking to get off the fundraising treadmill must resolve. Otherwise, they will never qualify for defragmented funding. Let me say it again:

> Nonprofits that can't prove they know how to continuously account for the use of and results gained from third-stage funding will never get any.

A few years back, George Overholser, founder and managing director of NFF Capital Partners (a division of the Nonprofit Finance Fund), wrote a seminal paper entitled "Building Is Not Buying,"[16] in which he explained that "a major reason why a market for nonprofit growth capital has failed to materialize" is that most nonprofits don't adopt sound accounting practices.[17] They commingle very different kinds of money they receive in ways that prevent them from funding long-term growth. Instead, all the money goes to immediate and short-term needs, leading to a hand-to-mouth existence. Professors Regina E. Herzlinger and Denise Nitterhouse put it perfectly: "They deplete the past and rob the future to finance the present."[18]

In the business world, money for current operations—revenue—is treated very differently from money to grow the business—capital. Revenue and capital come from different places and they're used for different purposes, so companies keep track of them separately on their books. Only in that way can they and their investors tell if each pot of money is being used effectively.

The accounting is so vital because companies spend the two kinds of money in very different ways. Revenue pays the ordinary expenses—employees' wages, supplies and operating costs—that companies need to make things they already make and provide services they

Exhibit 5.3 Revenue versus Growth Capital.

	Revenue	Growth Capital
What it is:	Flow of $	Pool of $
When it comes in:	Perpetual	Episodic
Where it comes from:	Paying customers (often "third-party payers")	Fed by investment, loans, and surplus revenue
What it's for:	Purchases the provisions of goods and services	Covers the deficit incurred on the way to sustainability

Source: Adapted from George Overholser, "Building Is Not Buying," www.nonprofitfinancefund.org/docs/Building%20is%20Not%20Buying.pdf.

already provide for customers they already have. That money flows in and out in a constant stream, which must be replenished constantly at levels sufficient to fund the firm's ongoing operations indefinitely. (See Exhibit 5.3.)

However, capital funds the growth of the business, either more of the same (expanded capacity) or the provision of additional products and services (extended lines of business). Capital is how companies build the capacity to do things they're not already doing and for which they don't already have customers, so it's riskier. While revenue flows in a more or less steady stream as customers buy what the company sells, capital arrives in large, infrequent blocks when companies raise it from investors.

Unlike revenue that must flow in forever (albeit subject to fluctuations in timing and amount), growth capital has a finite time horizon based on the planned achievement of specific strategic objectives. If the objectives are achieved, the investors celebrate their success and turn the funding of the company's enhanced level of operations over to customers who provide revenue through purchases of goods and services. If the objectives are not achieved, the investors acknowledge their failure and make an informed decision not to throw good money after bad. Exhibit 5.4 illustrates the same distinction in the case of nonprofit organizations.

Unfortunately, nonprofit accounting often doesn't distinguish revenue from capital. Instead, all funding is treated as revenue. This creates two potential problems. First, if revenue is diverted to long-term growth

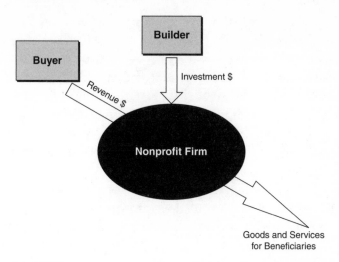

Exhibit 5.4 Investment Funds the Nonprofit; Revenue Funds Programs

Source: George M. Overholser, "Nonprofit Growth Capital: Defining, Measuring and Managing Growth Capital in Nonprofit Enterprises, Part One: Building Is Not Buying," www.nonprofitfinancefund.org/docs/Building%20is%20Not%20Buying.pdf.

initiatives, the nonprofit might not have enough cash flow to maintain its ongoing operations. If the nonprofit hasn't separated out the recurring funding it receives from customers from the occasional funds it receives from investors, it can't tell if it has sufficient and reliable revenue to be financially sustainable over the long term.

Second, as to capital, even if the enterprise has a multiyear growth plan, its accounting doesn't allow it to keep track of the relationship between the rate at which growth capital is depleted (called the "burn rate") and the progress on the plan. In that case, the organization can't tell if it's going to use up its growth funding before it finishes building the additional capacity it needs to grow (and generate more revenue). The enterprise needs to make sure it has enough money over the life of the growth plan—aside from revenue—to execute the plan.

What often happens is that nonprofits just continually raise money and use some of it for current operations and some of it for growth, and they hope they have enough to do both on any given day. When they find themselves running short on cash, as they often do, they delay or scale back their growth plans. They get trapped on the fundraising treadmill, spending what they raise and raising what they spend. This is not a recipe for sustained growth.

By keeping track of revenue and capital separately, social entrepreneurs can make sure, first, that their ongoing fundraising is large and steady enough to support current operations. If not, growth plans must be deferred while they improve their fundraising program by convincing their "customers"—donors and third-party payers—to help maintain programs at current levels.

Second, maintaining separate capital accounts would allow non-profits to track the progress of their growth plans. The basic idea is that nonprofits develop specific plans for growth, determine how much money they need to fund that growth, and then raise that amount of funding from "investors" (not customers) who are committed to help-ing the nonprofit achieve that growth. That's what a "capital campaign" is supposed to do. With separate capital accounts, social entrepreneurs can show investors whether their expenditures and strategic progress are in alignment. If not, the parties can have an informed discussion about ways to catch up, ways to reduce the rate of expenditures, whether to scale back, or whether to seek additional investment.

In that way, the investors hold the management team accountable, and the management team can make a case for additional investment if they've managed funds well but certain assumptions proved wrong, or circumstances beyond their control changed. By focusing on successful execution of the growth plan, the capital campaign can be adjudged a success or failure (either in whole or in part), and the nonprofit can be rewarded with additional investments for future growth plans, or penalized by withholding further investments:

> The Invested Growth Capital line includes only those funders who consider themselves, and are considered by the management team/board to be in the business of investing growth capital. They can be high-engagement philanthropists, and they can be contribu-tors to a specific growth capital fund drive. Their common trait is that they evaluate the success or failure of their investment based upon whether the enterprise expands, with high quality, to an enhanced level of operations, sustained by Ordinary Revenues.[19]

In either case, the capital market would begin to connect funding and performance, and channel money to social enterprises that could make the best use of growth capital. Without capital accounting, though, the investors can't determine whether the organization knows how to use growth capital effectively.

The absence of capital accounting helps explain why fragmentation occurs: funders don't know if nonprofits can put larger and longer grants to good use because potential grantees can't demonstrate competent financial control:

> Three activities enable good managerial control: (1) planning and budgeting to delineate intended results; (2) managerial accounting to measure actual results and analyze the reasons for the variances, if any, from the plan; and (3) motivating mechanisms to hold people responsible for attaining planned results and reward them for their accomplishment.[20]

As a result, funders keep grants at more modest levels with lots of strings attached commensurate with what they think nonprofits can handle. They err on the low side because they're making guesses in the dark.

It follows that third-stage funding will not materialize unless midcaps demonstrate their ability to align their use of cash with their growth plans. Third-stage funding presupposes a level of fiscal discipline that creates a kind of benevolent Catch-22: if you can't prove you know how to manage growth capital, investors won't give you any. But that's why they call it *accounting:* "accounting is the measurement, statement, or provision of assurance about financial information primarily used by lenders, managers, investors, tax authorities and other decision makers to make resource allocation decisions between and within companies, organizations, and public agencies."[21]

So Overholser's financial model isn't just about an arcane accounting issue. Rather, it's the second essential building block (the first being a compelling growth plan) in overcoming the fragmentation that's holding the social sector back. By recognizing growth capital as a separate and distinct source of funding, one that won't be raided whenever the nonprofit runs short of cash for ongoing operations, social entrepreneurs could break the glass ceiling that's preventing exponential growth.

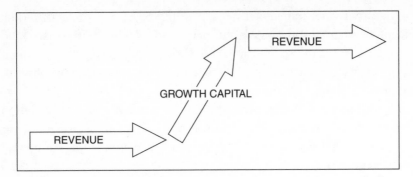

Exhibit 5.5 Growth Capital Step Function

Overholser calls this new equilibrium at which a higher level of operations is made possible by growth capital but is sustained thereafter by revenues, "take-off." After take-off, the enterprise can continue operations at the enhanced level indefinitely without additional growth capital because regular cash flow from revenue covers all ongoing expenses.

This combination of growth and stability works like a step function (see Exhibit 5.5) in which carefully managed growth capital raises nonprofit productivity to a higher scale, and carefully managed revenue sustains the higher level of operations. When the organization makes plans for the next stage of growth, it can show investors how it will deploy their capital effectively and how its revenues will support ongoing operations thereafter.

This step function can't be achieved without separating growth capital from ordinary revenue, and the nonprofit capital market can't finance mid-caps that are capable of significant expansion:

> ... imagine the case where each year's growth capital has been provided by a different investor. How would this look from the investors' point of view? Using the commingled data, investors would be "blind" to the fact that they had been contributing to one another's chronic bailouts. Thus, they would tend to conclude that they had been successful in promoting sustainable growth, rather than guilty of keeping an underperformer afloat with money that would have been better allocated towards building a sustainable enterprise.[22]

That's precisely what we have now: a status quo comprising "chronic bailouts" funded by "investments" that aren't being managed as growth capital. If we want to encourage the nonprofit capital market to shift from "hand-to-mouth fundraising" to geometric and sustainable growth, we need a capital market that can support the social entrepreneurs who manage their funding according to Overholser's model. And those forward-thinking social entrepreneurs need proactive investors to reward their disciplined management practices by funding them on the basis of demonstrable growth readiness, not galas and bake sales.

Mid-caps can't liberate themselves from oppressive fundraising burdens unless and until they liberate investors from the burden of figuring out whether grantees know how to manage larger sums of money for longer periods of time to achieve levels of operation well above those they currently support. It follows that mid-caps that want to attract new kinds of funding to cross the growth chasm will have to provide the kinds of financial information to which growth investors are accustomed. The homegrown spreadsheets that carried mid-caps to their current plateaus are not going to be enough to take them to the next level. Instead, they must achieve a level of sophistication that exceeds ordinary social sector practice.

Think of it this way. The private sector adopted double-entry bookkeeping long ago as the minimum standard for financial statements. Over time, commercial needs for consistency in reporting led to the adoption of generally accepted accounting principles (GAAP). No responsible financial investor would consider funding a company that doesn't conform to GAAP. Most recently, the Sarbanes–Oxley Act of 2002 imposed broad compliance standards in response to pervasive abuses in financial reporting by publicly traded corporations. Each advance in financial management enabled investors to nurture more adventurous business innovations from start-up to thriving enterprise to game changer.

Nonprofit financial management must evolve in similar fashion. The time has come for mid-cap nonprofits that aspire to "change the world" to prove their readiness to do so by adopting minimum accounting standards to achieve a threshold of transparency that risk-averse investors rightfully expect. Tools and methods of nonprofit capital accounting are well established and feasible for any mid-cap that aspires to game-changing growth. It is more expensive and requires greater expertise than paying for everything from the same checkbook, but it is the price of admission to the big leagues.

Notes

1. Christine W. Letts, William P. Ryan, and Allen Grossman, *High Performance Nonprofit Organizations: Managing Upstream for Greater Impact* (New York: John Wiley & Sons, 1999), p. 196.

2. Paul G. Schervish, Mary A. O'Herlihy, and John J, "Agent-Animated Wealth and Philanthropy: The Dynamics of Accumulation and Allocation Among High-Tech Donors," Havens Social Welfare Research Institute, Boston College, 2001, pp. 99–100.

3. Paul Wiefels, *The Chasm Companion* (New York: HarperBusiness, 2002), p. 131.

4. William Foster, "Money to Grow On," *Stanford Social Innovation Review* (Fall 2008): 50–55, www.ssireview.org/images/articles/2008FA_feature_foster. pdf.

5. William Foster and Gail Fine, "How Nonprofits Get Really Big," *Stanford Social Innovation Review* (Spring 2007), www.ssireview.org/articles/ entry/how_nonprofits_get_really_big/.

6. L. Schorr, *Common Purpose: Strengthening Families and Neighborhoods to Rebuild America* (New York: Anchor Books, 1998).

7. Sam Dillon, "2 School Entrepreneurs Lead the Way on Change," *New York Times*, 19 June 2008, p. A15, www.nytimes.com/2008/06/19/education/ 19teach.html?em&ex=1214020800&en=2a6e502365f8cf34&ei=5087%0A.

8. Bob Herbert, "Our Schools Must Do Better," *New York Times*, 2 Oct. 2007, www.nytimes.com/2007/10/02/opinion/02herbert.html?_r=1&oref=slogin.

9. Edward Skloot, "Slot Machines, Boat-Building and the Future of Philanthropy," inaugural address to the *Waldemar A. Nielsen Issues in Philanthropy Seminar*, Georgetown University, Washington, DC, 5 Oct. 2001, www.surdna. org/publications/publications_show.htm?doc_id=327788&cat_id=941.

10. Foster, "Money to Grow On," p. 50.

11. Gregory J. Dees and Beth Battle Anderson, "Scaling for Social Impact: Exploring Strategies for Spreading Social Innovations," *Pre-Conference Workshop*, North Carolina Center for Nonprofits, October 2003, www.fuqua. duke.edu/centers/case/documents/nc_center_master.ppt.

12. Paul N. Bloom and Aaron K.Chatterji, "Scaling Social Entrepreneurial Impact," Fuqua School of Business, Duke University, Working Draft, 2008,

www.google.com/url?sa=t&ct=res&cd=1&url=http%3A%2F%2Fwww.fuqua.
duke.edu%2Fcenters%2Fcase%2Fdocuments%2FSCALING%2520SOCIAL%
2520ENTREPRENEURIAL%2520IMPACT-%2520Bloom-Chatterji%
2520%2520(DRAFT).pdf&ei=-htcSLuhJaLSetHhqb0O&usg=AFQjCNG_
126b3CjEQmXya8DuzKQmqJvpDQ&sig2=3KsRrDym3MuvbevU-JGt4w.

13. Ibid.

14. www.rootcause.org/knowledge_sharing/business_planning_guide.

15. Regina E. Herzlinger and Denise Nitterhouse, *Financial Accounting and Managerial Control for Nonprofit Organizations* (Cincinnati: South-Western Publishing, 1994), p. 26.

16. George Overholser, "Building Is Not Buying," www.nonprofitfinancefund.org/docs/Building%20is%20Not%20Buying.pdf.

17. Ibid.

18. Ibid., p. 5.

19. Ibid., p. 7.

20. Hertzlinger and Nitterhouse, *Financial Accounting and Managerial Control for Nonprofit Organizations*, p. 247.

21. en.wikipedia.org/wiki/Accounting#cite_ref-0.

22. Overholser, ibid., p. 6.

Chapter 6

A Performance-Based Funding Market

The perfect is the enemy of the good.

—Voltaire

Markets are a great way to organize economic activity, but they need adult supervision.

—Bob Herbert, "Home Alone," New York Times

The Work of Markets

We've seen that the social sector cannot mount a sustained and robust campaign for transformative social impact without (1) a plentiful supply of third-stage funders that want to provide growth capital to high-performing mid-cap nonprofits and (2) a plentiful supply of growth-ready mid-caps that can demonstrate their ability to put third-stage funding to good use. The missing piece is (3) a market mechanism to connect the supply of and demand for third-stage funding.

The stubborn problem we encounter with the nonprofit capital market is that it doesn't act much like a market. A real financial market is supposed to allocate capital efficiently among the potential recipients based on the output that the constituent organizations produce, that is,

191

the results they achieve. Financial investors come to markets that host a large number of companies that compete for funding by providing extensive information about their accomplishments. The markets then facilitate the flow of capital by providing signals about the relative performance of those companies to help investors make informed choices. Those signals take the form of prices of securities (primarily stocks and bonds) that are traded on those markets.

Securities prices function as signals because they're dynamic. If, after watching CNBC, reading the *Wall Street Journal,* and reviewing corporate reports and analyst recommendations, investors think the asking price for a particular stock is too high, then investors who want to maximize the value of their portfolios at the lowest possible cost don't buy the stock (or they sell shares they already own) until its price falls. If investors think the price is too low, they buy the stock and the price goes up. When the price approximates what the market collectively perceives to be the fair value of the stock, investors hold onto the stock, supply and demand balance out, and its price stabilizes.

So financial markets provide *information* investors can use to compare alternative investment opportunities based on their performance, and they provide a *dynamic mechanism* for moving money away from weak performers and toward strong performers. Just as water seeks its own level, markets continuously recalibrate prices until they achieve a roughly optimal equilibrium at which most companies receive the "right" amount of investment. In this way, good companies thrive and bad ones improve or die.

The social sector should work the same way:

> [I]f charities did a good job of explaining [their] work and performing and meeting objectives, then they would continue to operate, and they would grow. If there were too many environmental groups on the Hudson River, they would merge, or some would go out of business. If there were not enough child development resources devoted to San Jose, then new nonprofits would develop, because the actors would be responding to needs, information, and proactive donor intent.[1]

But philanthropic capital doesn't flow toward effective nonprofits and away from ineffective nonprofits for a simple reason: contributors can't tell the difference between the two. That is, philanthropists just don't know what various nonprofits actually accomplish. Instead, they only know what nonprofits are *trying* to accomplish, and they only know that based on what the nonprofits themselves tell them. What SeaChange Capital Partners observes about "major donors" applies to charitable contributors of all sizes:

> Most major donors lack an efficient method for evaluating the relative effectiveness of various nonprofits. It's difficult for them to determine where their donations are likely to do the most good. They don't explore some opportunities to make meaningful contributions because research and data about the performance of one nonprofit versus another is not widely shared and therefore not available to them.[2]

As I said before, social entrepreneurs aren't trying to deceive anyone. Rather, it's exceedingly difficult and expensive to measure and report elusive concepts like "school readiness," "employability," and "violence prevention." So instead of reporting their *results*, nonprofits tell us about their *efforts*—such as how many more people participated in their programs, how many more volunteers they recruited, and how much more money they raised—all in the hope of attracting contributions.

In addition to enhancing the personal wealth of investors, financial markets produce an enormous amount of societal benefit by helping companies that create the most jobs and make the best products attract more investments than those that don't. Even with all the many grave problems associated with modern financial markets (as displayed so vividly beginning in late 2008), the long-term growth of the U.S. economy proves that the basic logic of the market fulfills its core function most of the time: channeling financial capital to the places where it can do the most good.

By contrast, the steady decline of social progress over the last 30 years attests to the failure of the nonprofit capital market (in tandem with a depleted public sector) at carrying out that same function. We're already seeing record levels of philanthropy and record growth in the rate of giving, but many social ills are worse than ever and becoming worse still.

The signs that the lack of social progress is linked to capital market dysfunctions are unmistakable: fundraising remains the number-one challenge of the sector despite the fact that nonprofit leaders divert some 40 to 60% of their time from productive work to chasing after money; donations raised are almost always too small, too short, and too restricted to enhance productive capacity; most mid-caps are ensnared in the "social entrepreneur's trap" of focusing on today and neglecting tomorrow; and so on. So any meaningful progress we could make in the direction of helping the nonprofit capital market allocate funds as effectively as the private capital market does could translate into tremendous advances in extending social and economic opportunity.

Indeed, enhancing nonprofit capital allocation is likely to improve people's lives much more than, say, further increasing the total amount of donations. Why? Because capital allocation has a multiplier effect.

The authors of *Philanthrocapitalism* provide the example of a Sudanese cell phone company:

> Celtel has arguably done more for the lives of ordinary Africans than much of the aid that has flowed over the decades from the rich governments of the West.... Mobile phones boost entrepreneurship and economic activity by reducing the cost of connecting with suppliers and customers.... Mobile phones are also being used in innovative ways to provide health care advice to remote communities, to help people to receive money from relatives abroad, and so on.[3]

We can't afford to increase nonprofit hiring by, say, 20%, but a corresponding decrease in the amount of time wasted on fundraising would have the same effect. If larger amounts of funds were donated for longer periods of time with fewer restrictions, just think how much more productive our best social enterprises could be. Such a shift from fragmented to defragmented funding could reduce turnover of seasoned nonprofit executives who otherwise suffer from fundraising burnout, decrease the need for "development" staff, and increase headcount in program and capacity-building positions. Indeed, "if, in aggregate, philanthropic grantmaking were to become 10 percent more effective ... or 30 percent ... such an improvement would convert the emerging wealth transfer into a social watershed."[4]

If we want to materially improve the performance and increase the impact of the nonprofit sector, we need to understand what's preventing it from doing a better job of allocating philanthropic capital. And figuring out why nonprofit capital markets don't work very well requires us to understand why the financial markets do such a better job.

The Illusion of Stock Prices

Many people suffer from the happy delusion that stock prices, unlike nonprofit contributions, represent the "real" value of the for-profit companies listed on the stock market. From this assumption, they infer that we know what businesses, unlike nonprofits, are "worth" because the market sets the "real" price to buy ownership shares. The reasoning is that companies report "actual" quantitative results, not qualitative approximations as nonprofits do, and those quantitative results are the basis for setting definitive prices for buying shares in the company. Multiply the share price times the number of shares outstanding and, *voilà*, that's the value of the business.

From these simplistic and erroneous assumptions, we conclude that there can't be anything equivalent or even similar to "price" in the nonprofit sector because, first, nonprofits generally don't sell anything and donors generally don't buy anything, and, second, social output isn't quantifiable. It follows that the nonprofit capital market cannot possibly allocate funding the way that financial capital markets allocate investments.

Virtually every premise of this argument is wrong and its conclusion is unjustified. First and foremost, the measurements that financial investors use are not in any sense definitive. John C. Bogle, founder of the Vanguard Group, inventor of the index mutual fund, and one of *Fortune*'s "Giants of the 20th Century," asks, "Is the price of a stock truly a consistent and reliable measure of the value of the corporation?" and answers, "Don't count on it!"[5]

If stock prices really were unambiguous, Wall Street wouldn't need armies of analysts, auditors, and rating agencies to set initial public offering prices, only to have the market prices jump by an average of 15% the day the stock went public.[6] As one recent example, Visa's stock price rose 29% on the first day of trading in March 2008.[7] Keep in mind, this was the largest IPO in U.S. history and its offering price was set by the finest minds on Wall Street, and, still, they were billions of dollars too low. Were the scores of investment bankers, underwriters, book runners, advisors, co-managers, brokers, dealers, researchers, analysts, corporate financiers, and all the rest who worked on the deal incompetent? No, they made their best prediction of the new stock's value and then they released it to the market for its independent determination. But a 29% margin of error doesn't look very much like an exact science.

Even before the 2008 Wall Street collapse, think of how many excuses, mulligans, and fudge factors the business news reports every day, including restated earnings, market "corrections," and corporate write-offs. Then there's a whole separate set of manipulations, sharp practices, and monkeyshines that ultimately led a reluctant Congress to enact the Sarbanes-Oxley Act in 2002 that required CEOs and CFOs to certify the accuracy and completeness of their SEC filings "under the pains and penalties of perjury." Bogle laments the advent of *"pro forma* earnings—that ghastly formulation that makes new use (or abuse) of a once-respectable term—that reports corporate results net of unpleasant developments." Consider this 2004 analysis by the respected *New York Times* financial columnist, Gretchen Morgenson, of a once-common but now-discredited business practice:

> Ask any chief executive officer if he or she practices the art of earnings management and you will undoubtedly hear an emphatic "Of course not!" Ask those same executives about their company's recent results, and you may very well hear a proud "we beat the analysts' estimate by a penny." While almost no one wants to admit to managing company earnings, the fact is, almost everybody does it. How else to explain the miraculous manner in which so many companies meet or beat, by the preposterous penny, the consensus earnings estimates of Wall Street analysts?...
>
> Over [a recent five-year] period, on average, almost half of the companies—46.1 percent—met consensus estimates or beat them by a penny. Pulling off such a feat in an uncertain world smacks of earnings management. "It is not possible for this percentage of reporting companies to hit the bull's-eye," said Bill Fleckenstein, principal at Fleckenstein Capital in Seattle. "Business is too complicated; there are too many moving parts."... The precision has a purpose, of course: to keep stock prices aloft.[8]

When all is said and done, securities prices are nothing more than convenient approximations that market participants accept as a way of simplifying their economic interactions, with a full understanding that market prices are useful even when they are way off the mark, as they so often are. In fact, that's the whole point of markets: to aggregate the imperfect and incomplete knowledge held by vast numbers of traders about how much various securities are worth and still make allocation choices that are better than we could without markets.

Philanthropists face precisely the same problem: how to make better use of limited information to maximize output, in this case, social impact. Considering the dearth of useful tools available to donors today, the solution doesn't have to be perfect or even all that good, at least at first. It just needs to improve the status quo and get better over time.

Much of the solution, I believe, lies in finding useful adaptations of market mechanisms that will mitigate the effects of the same lack of reliable and comprehensive information about social sector performance. I would even go so far as to say that social enterprises can't hope to realize their "one day, all children" visions without a funding allocation system that acts more like a market.

We can, and indeed do, make incremental improvements in nonprofit funding without market mechanisms. But without markets, I don't see how we can fix the fragmentation problem or produce transformative social impact, such as ensuring that every child in America has a good education. The problems we face are too big and have too many moving parts to ignore the self-organizing dynamics of market economics. As Thomas Friedman said about the need to impose a carbon tax at a time of falling oil prices, "I've wracked my brain trying to think of ways to retool America around clean-power technologies without a price signal—i.e., a tax—and there are no effective ones."[9]

Market Dynamics

As we look for ways to adapt market mechanisms to the social sector, let's explore more closely the idea that is most central to private capital markets and seems most foreign to social capital: price. The price of a stock is what it costs to buy a share of a publicly traded corporation, and, as everyone knows, you can't buy a share of a nonprofit. Since no one "owns" a nonprofit, logic suggests that the whole concept of price has no place in a nonprofit capital market.

In fact, financial markets use price as an *allocation mechanism*, as shorthand for what a security is "worth" at a given time. By representing the relative values of different securities, price becomes the linchpin for a dynamic system for moving money toward more productive uses. Even though ownership is a concept foreign to social enterprise, value is not. Since social impact investors also need to differentiate among nonprofits based on their relative levels of productivity, they also need some way to represent the relative value of different social investment opportunities. So it turns out that the seemingly foreign concept of price bears close consideration after all.

To explain how securities prices move investments around, I'm going to quote rather extensively from a 150-page treasure written by the former editor of the *Harvard Business Review,* Joel Kurtzman, entitled "How the Markets Really Work."[10] As the author explains, "the aim of this little book is to explain the *magic* of the markets and the thinking and the machinery that make that magic work." Kurtzman set out to answer the very same question that poses such difficulty for social impact investors: "Where should I put my money? And why?" To me, the book also explains convincingly why the term "nonprofit capital market" is not an oxymoron.

Kurtzman begins by asking the question "What the heck are prices, anyway?" Far from being some objective, quantitative fact, price is instead "a product of the mind, a construct, something we all must agree upon; it is not an absolute." Kurtzman observes (as we learned from Hayek in the last chapter) that "so little of what determines a price is under any single person's (or institution's) control." Rather, "prices are multi-level, multi-person, multi-organizational processes involving a host of different tangible and intangible elements all in a constant state of flux."[11] Price is the market's way of making sense out of an otherwise unmanageable mess of undefinable but relevant data that is by no means limited to "hard facts":

> But prices are also based upon soft information, like investor sentiment, mood, consumer confidence, and so on. Each additional item of hard or soft information is filtered through the millions of minds that make

up the market. It is as if prices were determined not by any "wisdom central," but by the mob of people you encounter when you stand in line to get a new passport or a driver's license, some of them wise, some of them, well, not so wise.

The totality of what is considered by the financial market is a mix of everything from corporate reports and news to the opinions of other investors, the views of high-priced analysts, TV pundits, cabdrivers, and the chairman of the Fed. It is as if decisions changing the course of the markets were a meal containing everything from truffles and caviar to shoe leather and old socks. No two investors look at the same information in quite the same way, nor do they weigh their perceptions equally, nor do they have the same objectives or needs. Information rattling around inside one set of minds prompts that group to think it is time to sell. The same information buzzing around inside another set of minds say the time is ripe to buy.[12]

That's why Kurtzman calls price a "process" and a "construct." Price represents the ever-changing consensus of what the market as a whole thinks the various items exchanged are worth at any given time. Seen from that rough-and-ready perspective, price sounds like an instrument that could well help tame the unruly chaos of nonprofit finance:

As a result, prices, economists like to point out, are a type of information that is a rich summary of all we know and *feel* about a stock, bond, or other financial product along with all we know about its issuer and the issuer's prospects at any given moment in time. Also contained within that summary is the market's assessment of risk as well as its general assessment of the future of a market sector, a market, and the world.[13]

Prices enable financial markets to work the way nonprofit capital markets should—by sending informative signals about the most effective organizations so that money will flow to them naturally:

Information, combined with capital and a distributed and informed investor community, changed the way the economy works. Rather than long periods of bearish sentiment, followed by a slow awakening into a world of new possibility, the growth of the capital markets has meant that a virtuous cycle now exists whereby good performance is rewarded by higher levels of capitalization, which enables the best performers to extend their reach further.[14]

So how could the nonprofit sector create such a clever thing for the millions of Americans who desperately need it to do a much better job rewarding and extending good performance?

Financial Value versus Social Value

As Michael Douglas's character, Gordon Gecko, memorably observed in the movie *Wall Street*, "The richest one percent of this country owns half our country's wealth, five trillion dollars. . . . We pick that rabbit out of the hat while everybody sits out there wondering how the hell we did it."[15] Joel Kurtzman agrees there's magic at work in the financial markets. Citing Peruvian economist Hernando de Soto, Kurtzman describes capital as a "mystery":

> It is a mystery because of its ability to transform the planet and the way we allocate everything we produce and consume. It is a mystery because of its ability to help organize our efforts. And it is a mystery because of the way in which it enables people to change the way they think about value.[16]

The nonprofit sector could use a dose of such powerful mystery. Indeed, as Kurtzman says, "Solve the mystery of capital and you solve many seemingly intractable problems along with it."[17] So let's solve the mystery of nonprofit capital—or at least give it our best shot.

Social Value

I submit that the output successful nonprofits produce has no less "value" than the output of businesses, but there's no obvious "price" by which the value of the work of one nonprofit can be compared to the value of the work of another. Nor is there a "medium of exchange," that is, currency, by which the amount of that value can be stored and traded later for other things of equivalent value. So, the economic problem of nonprofits is not lack of value per se but the difficulty of measurement and liquidity. That is no small thing, of course, and it has obvious implications for the different ways that business is conducted in the for-profit and nonprofit sectors.

If we want to develop nonprofit capital markets that can better support the growth of third-stage organizations, we need to be clear about what problems we need to address. The *existence* of value and its *amount* are two quite different things. Conflating them is dangerous, as the sociologist and pollster Daniel Yankelovich recognized long ago (albeit in the quite different context of the Vietnam War):

> The first step is to measure what can easily be measured. The second is to disregard what can't be measured, or give it an arbitrary quantitative value. This is artificial and misleading. The third step is to presume that what can't be measured easily isn't very important. This is blindness. The fourth step is to say that what can't be easily measured really doesn't exist. This is suicide.[18]

The obvious difficulty in measuring or even defining social "impact" does not, it seems to me, undermine the notion that donations given to more effective nonprofits have more "value" than comparable donations given to less effective ones. If I buy 100 shares of stock at a price of $100 per share, the initial value of my investment is $10,000, which I hope will grow by some increment if the company performs well. If the stock goes up to $110 per share, my investment is now worth $11,000, representing a 10% increase in value (let's not bother with taxes for this rudimentary exercise).

If I donate $10,000 to a nonprofit, the initial value of my investment is also $10,000. But if the nonprofit makes good use of the money and, let's say, brings the reading scores of 10 elementary school students up from below grade level to grade level, we can't say how much my initial investment is "worth" now. I could make the argument that the value has increased because the students have received a demonstrated educational benefit that is valuable to them. Since that's the reason I made the donation, the achievement of higher scores must have value to me, as well.

I could also make two alternative arguments. First, if I thought that the nonprofit accomplished exactly what I wanted and expected, no more and no less, then the value of my initial investment wouldn't have increased at all. It just changed from one form into another of equal value. That is, I made an even transaction of trading a specific amount of money for a corresponding amount of educational benefit. Under this view, I bought something, rather than invested in its growth.

But what if I thought that the nonprofit had not done as good a job as it could have, and that my $10,000 should have brought 15 students up to the reading levels for their respective grades instead of 10? In that case, I should think that I traded a specific amount of money and received a smaller amount of educational benefit in return than I had expected, so the value of my investment would have decreased. Of course, the opposite would be true if I expected my donation to help only five students.

My confusion is rooted in the fact that philanthropy doesn't fit neatly into established categories of "investment" on one hand and "consumption" on the other. Andrew Blau of the Global Business Network and Monitor Institute has shown that charitable donations are more like the former than the latter. For example, philanthropists (unlike investors) trade money for a nonprofit product or service (rather than for equity or debt), based primarily on immediate satisfaction (rather than financial gain over time), in a market that fosters choice (rather than transparency). In Blau's view, seeing donors as more like consumers than investors "allows us to make sense of behavior that is widely seen as puzzling and frustrating":

> For example, donors move slowly and seem risk averse in part because they have no way of managing risk the way real investors do. . . . Moreover, foundations and other donors are criticized for being easily distracted, for abandoning themes arbitrarily, for rarely learning from past experience, for rewarding weakness rather than strength, and for diffusing their interests rather than concentrating their attention.[19]

Lacking the system of rewards and penalties that guide financial investments, philanthropists have only weak "internal incentives . . . for the kinds of behavior that would seem obvious and 'natural' to even casual investors."

Also, most people don't realize that financial value and social value are two sides of the same coin: "nonprofits exist to bridge for-profit market deficiencies and thereby provide social value."[20] Like the Chinese concept of yin-yang, social value and financial value are opposing qualities that are rooted together; under the right circumstances, they balance and transform each other.[21] They are not independent.

Root Cause's Andrew Wolk explains how the seeming dichotomy springs from one source—markets:

> The social problems that social entrepreneurs address result from market failures—in which profitable markets are unavailable, insufficient, or underdeveloped and where the potential monetary gains for responding to a societal problem are less than the overall, society-wide positive impact of that response. Because of the lack of opportunity to generate profit, private-sector entrepreneurs—who succeed by finding market opportunities and maximizing profits—often leave these needs unaddressed. Traditionally, government responds in such cases by deploying public funds to address the unmet needs. Social entrepreneurship presents another option for addressing market failures—which can be considered the sources of the opportunities that social entrepreneurs act on.[22]

Just because market failures cause social problems doesn't mean that markets have no place in correcting social problems. To the contrary, it suggests that there are inherent connections between them and that market-based adjustments might well have a place in the production of greater social value.

Cash versus In-Kind

Let's look at another example involving two nonprofits engaged in similar activities. Goodwill Industries International, Inc., a quintessential large cap founded in 1902, is best known for its more than 2,000 thrift shops. As shown in Exhibit 6.1, Goodwill's main revenue source is retail sales ($1.8 billion in 2006), together with fees and grants ($365 million) and contributions ($49 million). Goodwill provides job training (931,000 trainees) that produces job placements (131,000) that generate salaries and wages ($1.9 billion), and provides contracted services (such as food, laundry, and janitorial service) to businesses that return revenue back to Goodwill ($567 million).[23] Inasmuch as Goodwill's

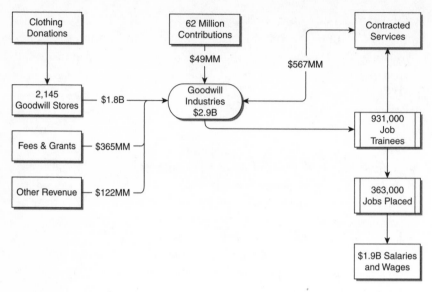

Exhibit 6.1   Goodwill Industries

results are expressed as employee income and sales of goods and commercial services, its performance can be readily assessed in largely economic terms.

Compare Goodwill with Cradles to Crayons (C2C), a small-cap social enterprise (and former employer of mine) founded in 2002 and based in Quincy, Massachusetts, with a $2 million budget for 2008 (together with a second site in Philadelphia opened in 2007). C2C targets some 282,000 poor and low-income children in Massachusetts aged 0 to 12 who lack basic and essential items they need to feel safe, warm, and ready to learn, such as baby equipment, clothing, school supplies, books, and toys. Like Goodwill, C2C collects donated goods, but unlike Goodwill, it does not sell them to generate revenue to fund social service programs. Instead, as shown in Exhibit 6.2, C2C collects new and "gently used" children's items from families, communities, and corporations (in bulk), trains thousands of volunteers to inspect, clean, sort, and package the items at its 12,000-square-foot warehouse, aptly named "The Giving Factory," and then distributes those packages back to the families through more than 300 social service agencies that placed online orders on their clients' behalf.

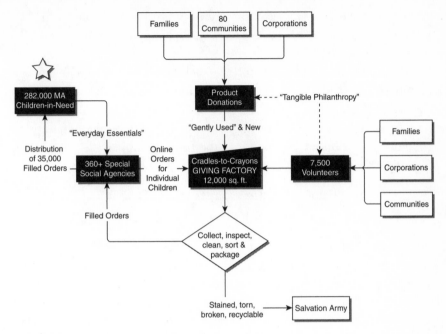

Exhibit 6.2   Cradles to Crayons

None of the value C2C creates is converted into cash. Instead, C2C is a machine that produces, enhances, and distributes in-kind value:

- A high-volume online ordering system that selects new and nearly new items for timely distribution of essential children's supplies
- A supply of inspected and packaged essential goods for social service agencies that is not covered by government budgets
- A large warehouse facility for collection, processing, storage, and distribution of donated goods
- Opportunities for "tangible philanthropy" for more than 7,500 volunteers annually from ages 5 to 85 in a safe, supervised environment

While economic value can be imputed to much of C2C's output (e.g., it costs C2C about $60 to produce one packaged order of used goods with an average value of about $300), almost all of the inputs are provided in-kind and the outputs are given away at no charge. Along the way, no money changes hands. So, although Goodwill and C2C are at opposite ends of the spectrum in terms of scale, their essential activities are quite similar in terms of value created from donated items. It makes no sense to treat one as economically valuable and one as economically inconsequential.

From the foregoing examples of a hypothetical $10,000 literacy donation and C2C's no-charge distribution of children's essentials, we can see that nonprofit goods and services have perceived value that can be difficult to measure. Surprisingly, things aren't really that different in the business world, at least some of the time. Consider these headlines from the *New York Times* business section from two consecutive days:

"iPhone Use Disappoints; Apple Slides" (July 25, 2007)

"Apple Profit Soars 73% as Sales Rise" (July 26, 2007)[24]

On the first day, "Apple's shares slumped 6 percent on Tuesday after AT&T said the early surge of iPhone buyers starting service on its network was smaller than some analysts had anticipated." The next day, Apple's shares rebounded by 9% on news that early iPhone sales had reached "a number that seemed to calm investors' fears." Thus, expectation setting had everything to do with the two-day roller-coaster ride, so that the perception of company performance directly affected its price. Because there's such a significant subjectivity factor figured into the pricing equation, the cost of buying and the return from selling Apple stock changed dramatically on July 25 and 26, 2007, far beyond the extent of any one-day change in Apple's underlying business performance.

Subjective perceptions influence stock prices over longer periods of time, as well. In fact, investors who use the "discounted cash flow" method to value stocks make estimates of corporate earnings *over the next 20 or 30 years,* which is surely a fanciful exercise in prognostication. To a very real extent, then, the values of corporate equity and debt reflect what different people think about the company's performance, particularly whether it was the same as, or better or worse than, they expected.

Up versus Down; More versus Less

Much the same can be said about nonprofit performance. Most people would think that a nonprofit that has raised more money, increased the number of people it has helped, and improved operational performance has "increased in value." It would be equally fair to think that the donations that funded those successes were more valuable now than they were at the time of the initial investment. Although we can't say how much performance had improved or how much more the donations were worth now, we would probably agree that both had "gone up." And we would say that both had gone up "more" if the performance scores had increased by, say, two grade levels than if they had increased by only one. Again, we wouldn't know how much more, but when it comes to social impact, more is better than less, and "more more" is better than "less more."

Perhaps we could reduce our discomfort about concepts like price by focusing on a more familiar idea: our shared impulse to maximize the social benefit that philanthropy produces. It seems self-evident that people who choose to give away some of their wealth for altruistic reasons would want their giving to provide as much help as possible. There doesn't have to be a perfect mathematical correspondence between the amount given and the results achieved, but it seems absurd to assume that philanthropically minded people are indifferent to "how much" good their money accomplishes. Writing in the March 9, 2008, issue of the *New York Times Magazine* dedicated to philanthropy, Jon Gertner offered a similar rubric:

> When Warren Buffett announced in 2006 that he would donate his billions to the Gates Foundation, the news of his gift eclipsed his dark observation at the same time that philanthropies are "tackling problems that have resisted great intellect and lots of money." But that resistance doesn't have to be permanent. Why shouldn't the world's smartest capitalists be able to figure out more effective ways to give out money now? And why shouldn't they want to make sure their philanthropy has significant social impact? If they can measure impact, couldn't they get past the resistance that Buffett highlighted and finally separate what works from what doesn't?[25]

If we accept the proposition that some nonprofits are more effective than others and that overall social progress would advance if more funds went to more effective nonprofits, then we must consider the prospect that some kind of market mechanism could improve the allocation of philanthropic capital. Once we abandon the false notions that financial markets are precision instruments for measuring unambiguous phenomena, and that the business and nonprofit sectors are based on mutually exclusive principles of value, we can deconstruct the true nature of the problems we need to address and adapt market-like mechanisms that are suited to the particulars of the social sector.

All of this is a long way (okay, a very long way) of saying that even *ordinal rankings* of nonprofit investments can have tremendous value in choosing among competing donation opportunities, especially when the choices are so numerous and varied. If I'm a social investor, I'd really like to know which nonprofits are likely to produce "more" impact and which ones are likely to produce "less." Just like financial investors, I want my money to create as much value as possible, even if it doesn't come back to me in the form of cash and even if we can't directly measure the quantity of value produced. So I would welcome information about which nonprofit investment opportunities—"stocks"—are likely to go "up" and which are likely to go "down," and I would also appreciate any information that could help me identify which ones are likely to go up "more" and which are likely to go down "less."

If we make the reasonable assumption that many social investors want to maximize the value of their philanthropy in terms of the amount of impact the recipient organizations produce, it follows that an effective nonprofit capital market should include a mechanism that can place nonprofits in some kind of order by some rational methodology in which we can have some level of confidence. Even though we can't attach adjustable quantitative values to nonprofit investment opportunities, investors should benefit individually, and the community of like-minded social investors should benefit collectively, if nonprofit capital markets could provide directional signals and relative rankings by which "smart money" could look for places to roost.

It isn't necessary to replicate the complex working of modern stock markets to fashion an intelligent and useful nonprofit capital allocation mechanism. All we're looking for is some kind of functional indication that would (1) isolate promising nonprofit investments from among the confusing swarm of too many seemingly worthy social-purpose organizations and (2) roughly differentiate among them based on the likelihood of "more" or "less" impact. This is what I meant earlier by increasing signals and decreasing noise. Any movement in the direction of performance-driven philanthropy should increase nonprofit productivity: more effective nonprofits would attract more money and less effective ones would attract less.

But how can we make conclusions about more and less if we don't know the starting quantities? And how can we make investment decisions if we can't measure how much more and how much less?

Collective Intelligence

Again, financial markets face the same problem. The derivation of business data is far from an exact science. As Kurtzman puts it, "because the economy is so complex, the data is not always meaningful or even accurate." But "how can [investors] make an intelligent decision regarding the prospects of a company unless they know its level of debt, its rate of growth, its overall expenses?" Ultimately, he asks, "How can you transact business if you don't really understand what is going on?"[26]

The answer he gives is that "the savviest investors and observers understand the odd principle that while the new data is almost always inaccurate, it must be treated as if it were correct."[27] Bogle observes that less astute investors who ascribe too much exactitude to reported financials "seem to be perfectly happy to take the risk of being precisely wrong rather than roughly right."[28]

This solves the "mystery" of capital Kurtzman posed earlier. No investor knows all the information he needs to invest wisely, and much of the information he does know is wrong much of the time. But by processing the incomplete and inaccurate information of all investors through the market, we can construct a set of prices that is sufficiently accurate to enable us to make reasonably intelligent decisions:

> Economists say that prices, because they are such complicated patterns of information, are really only "discovered" at the moment the parties agree to a sale and the only real "test" of a price is whether it receives a bid and the only real test of a bid is whether it is accepted. Since there are no disinterested parties in the market, everything aside from an accepted bid is either posturing, blathering, or a little of both.[29]

The same can be said of many macroeconomic statistics. James Surowiecki notes that unemployment statistics, which drive both government policy and Wall Street confidence, are "notoriously muddy" and, often, "numerical flimflammery." "The paradoxical truth about the jobs numbers," he wrote in the *New Yorker,* "is that they are much better than their critics say they are but nowhere near as good as investors believe them to be." All the more reason, he says, to use them:

> Flawed as they are, though, the employment numbers represent a dramatic and valuable economic innovation. The idea that the government can and should give the public a reliable picture of the economy is a surprisingly recent one. It wasn't until the Great Depression that the government began calculating a national employment rate, and it's only in the postwar era that employment data have been systematically and rigorously collected. And if the results are imperfect, that's because collecting up-to-date, accurate information about the U.S. economy, where millions of jobs are created and lost every year, is remarkably difficult.[30]

Financial markets work for an exceedingly simple but profound reason: they are, Kurtzman rightly observes, "a phenomenon of aggregation."[31] They collect a vast amount of imperfect and unreliable information held by myriad investors who don't agree on anything and extract a consensus, shifting and fleeting though it may be, that has significant power to differentiate up from down, more from less, and more more from less more. By constantly calling each other's bluffs, market participants "posture" and "blather" about the relative values of what they have and what they want to acquire, and they work out an accommodation through trading that they believe makes economic sense at a particular time by means of signals that guide the flow of resources to destinations that investors come to believe are the most productive. When new information arrives and circumstances change, which they always do, the market recalibrates and corrects itself dynamically in the same trial-and-error fashion to rediscover a new set of equilibrium prices.

If the financial markets didn't work, they'd have vanished long ago. As Benjamin Graham, the founder of "value investing," said, "in the short run, the stock market is a *voting* machine; in the long run it is a *weighing* machine."[32]

Joel Kurtzman offers good advice when he notes that "creating a market economy takes time and is given to trial and error."[33] In addition to physical and technological infrastructure, "the world of money also requires dozens of 'specialist' communities that in the aggregate constitute the larger global financial community."[34] These communities include "tens of thousands" of bank credit analysts, stockbrokers, bankers, technicians, stocks and bond analysts, fund managers, salespeople, bank and insurance risk managers, accountants, lawyers, regulators and rating agencies, financial and market economists, forecasters, teachers, trainers, professors, and journalists. These are the people who sort through all that imperfect information and trade more or less educated guesses about how much different securities are worth at any given time.

It's safe to say that the nonprofit capital market has very few of these "specialist communities." It does have a rather different kind of community, though, one that has the potential, if pointed in the right direction, of becoming enormously powerful in terms of its ability to inform the flow of philanthropy. This potential power of the millions of participants in the social sector resides in a characteristic that James Surowiecki described in his important book, *The Wisdom of Crowds*:

> Under the right circumstances, groups are remarkably intelligent, and are often smarter than the smartest people in them. Groups do not need to be dominated by exceptionally intelligent people in order to be smart. Even if most of the people within a group are not especially well-informed or rational, it can still reach a collectively wise decision. This is a good thing, since human beings are not perfectly designed decision makers. Instead, we are what the economist Herbert Simon called "boundedly rational." We generally have less information than we'd like. We have limited foresight into the future. Most of us lack the ability—and the desire—to make sophisticated cost-benefit calculations. Instead of insisting on finding the best possible decision, we will often accept one that seems good enough. And we often let emotion affect our judgment. Yet despite all these limitations, when our imperfect judgments are aggregated in the right way, our collective intelligence is often excellent.[35]

"Collective intelligence" is not like some kind of card trick with a roomful of people taking the place of the clever magician. As Barry

Schwartz points out in *The Paradox of Choice,* the reason it works is intuitive:

> We are all susceptible to making errors, but we're not each susceptible to making the *same* errors, because our experiences are different. As long as we include social interactions in our information gathering, and as long as our sources of information are diverse, we can probably steer clear of the worst pitfalls.[36]

The wisdom of crowds is rooted in a mathematically based set of scientific and economic principles that have become the subject of serious academic study. Its essential soundness has been confirmed by research conducted on throngs, swarms, and gaggles of all kinds that, as Surowiecki chronicles, made astonishingly accurate collective judgments about the weight of an ox, the location of a submarine that sank somewhere in "a circle twenty miles wide and many thousands of feet deep," the numbers of jelly beans in countless jars, election results, box-office sales for the opening weekends of new movies, the best weekend night to avoid crowds at a certain Santa Fe bar, and how to efficiently and effectively coordinate worldwide scientific research at 11 independent and competitive laboratories to discover the cause of an emerging contagious disease.

Crowd wisdom can extract useful information from a jumble of data of widely differing reliability. Let's consider what kinds of systems can be developed to derive collective intelligence from heterogeneous crowds.

Notes

1. William F. Meehan, Derek Kilmer, and Maisie O'Flanagan, "Investing in Society: Why We Need a More Efficient Social Capital Market—and How We Can Get There," *Stanford Social Innovation Review* (Spring 2004), www.ssireview.org/articles/entry/investing_in_society.

2. Background, SeaChange Capital Partners, www.seachangecap.org/background.html.

3. Matthew Bishop and Michael Green, *Philanthrocapitalism: How the Rich Can Save the World* (London: Bloomsbury Press, 2008), pp. 106–107.

4. Thomas J. Tierney, "Higher-Impact Philanthropy: Applying Business Principles to Philanthropic Strategics," Philanthropy Roundtable, 14 Feb. 2007, www.philanthropyroundtable.org/article.asp?article=1453&cat=147.

5. John C. Bogle, "Don't Count on It! The Perils of Numeracy," keynote address before the *Landmines in Finance* Forum of the Center for Economic Policy Studies, Princeton University, 18 Oct. 2002, www.vanguard.com/bogle_site/sp20021018.html.

6. "Who Profits from IPO Underpricing?" Knowledge@W.P. Carey, 26 March 2008, http://knowledge.wpcarey.asu.edu/article.cfm?articleid=1578.

7. Ben Sterverman, "Visa's IPO Victory," *Business Week,* 20 March 2008, www.businessweek.com/investor/content/mar2008/pi20080319_477132.htm.

8. Gretchen Morgenson, "Pennies That Aren't from Heaven," *New York Times,* 7 Nov. 2004, www.nytimes.com/2004/11/07/business/yourmoney/07watch.html?pagewanted=1&_r=1&ei=1&en=357a25b46b37d0e3&ex=1100927512&oref=slogin.

9. Thomas L. Friedman, "Win, Win, Win, Win, Win..." *New York Times*, 28 Dec. 2008, p. 8, www.nytimes.com/2008/12/28/opinion/28friedman.html?em.

10. Joel Kurtzman, *How the Markets Really Work* (New York: Crown Business, 2002).

11. Ibid., p. 21.

12. Ibid., pp. 24–25.

13. Ibid., p. 27.

14. Ibid., p. 46.

15. Stanley Weiser and Oliver Stone, *Wall Street,* www.imsdb.com/scripts/Wall-Street.html.

16. Kurtzman, *How the Markets Really Work,* p. 68.

17. Ibid., p. 69.

18. "Adam Smith" (George G. W. Goodman), *Paper Money* (New York: Summit Books, 1981), p. 37.

19. Andrew Blau, "Why Donors Are Not Investors," Monitor Company Group, 2005, pp. 3–4, www.futureofphilanthropy.org/files/donors.pdf.

20. Clara Miller, "The Equity Capital Gap," *Stanford Social Innovation Review* (Summer 2008): 42, www.nonprofitfinancefund.org/docs/2008/ssir_summer_2008_equity_capital_gap.pdf.

21. "Yin and Yang," Wikipedia, http://en.wikipedia.org/wiki/Yin_and_yang.

22. Andrew M. Wolk, "Social Entrepreneurship & Government: A New Breed of Entrepreneurs Developing Solutions to Social Problems," from *The Small Business Economy: A Report to the President, Small Business Administration* (SBA), Office of Advocacy, 2007, p. 17, www.rootcause.org/sites/rootcause.org/files/files/SE_and_Gov_Wolk.pdf.

23. Goodwill Industries, "FAQ About Goodwill," www.goodwill.org/c/document_library/get_file?folderId=102122&name=DLFE-2245.pdf.

24. www.nytimes.com/2007/07/25/technology/25phone.html?scp=2&sq=apple +iphone&st=nyt, www.nytimes.com/2007/07/26/business/26apple.html?scp =3&sq=apple+iphone&st=nyt.

25. Jon Gertner, "For Good, Measure," *New York Times Magazine,* 9 March 2008, www.nytimes.com/2008/03/09/magazine/09metrics-t.html.

26. Kurtzman, pp. 125-127.

27. Kurtzman, p. 128.

28. John C. Bogle, "Don't Count On It! The Perils of Numeracy," speech before The "Landmines in Finance" Forum of The Center for Economic Policy Studies, Princeton University, Princeton, NJ, 18, Oct. 2002, www.vanguard.com/ bogle_site/sp20021018.html.

29. Kurtzman, *How the Markets Really Work,* pp. 32–33.

30. James Surowiecki, *The Wisdom of Crowds* (New York: Random House, 2005), pp. xiii–xiv.

31. Kurtzman, *How the Markets Really Work,* p. 95.

32. CASTrader blog, www.castrader.com/2007/03/the_stock_marke.html.

33. Kurtzman, *How the Markets Really Work,* p. 72.

34. Ibid., pp. 73–74.

35. Surowiecki, *The Wisdom of Crowds,* pp. xiii–xiv.

36. Barry Schwartz, *The Paradox of Choice* (New York, Harper Perennial, 2004), p. 60.

Chapter 7

Prediction Markets

Nobody knows anything. But everybody, it turns out, may know
something.
—James Surowiecki, "The Science of Success"

An ordered list is a beautiful thing.
—Adam Siegel, Inkling Markets

A financial investment or charitable contribution is an expression
of expectation about future organizational performance: that
over some period of time, the company's profits will increase
or the nonprofit will produce more social benefit. One focus of capital
markets, whether financial or nonprofit, is to provide investors with
intelligence about prospective performance for the purpose of informing
investment decisions.

There are any number of ways to make assessments about the future.
ForecastingPrinciples.com, sponsored by the International Institute of
Forecasters, identifies 17 categories of forecasting methodologies with
such intriguing names as "conjoint analysis," "judgmental bootstrap-
ping" and "neural nets."[1] In recent years, a great deal of academic study
and corporate experimentation has focused on another compelling way
to gather crowd wisdom called a prediction market: "markets that are
designed and run for the primary purpose of mining and aggregating

information scattered among traders and subsequently using this information in the form of market values in order to make predictions about specific future events."[2]

An Illustration

Charter schools are a prime example of social entrepreneurship. With more than 1 million enrolled students, the U.S. charter school movement has grown from toddlerhood to adolescence. A common set of defining characteristics can be distilled from the rich diversity of some 3,500 locally run charter schools:

> Charter schools are nonsectarian public schools of choice that operate with freedom from many of the regulations that apply to traditional public schools. The "charter" establishing each such school is a performance contract detailing the school's mission, program, goals, students served, methods of assessment, and ways to measure success. The length of time for which charters are granted varies, but most are granted for 3 to 5 years. At the end of the term, the entity granting the charter may renew the school's contract. Charter schools are accountable to their sponsor—usually a state or local school board—to produce positive academic results and adhere to the charter contract. The basic concept of charter schools is that they exercise increased autonomy in return for this accountability. They are accountable for both academic results and fiscal practices to several groups: the sponsor that grants them, the parents who choose them, and the public that funds them.[3]

To understand how a prediction market might inform philanthropy, I'll use the following hypothetical and simplified illustration. It's the first quarter of 2007 and a national education foundation has asked a geographically dispersed group of 250 business executives, community leaders, parents, teachers, and school administrators to advise the foundation about potential investments in two charter high schools named Able and Baker. Able was started by an established charter managed organization (CMO) that runs five charter schools in three other states, while a local nonprofit formed by parents who were dissatisfied with their district's public high school founded Baker. Both schools opened three years earlier and each has about 200 students of comparable family income and racial and ethnic composition.

The foundation wants to support charter schools that improve student graduation rates. High school dropouts face substantially increased rates of violence, unemployment, drug abuse, and imprisonment, and their long-term social and economic prospects are poor. In the communities where Able and Baker students live, one-third of public high school students don't finish high school in four years. Both schools have set a two-year goal of increasing graduation rates from 67% to 75% and reducing dropout rates from 33% to 25%.

The advisors created a password-protected online market to track their assessments of both schools over the course of two years. The market offered two virtual stocks and traders could bid on one or both. The first stock claimed "Able will increase graduation rates from 67% to 75% by the end of the 2009 school year." The second stock made the same claim for Baker.

The market was structured to forecast the collective probability on a scale from 0% to 100% that each school would achieve the targeted graduation rate. The initial price of both stocks was set at $0.50, signifying a neutral 50–50 view of each school's prospects. As trading progressed, prices above $0.50 meant that, as a group, the advisors thought that school's probability of success was better than 50–50, and prices below $0.50 meant the opposite. For example, a Baker stock price of $0.54 at the end of the first year (2008) meant that the market thought there was a 54% chance at that particular time that at least 75% of Baker seniors would graduate at the end of the second year (2009).

When the market closed in two years, there were two possible outcomes for each stock: either the school would have a graduation rate of at least 75% or it would not. At that time, the probability of success would be either 100% or 0%. The market would "pay" $1 for each share of stock for either school that graduated at least three-quarters of the senior class and $0 for stock in a school that did not.

Each advisor was given 100 virtual dollars to trade, and each was instructed to try to maximize his or her virtual "profits." The market mechanism afforded two strategies for maximizing profits: the timing of trades and the size of trades.

Exhibit 7.1 Stock Price, Probability, and Profits
Source: Adapted from "Short Selling Explained," Inkling Markets,
http://home.inklingmarkets.com/help/shortselling.

Any shareholders who thought that either or both schools would meet the graduation goal should be interested in buying those shares if the price was below $1, since they would make a virtual profit when the market closed. The lower the price they paid for each share of "winning" stock would increase their profit, so the market provided an incentive for discovering relevant information as quickly as possible and buying shares before other traders bought shares and drove the price up. (Of course, the incentives ran the other way for virtual losses. Shareholders would look to sell shares of either school that they thought would fall short of the 75% target and have no value, and they would look to sell what they believed would become "losing" stock as quickly as possible to reduce their losses.) See Exhibit 7.1.

Traders could also increase their profits (and reduce their losses) by buying more of a given stock if they held stronger beliefs that the stocks would rise (and selling more if they were confident about price declines). In that way, the number of stocks traded reflected the intensity of the market's assessments. Thus, the market encouraged traders to acquire information and trade early, and to reveal their levels of confidence through trading volume.

The online marketplace provided each participant with a "dashboard" that displayed this information:

- The number of shares held of each stock
- The current price of each stock
- The current value of the portfolio and the balance of virtual dollars available for trading
- A history of the price of each stock over the last week, month, and year as well as the corresponding increase/decrease in the value of the trader's portfolio over the same periods of time

Stockholders could "buy" and "sell" shares at any time over the course of two years to reflect their current assessments of each school's performance. All trades were posted as they were made, and shareholders could set "alerts" on their computers or mobile devices to inform them of price changes (up or down) that exceeded some preset threshold (say, 5%). All advisors knew something about both schools, but different advisors knew different things about each school when the market began, and they had access to different sources of information throughout the contest. Traders could post comments on the Web site with their trades, ask and answer online questions, and insert links to relevant Web sites and documents. The Web site also included an automated RSS news feeder that posted updated links to articles about the schools whenever they appeared on the Internet.

Advisors could adjust their portfolio holdings at any time based on information they received about the schools along the way. A shareholder who learned that Able had instituted a program to identify students with repeated truancies and assign a trained adult volunteer to mentor those students might buy some Able shares at $0.55, post a comment about the program, and watch the price rise to $0.60. Another group of local traders might have heard that the program was having trouble recruiting volunteers and decided to hold off. If the mentoring program fizzled out, the price might drop back to $0.50, and those cautious investors would have avoided a loss.

The comments could provide an ongoing forum in which relevant developments would be brought to the timely attention of both other traders who didn't have other sources of information about the truancy intervention program and school officials who might not be fully aware of factors (such as volunteer perceptions) outside their control. Other participants who were tracking these trades might be induced to investigate to see whether their own holdings were out of balance in view of the various repricings.

At any given time, the market price would reflect the consensus prediction of all advisors about the probability that each school would hit the graduation target. Exhibit 7.2 provides a chronology of relevant events over the two-year trading cycle and the closing prices for each stock at the end of every quarter. Exhibit 7.3 graphs the quarterly closing prices.

How might the hypothetical education foundation use these market results? There's no unambiguous answer. Baker got off to a strong start

Exhibit 7.2 Trading Two Charter School Stocks.

Quarter	Event	Able Price	Baker Price
1Q07	Market opening.	$0.50	$0.50
2Q07	Both schools start the school year smoothly, but Able receives unfavorable media coverage from local community leaders who call the school's founders "outsiders."	$0.45	$0.60
3Q07	Able holds a series of open houses to educate parents and students about its approach and track record at its other schools.	$0.54	$0.60
4Q07	Both schools distribute newsletters about school activities and student progress during Year 1.	$0.56	$0.61
1Q08	Baker conducts a survey of parents and students, which reports increased satisfaction compared with prior public school experience. Some investors read news accounts of a racial incident at one of the other schools run by Able's CMO.	$0.45	$0.64
2Q08	Baker holds a poorly attended fundraiser and its bookkeeper tells the board of directors that available cash is lower than budgeted. Able's CMO is featured in a favorable article about charter schools in the *Wall Street Journal*.	$0.60	$0.49
3Q08	Baker's cash position doesn't improve and teachers complain about announced cutbacks. Able has a spike in student dropouts.	$0.57	$0.40
4Q08	Baker receives a one-time cash donation from a community foundation, while Able's dropout rate returns to normal.	$0.60	$0.43

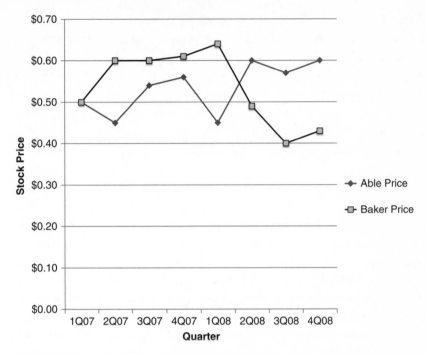

Exhibit 7.3 Quarterly Closing Prices for Charter School Stocks

before running into financial difficulties. Does the foundation think the recovery is tentative or durable? Is the foundation looking for promising community-supported charters? Perhaps the foundation believes that its funding model is well suited to helping such schools through lean times. Based on its experience with other schools, it might consider the steepness of the decline during the second and third quarters of 2008 to be within the expected range for locally sponsored start-ups, giving the foundation confidence that Baker could put its financial assistance to good use. Or the price swings might encourage the foundation to make its funding decision either sooner or later than it otherwise would, depending on whether it interpreted the information as signaling the need for urgency or caution.

Able, however, had steady progress over the entire review period, except for two challenging quarters. Perhaps the foundation has supported other schools the same CMO manages and thinks Able's outlook is encouraging. Or the foundation might engage in a more focused conversation with the CMO to better understand what led to those troughs and how the foundation could help prevent future reoccurrences.

This hypothetical has been artificially structured so that the foundation would make a simple favorable/unfavorable decision only at the end of the two-year market cycle. In the real world, prospective funders could consider interim market information at any time about the progress that social entrepreneurs seemed to be making in accomplishing long-term goals. This could be particularly useful if funders had made an initial investment and were considering if and when additional investments should be made over the course of, say, a five-year strategic growth plan.

Investment decisions are always personal and specific to a complex set of circumstances. The results from the charter school prediction market would probably not be the foundation's sole or even primary factor in making its funding decision, but instead would be considered in conjunction with other relevant information from other sources. If the market confirms other data or raises new questions, the funder would benefit, especially if some traders outside the foundation's usual circles had access to site-specific information that the distant institution did not.

Behind the Curtain

When traders study the stocks and current prices posted on a prediction market, they ask themselves two important questions: "What does the market know that I don't know, or what do I know that the market doesn't know?"[4] Well-designed prediction markets elicit meaningful responses because markets encourage traders to (1) gather information, (2) reveal their true beliefs, and (3) reveal the levels of confidence with which they hold those beliefs. In our hypothetical case study of two charter schools competing for funding, traders performed formal and informal research to understand why stocks moved in ways they hadn't expected, they made new trades only when they thought the market was wrong, and they sized their trades based on the strength of their convictions.

Like other kinds of markets, prediction markets are designed to provide participants with incentives to act in their perceived self-interest. In the case of the charter school scenario, the foundation enlisted a diverse range of market participants whose professional and community interests would naturally motivate them to offer their best judgments to help the funder make a more informed decision. Perhaps the foundation marketed the advisory board in ways that would enhance the prestige of its members or create excitement about the innovative experiment. A promised invitation to the foundation's annual gala to celebrate the winning school also might have been alluring.

Of the many potential traders in Able and Baker stocks, there would likely be some partisans who would make trades for the purpose of helping their favored school "win" rather than expressing their honest opinions about which school was performing better over the test period. However, if there were a sufficient number of disinterested traders, they should be able to drown out the rigged voting of the would-be manipulators. In that event, dishonest traders should lose "money" (or other market rewards, such as points or bragging rights) if their preferred school lost, and their awards should be diminished if their school won. In either case, prediction markets can be designed to prevent manipulation from affecting the outcome.

The net effect should be that well-constructed markets can do a better job of extracting meaningful insights from widely dispersed information of varying quality than many other forecasting methods. For example, although political polls have the statistical virtue of random selection, they also solicit opinions from people who might have little information about or interest in a future election, and there's no downside to casually answering a pollster's question. So polls sometimes produce statistically valid measures of unreliable data. By contrast, market participants are self-selected based on their knowledge and interest, so they do not fairly represent the population at large. But they trade only when they care about the outcome and think they have information that gives them an advantage over others.

Thus, markets can derive information that would not otherwise be available without incentives for self-interested disclosure. Consider this example involving a software development project:

> The benefit of a prediction market does not lie exclusively in better quantification of a forecast. Unearthing the reasons behind the forecasts may be of even greater value. A prediction-market pilot at Microsoft

in 2005 was designed to forecast the probability of on-time release for several products. To management's surprise, the stock price representing on-time release dropped to zero, despite the staff's prior assurance that on-time release was likely. The ensuing conversation uncovered the true beliefs of the programmers, a much more valuable result than simply knowing whether the release date would be missed.[5]

The value of discovering and sharing inaccessible information is magnified in the nonprofit sector, where reliable information about nonprofit performance is so scarce. As it is so difficult, expensive, and inexpedient for nonprofits to produce meaningful and comparable reports about their successes and failures, a mechanism that can extract and process lots of scraps from which an insightful mosaic can be assembled could be a real boon to social impact investors. The potential size, diversity, and passion of the crowd that knows something about social purpose organizations could give rise to an unusually robust information market.

New Tools Proliferate

The first real-world application of prediction markets arrived in 1988, brought to us by the University of Iowa Henry B. Tippie College of Business. The Iowa Electronic Markets (IEM) is a research tool originally designed to see if collective intelligence could work better than polls in predicting the outcomes of elections. In March 2008, the IEM published research comparing its predictions to the reported results of 964 public opinion polls in every presidential election between 1988 and 2004, which showed that the IEM made more accurate predictions 74% of the time.[6]

Prediction markets have been used to shed light on all kinds of future events. In 2004, Google held a rather unusual auction for its initial public offering in an attempt to avoid the usual problem of underpricing new stocks. The auction set the initial stock price at $85. When the stock went on sale, it opened at $100 and closed at $100.34, so the auction was off by $15.34. But an IEM prediction market pegged the closing price at $104.34, which was off by only $4.00. Thus, the prediction market was 3.84% too high, while the auction market was 15.3% too low.[7]

This is not an isolated example. Hewlett–Packard conducted internal prediction markets that beat official corporate forecasts of printer sales 15 out of 16 times.[8] The Hollywood Stock Exchange (owned by the financial services firm Cantor Fitzgerald) did a better job picking Oscar winners than four out of five columnists.[9] Eli Lilly conducted prediction markets that correctly identified the three most successful candidates for new drugs.[10] The U.S. Centers for Disease Control and Prevention conducted a pilot project with IEM that predicted the beginning, peak, and end of the influenza season two to four weeks ahead of disease reports from the field.[11] Intel developed a prediction market that outperformed traditional corporate forecasts in estimating customer product demand:

> In terms of accuracy, the markets are producing forecasts at least the equal of the official figures and as much as 20% better (20% less error), an impressive result given that the official forecasts have set a rather high standard during this time period with errors of only a few percent. In the longest sample to date, six of eight market forecasts fell within 2.7% of actual sales [versus the corporate goal of ±5%].[12]

Corporate prediction markets have become a serious tool for making better business decisions. More and more blue-chip companies are conducting internal prediction markets to inform and improve business forecasting, strategic planning, and marketing decisions, including Abbott Labs, Arcelor Mittal, Best Buy, Corning, EA, France Telecom, Frito Lay, Fuse Networks, GE, HP, Institute for the Future, InterContinental Hotels, Lionsgate Studios, Masterfoods, Microsoft, MGM, Motorola, Nokia, Pfizer, Qualcomm, Siemens, Starwood Hotels, and TNT.

Also, there's an explosion of online prediction market providers, including Ask Markets, Foresight Exchange, NewsFutures, Bet 2 Give, Global Betting Exchange, Betdaq, HedgeStreet, Pop Sci Prediction Exchange, BetFair, HedgeStreet Mock Trader, Prediction Xchange, Bet-Fair, Hollywood Stock Exchange, Reality Markets, Cenimar, HubDub, Red Monitor, Inkling Markets, SpreadFair, The Sim Exchange, InTrade, TradeFair, TradeSports, CNN Political Market, Iowa Electronic Markets, Eurex, U.S. Futures Exchange, Financial Times Predict, Media Predict, and Wall Street Journal Political Market. There's also tremendous growth in the number of companies offering information market software and

Open Innovation Markets

Open Innovation Markets enable crowd sourcing, crowd ranking and crowd analysis of innovations.

 Multiple innovations are submitted by invited participants or the public. These ideas can be open, "What should the organization develop?", or related to a particular question, "How could we solve this client problem?".

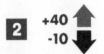 Using a simple up / down voting mechanism, the crowd ranks the ideas. This enables focus on the most promising innovations. Using a comments system, the innovator gains feedback.

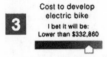 For the most promising ideas, the crowd bets on the accuracy of the key forecasts. Using the Xpree Forecast Markets toolset, accurate, unbiased forecasts of key metrics are generated.

 Armed with accurate forecasts and ranking of ideas, the organization can select innovations to develop. Based on the unbiased forecasts of the key metrics, development teams set reasonable targets, rather than being saddled with impossibly optimistic development timelines and success criteria.

Exhibit 7.4   Xpree's Open Innovation Markets
Source: www.xpree.com/open_innovation.png.

services, including Ask Markets, Consensus Point, HSX Virtual Markets, Inkling Markets, Microsoft PredictionPoint, NewsFutures, Xpree, and Zocalo. Exhibit 7.4 illustrates Xpree's "Open Innovation Markets."

The once-moribund *Industry Standard* business magazine relaunched on February 4, 2008, as an online prediction market:

> The Standard aggregates community knowledge in a quantified fashion, thereby ranking both the knowledge of the individual community members themselves, as well as the value of the information the community provides as a whole. This system is built as a prediction market, intersected with a reputation-based social network.[13]

The MIT Center for Coordination Science recently published "Harnessing Collective Intelligence to Address Global Climate Change," which argues that

> it is now possible to harness computer technology to facilitate "collective intelligence"—the synergistic and cumulative channeling of the vast human and technical resources now available over the internet—to

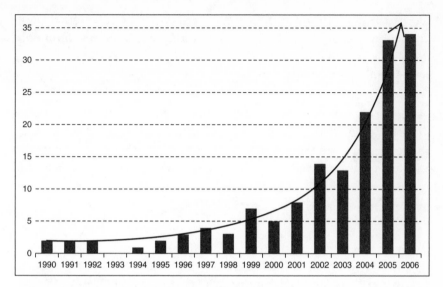

Exhibit 7.5 Number of Prediction Market Articles per Year
Source: George Tziralis and Ilias Tatsiopoulos, "Prediction Markets: An Extended Literature Review,"
Journal of Prediction Markets (February 2007),
http://gtziralis.googlepages.com/PredictionMarkets_AnExtendedLiteratureReview_
TziralisTatsiopoulos.pdf.

address systemic problems like climate change. What is needed, we
believe, is a new kind of web-mediated discussion and decision-making
forum.[14]

Scholarly research about prediction markets has increased dramatically (Exhibit 7.5). And last but not least, the adoption of prediction
markets has advanced sufficiently that the federal government, specifically
the Commodity Futures Trading Commission (CFTC), is considering
whether such markets should be regulated.[15] Supporters hope that CFTC
oversight might encourage the growth of prediction markets by extending the permission granted to the Iowa Electronic Markets to offer markets in which traders can bet real money (in the case of IEM, up to $500).

Kinds of Markets

I divide prediction markets into two broad categories: determinate and
indeterminate. In determinate markets, the outcome becomes known
at some point, so it's possible to compare the market prediction with

the actual result. In indeterminate markets, the outcome is either never known (or not known until the too-distant future), or more commonly, the market is used to make an either/or decision, or to make one choice among multiple mutually exclusive alternatives, so that the effect of other possible decisions that were not chosen can't be assessed.

Determinate markets have been studied extensively, and the results show that they "work" in the sense that they make predictions that are about as good as, and sometimes even better than, other more commonly accepted methods, such as polls, opinion surveys, expert panels, and corporate forecasts. Robin Hanson, the founding father of prediction markets, has summarized their track record:

> Such markets (at least the hard cash versions) have so far done well in every known head-to-head field comparison with other social institutions that forecast. Orange juice futures improve on National Weather Service forecasts, horse race markets beat horse race experts, Academy Award markets beat columnist forecasts, gas demand markets beat gas demand experts, stock markets beat the official NASA panel at fingering the guilty company in the Challenger accident, election markets beat national opinion polls, and corporate sales markets beat official corporate forecasts.[16]

By comparing predicted to actual events, well-designed determinate markets estimate the probability of future events at levels of accuracy that equal or exceed those of established forecasting methods.

What about indeterminate markets, where the market suggests one choice from a mutually exclusive set that precludes alternative choices, thereby preventing any comparison to an alternative "event" that did not occur? If, for example, a prediction market concludes that product A would outsell product B, a company that then decides to make product A and not product B wouldn't be able to later compare the actual sales of both products to assess the accuracy of the market predictions.

It turns out that well-designed indeterminate markets are useful for making better *decisions* in the face of uncertainty for the same reasons that they're useful for extracting wisdom from crowds about future *events*. To be sure, predictions derived from indeterminate markets are inherently fuzzier and, therefore, less confidence-inspiring than markets that produce specific answers to specific questions, the accuracy of which can be measured after the fact.

But information markets designed to improve the quality of making inexact decisions are gaining corporate acceptance precisely *because* they face indeterminate problems for which reliable forecasting methods are lacking. Such "decision support" markets are being used to help far-sighted companies identify new product ideas worthy of development, allocate limited resources, and forecast market demand. They are based on the simple but profound circumstance that they might just work better than traditional methods. Given that no one can tell whether any strategic decision was "correct"—even if the decision turned out well, it's always possible that a different choice would have produced a superior result—why not extract the wisdom of an informed crowd, if for no other reason than to provide a comparison to, or perhaps a confirmation of, management's chosen course?

This would seem to be particularly true in the case of nonprivate decisions of significant consequence. Many of the $100 million problems that social enterprises work on were once considered the exclusive province of government for which democratically elected officials or their appointees were responsible. Just as the accepted role and scope of government changed significantly beginning with the New Deal, the United States has been quietly but inexorably evolving toward the "governing by network" model advanced by Goldsmith and Eggers (see Chapter 2). As the once-impervious boundaries among the public, private, and nonprofit sectors become increasingly porous, it makes sense to add collective intelligence to decisions about allocating philanthropic resources. The fact that charitable donations divert precious tax revenues reinforces the point.

Consider some examples of indeterminate corporate predictions markets. Siemens developed an internal information market to provide early warnings of schedule delays in software development projects. Motorola created an internal market to screen 8,500 new product ideas and identify the most promising prospects for development. GE created "imagination markets" that generated and ranked 63 ideas for new technologies. A customer of Consensus Point, Inc. (identified as a "large computer manufacturer") used employee markets to answer such questions as "How much of each product should we build?" and "Will the addition of feature 'XYZ' lead to stronger sales in the telecom industry?" Microsoft is researching markets to "generate business value with new forecasts where no previous forecast was practicable." Dentsu, Japan's largest advertising agency, is using information markets as internal fore-casting tools to spot consumer trends.[17]

Best Buy has one of the most advanced programs of internal infor-mation markets. After successful pilots in 2006 and 2007 showed that employee-based predictions beat corporate forecasts, Best Buy launched an internal prediction market called "TagTrade" to support forecasting, project management, new product/service development, and new busi-ness ideas. TagTrade's criteria for "stock ideas" show how indeterminate markets can shed light on murky business decisions:

- Where is information potentially distorted, delayed, or diluted on its way to [senior] management?
- Where does management want/need a better gauge of employee sentiment/confidence?
- What businesses are most challenging (least conducive) for tradi-tional forecasting methods?
- What initiatives/outcomes require increased visibility by a broad audience?
- What economic assumptions require better input from those closest to customer?
- For what major initiatives do leaders require a more accurate health check?[18]

Of course, nonprofits encounter similar challenges.

Good Enough

The ambiguity and uncertainty of nondefinitive information often leads people to conclude—wrongly, I believe—that because social outcomes and their causes are inherently debatable, marketlike mechanisms aren't useful for making decisions about social choices. Certainly, formidable obstacles to the effective use of prediction markets remain. I'm not aware of any prediction market experiments involving nonprofit organizations.

But the nonprofit sector is not in any position to allow an illusory perfect solution to become the enemy of an available good one.

Today, donated funds are flooding into the social sector with virtually no intelligent means of making informed choices among a bewildering array of seemingly equally worthy recipients. Little has changed since Andrew Carnegie observed in 1889 that "one of the serious obstacles to the improvement of our race is indiscriminate charity."[19] Today, nonprofits proliferate like weeds, starving more mature seedlings of the sustained nourishment they need to grow. The net result certainly does not inspire confidence that the status quo is anything approaching optimal. The cost-benefit boundaries of more effective nonprofit capital allocation have not changed since Harvard's Allen Grossman framed them nearly ten years ago:

> Is there a significant downside risk in restructuring some portion of the philanthropic social capital markets to test the effectiveness of performance driven philanthropy? The short answer is, "No." The current reality is that most broad-based solutions to social problems have eluded the conventional and fragmented approaches to philanthropy. It is hard to imagine that experiments to change the system to a more performance driven and rational market would negatively impact the effectiveness of the current funding flows—and could have dramatic upside potential.[20]

As it turns out, the many shortcomings of nonprofit capital markets are the very things that make them so well suited to prediction markets. And the unmet conditions that have kept prediction markets from gaining wider acceptance are the very ones nonprofit capital markets uniquely satisfy. Three primary conditions must be satisfied:

> that there are enough traders in the market (critical mass); that those traders represent the peer group that is knowledgeable about the issues the market seeks to address; and that there are sufficient incentives to motivate participants to trade and generate useful information.[21]

Think how well a virtual nonprofit stock market could meet these requirements of having a critical mass of knowledgeable and motivated traders. Online giving is finally catching on, with the largest North

American platform, Network for Good, attracting 160,000 individual donors in 2006 alone.[22] Our golden age of philanthropy is marked not only by an increase in the amount of giving, but in the number of givers, too. The number of taxpayers who filed itemized federal tax returns with charitable deductions increased from 29.6 million in 1992 to 40.2 million in 2002.[23] Active participation in social purpose organizations is rising significantly, too, with unprecedented levels of volunteering and formation of new nonprofits. A September 10, 2007, *Time* magazine cover story, "The Case for National Service," reported that more than 61 million Americans dedicated 8.1 billion hours to volunteerism in 2006, an increase of more than 6 percentage points since 1989, representing 27% of Americans who volunteer.[24]

These millions of donors, social entrepreneurs, and volunteers are passionately engaged in issues they follow closely, from education reform to climate change, from women's health to poverty. I'm not besotted by starry-eyed prospects for a utopian future, but there is a large, engaged, and informed social sector that potentially could be enticed to help bring about a more robust kind of philanthropy that rewards strong performance and magnifies results. If indeed "the future is not invented; it is co-evolved by a wide class of players," the nonprofit sector seems like fertile ground.[25]

In *How to Measure Anything: Finding the Value of Intangibles in Business,* Douglas W. Hubbard analyzes measurement in terms of "uncertainty reduction": "what really makes a measurement of high value is a lot of uncertainty combined with a high cost of being wrong."[26] He offers the case of social services programs as one that's ripe for error-reduction measurements:

> If we insist on being ignorant to the relative values of various public welfare programs (which is the necessary result of a refusal to measure their value), then we will almost certainly allocate limited resources in a way that solves less valuable problems for more money. This is because there is a large combination of possible investments to track such things and the best answer, in such cases, is never obvious without some understanding of magnitudes.[27]

We don't need to eliminate all the uncertainty, or even 90% of it, as statistical conventions often require. Advancing social progress is not an academic exercise reserved only for interventions that can be shown to be "statistically significant." Glen Whitman wisely observes that "the decision rules of pure science should not be confused with the decision rules of life."[28] He offers the example of studies investigating the hypothesized connection between minimum wage laws and unemployment: "if studies fail to show the minimum wage causes unemployment, the appropriate conclusion is not that there isn't a relationship, but that we just can't say so with much confidence." Social science often fails to prove the existence of cause-and-effect relationships, but as Carl Sagan famously said, "The absence of evidence is not evidence of absence."

When we throw up our hands and say that social outcomes can't be measured, we're guilty of measurement snobbery, insisting that only the highest forms of exactitude are valid. It is past time to acknowledge that different types of measurement are suited to different uses.

In his seminal 1946 article, "On the Theory of Scales of Measurement," Stanley Smith Stevens spelled out four "levels of measurement": nominal, ordinal, interval, and ratio.[29] Nominal measurements are just categorical groupings, such as male/female, and animal/vegetable/ mineral. Nominals are useful in distinguishing one thing from another when the categories are defined by mutually exclusive criteria. Interval and ratio measurements are what we think of as precise forms of measurement that produce results we can analyze mathematically because their values are constant. For example, four is always twice as much as two and six is always halfway between three and nine.

Ordinal measurements tell us whether one thing is "more" or "less" of some value than other things, but not how much more or less. So ordinal measures enable us to rank objects based on their order relative to a value scale, but we can't add or subtract ordinals.

Rank Intelligence

Even with their limitations, though, ordinal measurements are used all the time to help guide real-world decisions. The Google search engine is one gigantic ordinal measuring device based on a mathematical algorithm called "PageRank." In 1998, Google's founders described their ranking methodology in terms that are similar to the challenging ranking problem we face here:

> The importance of a Web page is an inherently subjective matter which depends on the reader's interests, knowledge and attitudes. But there is still much that can be said objectively about the relative importance of Web pages. This paper describes PageRank, a method for rating Web pages objectively and mechanically effectively measuring the human interest and attention devoted to them.[30]

Google search results reflect the relative "importance" of Web site pages based, in the first instance, on the number of other pages that link to each page:

> PageRank relies on the uniquely democratic nature of the Web by using its vast link structure as an indicator of an individual page's value. In essence, Google interprets a link from page A to page B as a vote, by page A, for page B. But, Google looks at more than the sheer volume of votes, or links a page receives; it also analyzes the page that casts the vote. Votes cast by pages that are themselves "important" weigh more heavily and help to make other pages "important."

Google describes its ranking algorithm as "recursive," meaning that one of the steps in the procedure is to run the procedure again. (The standard instructions for using shampoo are the most familiar example of a recursive procedure: "lather, rinse, repeat.") A Google search is recursive because it takes the results and plugs them back into the algorithm and runs it repeatedly until the value of additional rounds diminishes essentially to zero.

A prediction market is also recursive because traders change their rankings based on the rankings of other traders. This dynamic process continues until the market closes, forcing traders to place their most confident bets as the deadline approaches, just as bids converge rapidly on eBay auctions as time expires.

Internet surfers don't need to know if one site is "twice" as important as some other site; they just want to be able to see the pages that are most relevant to their inquiry first and present them in some legitimate order of relevance. When they review the search results, higher-ranked sites are far more likely to be what they're looking for than lower-ranked sites. Google's rankings aren't perfect, but they're the best available the vast majority of the time.

For search engines, "better" equates with relevance, so focusing on "human interest and attention" as a measure of "importance" makes sense. For social investment choices, "better" translates to effectiveness, so the market must aggregate information about performance. A nonprofit ranking system that might produce useful, albeit imperfect, intelligence would begin to take philanthropy in the right direction of funding better performance.

Polls and beauty contests ask a fundamentally subjective question, "Whom do you want to win?" Prediction markets ask something quite different: "Whom do you think will win?" Philanthropists should take a lesson from Google's founders and recognize that, much like the quality of billions of disparate Web pages, "there is still much that can be said objectively" about nonprofit performance.

When high school students start thinking about one of the most consequential decisions they face, where to go to college, they consult published school rankings to narrow their choices based on criteria that matter to them. For example, the annual rankings of *U.S. News & World Report* slice and dice data on a host of parameters, including location, size of student body, religious affiliation, majors, sports programs, and best financial value. The rankings are based on a combination of nominal and ordinal information:

> To rank colleges, *U.S. News* first places each school into categories based on mission (research university or liberal arts college) and, for universities offering a range of master's programs and colleges focusing on undergraduate education without a particular emphasis on the liberal arts, by location (North, South, Midwest, and West). Universities where there is a focus on research and that offer several doctoral programs are ranked separately from liberal arts colleges, and master's universities and baccalaureate colleges are compared against other schools in the same group and region. Second, we gather data from and about each school in 15 areas related to academic excellence. Each indicator is assigned a weight (expressed as a percentage) based on our judgments

about which measures of quality matter most. Third, the colleges are ranked based on their composite weighted score. We publish the numeric rank of roughly the top half of schools in each of the 10 categories; the remaining schools are placed into the third and fourth tiers, listed alphabetically, based on their overall score in their category.[31]

Fully 25% of the *U.S. News* rankings are based on "a peer assessment survey" in which "*U.S. News* asks the president, provost, and dean of admissions at each school to rate the quality of the academic programs for schools in the same category, including their own." Although there has been a good deal of criticism directed at the *U.S. News* rankings, millions of students and parents use them, if for no other reason than to help them narrow down the overwhelming number of choices.

Much of social science also depends on ordinal ranking systems. Psychological measurements, in particular, lend themselves to ordinal rather than absolute comparisons:

> Since many mental constructs within psychology cannot be observed directly, most measures tend to be ordinal. Attitudes, intentions, opinions, personality characteristics, psychological well-being, depression, etc., are all constructs which are thought to vary in degree between individuals but tend only to allow indirect ordinal measurements.[32]

Physical medicine uses ranking systems for making assessments about such elusive concepts as degrees of pain. Thus, even with recognized limitations in the underlying data, health professionals use ordinal rankings to make critical decisions about diagnosis, treatment and recovery.

With all their imperfections, ordinal rankings often have the profound virtue of being better than the alternative. Professor Stevens called this "a kind of pragmatic sanction: In numerous instances it leads to fruitful results." In the case of assessing alternative nonprofit investments, I believe the prospects are similarly promising.

Notes

1. Methodology Tree, "Evidence-Based Forecasting," www.forecastingprinciples.com/methodologytree.html.

2. Tzu-Chuan Chou, Georgios Tziralis, and Ilias Tatsiopoulos, "Prediction Markets: An Extended Literature Review," *Journal of Prediction Markets* (February 2007), http://gtziralis.googlepages.com/PredictionMarkets_AnExtended LiteratureReview_TziralisTatsiopoulos.pdf.

3. Overview, U.S. Charter Schools, www.uscharterschools.org/pub/uscs_docs/o/index.htm.

4. Todd Proebsting, "Tee Time with Admiral Pointdexter (Markets at Microsoft)," presentation at 2005 *DIMACS Workshop on Markets as Predictive Devices* (Information Markets), http://dimacs.rutgers.edu/Workshops/Markets/slides/proebsting.ppt.

5. Carol Gebert, "Prediction Markets—A Guide to Practical Adoption in the Pharmaceutical Industry," *Foresight* 9 (Spring 2008): 27.

6. Joyce E. Berg, Forrest D. Nelson, and Thomas A. Rietz, "Prediction Market Accuracy in the Long Run," *International Journal of Forecasting* 24, no. 2 (April–June 2008): 283–298, www.sciencedirect.com/science?_ob=ArticleURL&_udi=B6V92-4SCTMTB-1&_user=440026&_rdoc=1&_fmt=&_orig=search &_sort=d&view=c&_acct=C000020939&_version=1&_urlVersion=0&_userid=440026&md5=b71e3eb286285017763be79dd7cb9209.

7. Joyce E. Berg, George R. Neumann, and Thomas A. Rietz, "Searching for Google's Value: Using Prediction Markets to Forecast Market Capitalization Prior to an Initial Public Offering," August 2008, http://papers.ssrn.com/sol3/Delivery.cfm/SSRN_ID1260105_code23269.pdf?abstractid=887562& mirid=1.

8. Kay-Yut Chen and Charles R. Plott, "Prediction Markets and Information Aggregation Mechanism: Experiments and Application," California Institute of Technology, Department of Social Science, 1998.

9. David M. Pennock, Steve Lawrence, Lee C. Giles, and Finn Arup Nielsen, "The Real Power of Artificial Markets," *Science* 291, no. 5506 (9 Feb. 2001): 987–988, http://artificialmarkets.com.

10. Ibid.

11. Philip M. Polgreen, Forrest D. Nelson, and George R. Neumann, "Use of Prediction Markets to Forecast Infectious Disease Activity," *Clinical Infectious Diseases* 44 (2007): 272–279, www.journals.uchicago.edu/doi/full/10.1086/510427?cookieSet=1.

12. Jay W. Hopman, "Using Forecasting Markets to Manage Demand Risk," *Intel Technology Journal* 11, no. 2 (2007), www.intel.com/technology/itj/2007/v11i2/4-forecasting/6-results.htm.

13. The Industry Standard, www.thestandard.com/about.

14. Thomas W. Malone and Mark Klein, "Harnessing Collective Intelligence to Address Global Climate Change," *Innovations* (Summer 2007): 1–2.

15. Commodity Futures Trading Commission, "Concept Release on the Appropriate Regulatory Treatments of Event Contracts," *Federal Register* 73, no. 89 (7, May 2008): 25669.

16. Robin Hanson, "Decision Markets for Policy Advice," in Alan S. Gerber and Eric M. Patashnik, eds., *Promoting the General Welfare: New Perspectives on Government Performance* (Washington, DC: Brookings Institution Press, November 2006).

17. Conference on Corporate Applications of Prediction/Information Market, 1 Nov. 2007, http://people.ku.edu/~cigar/PMConf_2007/.

18. Dawn Keller, Best Buy Prediction Markets Conference, Kansas City, 1 Nov. 2007, p. 30, http://people.ku.edu/%7Ecigar/PMConf_2007/DawnKeller %28Prediction%20Market%20Conference%20110107_Best%20Buy_for %20web%29.pdf.

19. Andrew Carnegie, "Wealth," *North American Review* 148, no. 391 (June 1889), www.swarthmore.edu/SocSci/rbannis1/AIH19th/Carnegie.html.

20. Allen Grossman, "Philanthropic Social Capital Markets: Performance Driven Philanthropy," Social Enterprise Series 12, Harvard Business School, 1999, p. 12, www.hbs.edu/socialenterprise/pdf/SE12SocialCapitalMarkets.pdf.

21. Ajit Kambil and Eric van Heck, *Making Markets* (Boston: Harvard Business Press, 2002), p. 155.

22. David Bonbright, Natalia Kiryttopoulou, and Lindsay Iversen, "Online Philanthropy Markets: From 'Feel-Good' Giving to Effective Social Investing," Keystone, 2008, www.keystoneaccountability.org/files/Keystone_ Online%20Philanthropy%20Markets.pdf.

23. Urban Institute, Center on Nonprofits and Philanthropy, National Center for Charitable Statistics, Profiles of Individual Charitable Contributions by State, 2002, Appendix A: Data on 2002 Itemized Charitable Contributions from the IRS Statistics of Income, nccsdataweb.urban.org/kbfiles/421/stgive_02.pdf; Urban Institute and Independent Sector, *The New Nonprofit Almanac and Desk Reference* (San Francisco: Jossey-Bass, 2002), Table 3.8, p. 67.

24. Richard Stengel, "The Case for National Service," *Time*, 10 Sept. 2007.

25. Katherine Fulton and Andrew Blau, "Cultivating Change in Philanthropy," Monitor Group, 2005, p. 16.

26. Douglas W. Hubbard, *How to Measure Anything: Finding the Value of Intangibles in Business* (Hoboken, NJ: John Wiley & Sons, 2007), pp. 22, 34.

27. Ibid.

28. Glen Whitman, "The (in)Significance of Significance," Agoraphilia: The Center for Blurbs in the Public Interest, 14 July 2004, http://agoraphilia. blogspot.com/2004/07/insignificance-of-significance.html.

29. S. S. Stevens, "On the Theory of Scales of Measurement," *Science,* 7 June 1946, pp. 677–680, DOI: 10.1126/science.103.2684.677, www.sciencemag.org/cgi/pdf_extract/103/2684/677.

30. Lawrence Page, Sergey Brin, Rajeev Motwani, and Terry Winograd, "The PageRank Citation Ranking: Bringing Order to the Web," 1998, http://dbpubs.stanford.edu:8090/pub/showDoc.Fulltext?lang=en&doc=1999-66&format=pdf&compression=.

31. *U.S. News & World Report*, "Best Colleges, Frequently Asked Questions," www.usnews.com/articles/education/best-colleges/2008/08/21/2009-frequently-asked-questions.html.

32. Marie Glynis Breakwell, Sean Hammond, Jonathan A. Smith, and Chris Fife-Schaw, *Research Methods in Psychology,* 3rd ed. (Bakersfield, CA: Sage, 2006), p. 55.

Chapter 8

The Impact Index

We need a way to rank nonprofit groups according to results—
not budget size or organizational reach.
    —*Leslie R. Crutchfield and Heather McLeod Grant, "Rankings Should
    Reflect Results, Not Donations"*

Many people have been thinking about the creation of a social
stock market, but as yet no standard or platform exists as a marketplace or clearinghouse.
    —*Brian Trelstad, Acumen Fund, "Simple Measures for Social Enterprise"*

What would a virtual nonprofit stock market look like, and how would it work? The honest answer is that, beyond some general observations, we don't really know yet. A nonprofit stock market would be a social institution that would evolve from some plausible starting point in whatever direction the participants' organic decisions took it. As Steven Johnson observed in *Emergence: The Connected Lives of Ants, Brains, Cities, and Software,* "It is both the promise and the peril of swarm logic that the higher-level behavior is almost impossible to predict in advance. You never really know what lies on the other end of a phase transition until you press play and find out.... And then you see what happens."[1]

Woody Allen offered a somewhat different formulation: "If you want to make God laugh, tell him about your plans."

Just as financial "market participants will choose the ownership struc-ture that maximizes their benefits and profit potential,"[2] so, too, will the participants of the nonprofit stock market choose whatever self-organizing mechanisms they deem most beneficial. As Harvard's Allen Grossman put it, under the right conditions "metrics that had increasing relevancy and accuracy would evolve."[3] After all, the mighty New York Stock Exchange began as 24 brokers gathered under a buttonwood tree in lower Manhattan in 1792.

In the remaining two chapters of this book, I'll describe what I think it will take to implement a working nonprofit prediction market. This chapter focuses on the Impact Index (IMPEX) itself in terms of the parameters of its design and the responsibilities of the organization that would build and manage it. The next (and final) chapter will bring the discussion back full circle to the question raised earlier about what kind of "whole product solution" must be developed to help steer growth capital to mid-cap nonprofits so that they might effectively attack $100 million problems on the way to producing transformative social impact. Many elements of that solution are likely to come from collaborators out-side the IMPEX itself, such as independent researchers and government agencies, working together to form an ecosystem of performance-driven philanthropy.

Designing the IMPEX

Professor Robin Hanson of George Mason University devised the field of information markets back in the early 1990s, and we are fortunate that prediction market science has advanced sufficiently in the ensuing years that a consensus has formed around a well-defined set of criti-cal success factors. I am privileged to have made the acquaintance of Carol Gebert, who not only founded one of the first prediction market providers nearly a decade ago but also boiled those factors down in a recent *Foresight* magazine article entitled "Prediction Markets—A Guide to Practical Adoption in the Pharmaceutical Industry."[4]

While Gebert began her work in this field by bringing prediction markets to Eli Lilly, her insights are not confined to that industry. She identifies three barriers to the effective adoption of prediction markets:

defining the prediction, creating a community of traders, and providing adequate incentives to participation. Let us consider each in turn.

Defining the Prediction Event

As we saw in the charter schools example in the previous chapter, the market prediction is generally framed as a question or a claim, such as whether something—for example, the election of a candidate or the debut of a new product—will happen by a certain date, or how big something else will get—for example, the sales of a book or the price of a commodity—by a certain date. These questions or claims are called "stocks" or "contracts" because they're traded on a market and because they promise to pay a certain amount (in either real or "play" money) depending on the ranking assigned by the market. The ranking is usually expressed either as a binary outcome—"winner take all"—or as a ratio— "share of the vote."

Gebert identifies five rules for defining predictions effectively:

1. The cardinal rule is that the *stock*—the event being predicted—must be clearly and precisely defined.
2. The stock must be valuable.
3. Timeframes should be short enough to maintain trader interest.
4. Proper consideration needs to be given to the sensitivity of the prediction.
5. The best stock definitions are those for a prediction worth making.

Clarity and Precision All participants must understand and agree on the possible outcomes they're forecasting. Not only is this necessary to insure that everyone agrees on the results when the market closes, but also to insure that the prices and the trades that influence those prices relate to the same thing.

For the IMPEX, this means that the market sponsor must frame unambiguous questions, such as "How many volunteers will Jumpstart for Young Children recruit in 2009?" and "Will the KIPP Foundation win a *Fast Company* Social Capitalist Award this year?" Counterexamples would be "Will nonprofit mergers increase this year?" and "Will the IRS crack down on charities engaged in political activity?"

Although the questions for indeterminate stocks are more difficult to frame than determinate ones, it's not impossible, and I'm sure we'll get better at it with time. The president of the X Prize Foundation (and former head of the Gates Foundation) is right when he says, "Anything worth achieving can be stated as a goal and measured."[5] As always, the trick is to focus on what's ascertainable. For example, rather than asking "How can ABC Nonprofit improve its performance?" try something like "Would ABC Nonprofit help more kids by opening new sites or increasing enrollment at its existing sites?"

For example, the Iowa Health Prediction Market (an IEM project) tries to help public health agencies make better decisions about resource allocation by creating markets that ask "Will the number of new World Health Organization–confirmed cases of H5N1 [avian flu] in humans during month B be greater than or equal to the total number of cases during month A?"[6] The answer could help inform choices about optimal times for intervention and the rates of expenditures for disease control.

Emulating financial stock markets, many prediction markets prepare a prospectus that provides traders with baseline information about the market. A typical prospectus explains the contract (i.e., stock) definitions, how "liquidation values" will be determined, when the market will close, and how traders can participate. The market maker often also provides common background information about the market, such as current and historical prices, and links to relevant Web resources, such as each candidate's sites in an election prediction market.

Valuable Stocks   Gebert stresses the need for predictions that matter:

> Prediction markets created around unimportant events are bound to fail. If the outcomes are not important, the stock will not attract active trading. Without active trading, there is no market.

The need for important markets is particularly acute in the case of nonprofit stocks because, in most cases, there won't be any pecuniary return from trading. So nonprofit contracts must be fashioned to highlight their intrinsic value. Particularly when the IMPEX is starting out, attention should be drawn to questions of self-evident significance, so that large numbers of knowledgeable traders will readily understand how

much their "votes" matter. Consider this description of the IEM's bird
flu market:

> Recent cases of avian influenza (H5N1) in birds and humans have led
> many to fear that this strain of the "bird flu" may produce the next
> worldwide influenza pandemic.... Despite considerable uncertainty,
> information does exist that may help predict when and if the next pan-
> demic will be caused by an H5N1 strain. For example, an increase in the
> number of human clusters might suggest an increase in the likelihood
> of an H5N1 pandemic. Collection and analysis of such information is
> difficult because it is geographically dispersed and not always shared
> among health professionals (e.g., epidemiologists, clinicians, basic sci-
> entists). Currently available methods do not efficiently collect and
> interpret these data. We believe that a Web-based prediction market
> designed to collect disparate information from widely dispersed health
> care professionals can serve as an avian influenza "barometer.".... The
> probabilities generated by this market could help policymakers and
> public health officials coordinate resources, facilitate vaccine produc-
> tion, increase stockpiles of antiviral medications, and plan for allocation
> of personnel and resources.[7]

Timeframes   Gebert endorses conventional wisdom when she says that
the length of markets "should be short enough to maintain trader interest," for which she offers compelling commonsense explanations: "time
scales extending years into the future make participation in the market
unattractive to traders" and "knowledge contributing to a good prediction market may simply not exist that far in advance." Gebert claims, not
unreasonably, that "time scales of three to six months probably supply the
best balance of trader interest, available knowledge, and foresight value."

Under the most favorable conditions, prediction markets have yet to
achieve widespread adoption, and the idea of using them as a virtual nonprofit stock market is certainly more exotic than, for example, predicting
next quarter's widget sales. At the same time, I hope I have convinced
readers that there is a compelling case for using prediction markets to
inform certain kinds of social investment decisions. The place to begin,
then, is with the user-friendliest predictions of the most obvious importance whose unambiguous results can be determined within comfortably
short timeframes that won't try anyone's patience.

For the record, I note that some kinds of $100 million problems—climate change comes to mind—invite predictions of significantly longer duration, and that a small amount of encouraging research has been conducted on such markets.[8] Just as indeterminate markets might prove particularly valuable because fewer alternatives are available, the time could come for long-term markets. As Warren Buffett has said, when it comes to philanthropy, "You have to have a longer view than that. You have to take delayed results in many cases."[9] In the meantime, though, prudence counsels that we make sure we can walk before we attempt to run.

Sensitivity Sensitivity has special salience for nonprofit investing. In many ways, the nonprofit sector, for all its innovation, is a tradition-bound fellowship that generally does not collect performance data, does not condition funding on performance, and does not publish or share internal performance assessments. And here I am proposing that donors consider artificial, public market predictions of future organizational performance to inform some of their philanthropy. It is safe to assume that there might be some resistance to the idea.

Inevitably, the introduction of prediction markets to philanthropy will entail a good measure of trial and error. Once the initial design glitches are discovered and tweaked—who can say how long that will take?—the best we can probably hope for early on is that the markets will signal some broad, directional consensus around relatively stronger and relatively weaker performers that some small set of "early adopter" investors might consider worthwhile information. When we try to apply such tentative results to the highest-stakes activity that social entrepreneurs undertake—fundraising—the place to start is probably behind closed doors.

Of course, the sensitivity problem is not unique to nonprofits. Published research about corporate prediction markets provides analysis, for example, of how prediction market forecasts of product sales compared to management's predictions, but companies don't disclose confidential information that might interest their competitors or give their investors heartburn.

Sensitivity provides another reason why I recommend later in this chapter that initial experiments with nonprofit prediction markets should be conducted with full confidentiality under controlled conditions.

Open public markets should be reserved until such time as the pluckiest nonprofits begin to see that there might be something in it for them.

Actionable Predictions Gebert wisely observes that "the value of information is eroded if no action can be taken as a result of having that information." Such markets will not "be valued by the corporate leadership and attractive to traders."

It is interesting to note that after being largely relegated to academic circles for nearly 20 years, prediction markets have only recently gained traction with corporate clients. Political markets received a good amount of TV and Internet exposure for the first time during the 2008 U.S. presidential campaign, notwithstanding the fact that IEM has been running them for two decades. Exhibit 8.1 shows how the use of "Intrade," the leading provider of prediction market services, jumped as a Google search term early in 2008, with spikes at the Super Tuesday primaries and from the August conventions through the November 4 election. (The spike in April–May coincides with the intense press coverage leading up to the Pennsylvania Democratic primary of Barack Obama's recorded remarks about rural voters who "cling to guns or religion."[10])

The point of the IMPEX would be to become a useful source of information for social impact investors looking for insight about the relative performance of mid-cap social enterprises. Just as financial investors

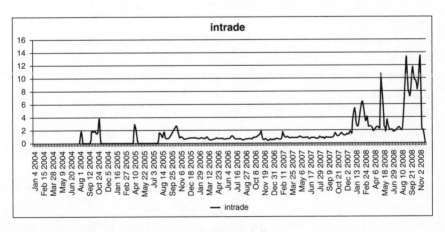

Exhibit 8.1 Search Volume Index for "Intrade"
Source: Google Trends, www.google.com/trends?q=intrade&ctab=0&geo=all&date=all&sort=0, search conducted by the author on 29 Nov. 2008.

consider stock prices in conjunction with other information about prospective investments, it is highly unlikely that the IMPEX would ever become the sole or even primary driver of social investment decisions. The value of IMPEX data should increase, however, if it helps move the nonprofit capital market as a whole in the direction of performance-based funding and generates more reliable information as participation increases over time and the ranking engine becomes more refined. In that way, it could play an essential role in the formation of a more effective sector: "A vital role for infrastructure is to provide the information and connecting channels needed to overcome the problems of fragmentation and isolation, and to be a force of synthesis and aggregation."[11]

Creating a Community of Traders

An enormous amount of digital ink has been spilled over the question of how many traders are needed to produce reliable predictions, and the problem of "thin" markets is the subject of much consternation and research. Although accurate predictions can be produced under the right conditions with just a few dozen traders, the attention devoted to the thin-market problem is a testament to the challenge of attracting large numbers of active traders over extended periods of time.

I think it is not too much to say that the ability to engage sizable crowds to the IMPEX should be the acid test of whether this is a worth-while endeavor. As noted, the nonprofit sector is populated by millions of energetic donors, volunteers, employees, and beneficiaries from all manner of community, family, religious, cultural, and corporate groups, the vast majority of whom choose to do so voluntarily, often for largely altruistic reasons. This is a knowledgeable, motivated, and diverse uni-verse of people who care deeply about the organizations they support and who might well be receptive to new kinds of participation that could substantially increase the bang-per-donated-buck and really move the needle of social change.

Active participation in nonprofit prediction markets will not emerge spontaneously. Assuming that successful pilot projects can be conducted discretely with small groups of innovators under controlled conditions, I believe a coordinated and muscular effort to develop a committed coalition of foundations, social entrepreneurs, and thought leaders can be followed by a well-funded marketing campaign to educate the public at large about the potential importance of the enterprise. But if the initial results of nonprofit prediction markets look promising, the conditions favorable to recruiting an impressively large community of diverse, informed, and active traders could place the IMPEX in a class by itself among prediction markets.

Incentives and Rewards

Incentives to participate could also be a strong suit of the IMPEX, although creative approaches will be necessary. Large numbers of ostensible traders are not sufficient; instead, participants must trade both actively and rationally.

Prediction markets work only when stock prices move up and down in response to traders' dynamic assessments of what the market is thinking in relation to their own knowledge. When market prices change infrequently, trading languishes in a downward spiral of indifference and uncollected information. Such markets lose the spark that drives participants to gather information, reveal their true belief, and reveal the levels of confidence with which they hold those beliefs. Passive crowds don't produce collective intelligence.

Nonprofit prediction markets have inherent advantages and disadvantages when it comes to incentives. The folks who devote considerable time, resources, or both to social-purpose organizations tend to be passionate about their involvement. The prospect of dramatically enhancing social impact just by playing an online social stock market game should be naturally enticing.

Yet Gebert is probably correct when she says that, "in most settings, real money rewards are required, but the dollar amount doesn't need to be high." There has been some research showing that nonfinancial incentives (often called "play money" in the literature) can drive workable prediction markets,[12] but the absence of financial payoffs is likely to make it that much harder to overcome trader inertia, especially in successive markets. On the other hand, competing for financial prizes—gambling—is generally illegal in the United States.

"The essential ingredient seems to be a motivated and knowledgeable community of traders, and money is just one among many practical ways of attracting such traders."[13] There are two aspects of incentive systems to consider:

> What are the sources of the motivation: are the incentives targeted primarily at the intrinsic or the extrinsic motivation of the participants? And how is the incentive system structured: what is the system performance based on? Is it for instance, a rank-order-tournament, or e.g. an unconditional lottery?[14]

All kinds of incentives have been tried with varying levels of success: published rankings (leaderboards), T-shirts, trophies, bragging rights, tchochkes and trinkets, play money (redeemable for prizes of nominal or modest value), nonmonetary prizes, and more. There can be a single winner, prizes for the top three traders, or any other arrangement that encourages participation. Just as law enforcement doesn't seem to care all that much about March Madness office pools, it is at least theoretically conceivable that there might be more latitude for nontrivial financial incentives for private prediction markets confined to an organization's own employees. I wouldn't care to speculate.

Fashioning effective incentive systems would seem to present another surmountable marketing challenge for the IMPEX. Given the altruistic motivations of most social sector participants, the imprimatur of good citizenship is probably the core idea by which high levels of active engagement could be encouraged.

For example, about 8 million people donate life-saving blood every year, even though it's a time-consuming and mildly uncomfortable procedure. After about an hour or so, they get some cookies, some juice, and a Red Cross sticker that a surprisingly large number of donors wear saying "Be nice to me. I gave blood today!"

The IEM Influenza Prediction Markets gives three answers to the frequently asked question, "Why do the traders participate?"

> **1.** They are interested in influenza and have information about its activity. Traders are interested in volunteering information in the same way that they are when filling out any other medical survey.

2. Unlike surveys, prediction markets allow participants to view what other participants think in real-time. This encourages traders to keep participating.

3. Surveys often provide a small financial incentive for participants to respond, but with prediction markets the amount of the incentive depends upon the accuracy of the participants' predictions. If participants do well, their account grows; if their predictions are inaccurate, their account shrinks. This performance feedback tends to spur further participation.[15]

Recall that prediction markets often provide better forecasts because they promote the discovery and revelation of disparate information that would not otherwise become available to experts, focus groups, or executives. Even though a virtual nonprofit stock market would be handicapped by the lack of financial return, it might have other advantages by virtue of community commitment and expertise: "Theory suggests that real money may better motivate information discovery, while in play money markets those with substantial wealth are those with a history of successful prediction, suggesting potential for more efficient weighting of individual opinions."[16]

Determining Eligibility

Almost all prediction markets have been conducted with at most a handful of stocks at any one time, for obvious reasons. The design and administration of these artificial markets are challenging enough without adding the complexity of dozens of stocks moving in different directions at once. To encourage active, ongoing participation, trading must be a casual and preferably fun activity that doesn't require a lot of time, effort, or attention span. The IMPEX will never catch on if only quant jocks chugging Red Bulls in front of Bloomberg terminals can trade.

More fundamentally, the thesis of this book is that third-stage funders need capital market mechanisms to find and fund growth-ready mid-cap social enterprises that have the potential of producing transformative social impact. So the virtual stock market needs to help identify the nonprofits that might have what it takes and then compare their prospects for strong performance at much higher levels of growth funding. Even if we exclude the more than 1 million small caps (see Exhibit 4.2), we'd still have to sort through more than 50,000 mid- and large-cap nonprofits with annual revenues greater than $5 million. By way of comparison, the New York Stock Exchange and Nasdaq each list only about 3,200 companies.

It is too soon to say how many organizations might ultimately be listed on a mature IMPEX, but I anticipate that the development of the IMPEX would proceed in three stages:

1. A controlled laboratory experiment would be conducted in private with handpicked participants trading one to three fictional stocks using hypothetical scenarios like my charter schools illustration.
2. A handful of brave social entrepreneurs would volunteer for a pilot project (probably also conducted in private, at least initially) using real data.
3. Some number—dozens?—of qualified nonprofits would sign up for the real thing.

Practicable eligibility criteria would become important in the design of the second and third phases to insure manageable trading and meaningful rankings. It might make sense to conduct multiple pilots, so separate markets could be run in different fields—for example, K–12 education, public health, and housing—each containing an appropriate number of stocks.

One of the responsibilities of the organization developing and managing the IMPEX, which I refer to later by the generic name, "IMPEX.org," would be to implement a workable qualification and screening system. I suspect this would be a fairly labor-intensive activity early on, requiring challenging decisions about growth readiness, transparency, metrics, and fairness in the event that more social enterprises are interested in participating than the IMPEX can handle at the outset. One useful model might be the hands-on methodology used by the Monitor Group to select recipients for *Fast Company*'s Social Capitalist Awards, which considers five criteria—Social Impact, Aspiration & Growth, Entrepreneurship, Innovation, and Sustainability:

Our process balances the need to collect a robust, detailed set of data from each organization with a desire to make the process as open and straightforward for applicants as possible. Any non-profit organization can register for the Social Capitalist Awards online at the Fast Company website. We also accepted outside nominations. The application itself is a one-step written application that consists of a focused, personal essay from the CEO or Executive Director, a 30-question survey about strategic and organizational specifics, copies of the organization's mission statement and board of directors list, key leadership bios, organizational charts, and copies of the last two years' audited financial statements and 990 tax forms.[17]

Ranking Nonprofit "Stocks"

Once eligibility requirements have been established, the IMPEX would publicize the markets, including opening and closing dates, contract definitions, trading rules, method for determining results, liquidation values, and other important terms of participation. The goal would be to conduct transparent markets that foster the energetic discovery and exchange of relevant information about nonprofit performance among a large and diverse group of engaged traders so that market prices yield insightful rankings of alternative investment opportunities.

It is safe to assume that this will be easier said than done. The potential objections to each of the foregoing elements could become overwhelming, contributing to an atmosphere more suited to a debating society than a marketplace. It will be the responsibility of the organizers and sponsors of the IMPEX to maintain discipline and focus in the hope that the frustrations of herding so many opinionated cats will be worth the effort if a significantly more robust nonprofit capital allocation system might result.

The IMPEX is not intended to tame or homogenize the splendid chaos of social enterprise (which would surely be a fool's errand in any case). Much of what makes social entrepreneurship such a worthwhile place to spend one's time—the encouragement of creativity and experimentation, the diversity and enthusiasm of the people, the need for dynamic improvisation, the lack of bureaucracy and authoritarian management—is inimical to the whole notion of ordered rankings.

There is, however, a compelling need for "adult supervision" when it comes to the conversion of billions of philanthropic dollars into exponentially greater social impact. The impetus for shifting in a more serious direction will have to come from hard-nosed investors. As is often the case, "The Money"—capital "T," capital "M"—probably will have to lead the way, But they should be followed shortly thereafter by farsighted nonprofit leaders (and their boards) who are prepared to accept the risks of market-based rankings with the understanding that performance-driven philanthropy might stop at least some of the madness associated with accepted but nonetheless daft norms of fundraising.

IMPEX.org

Although I am personally agnostic about whether the IMPEX is run by a for-profit or nonprofit organization, I make the assumption that it will be a nonprofit, primarily for cultural reasons. For-profit status would probably confuse, and quite possibly alienate, large numbers of potential stakeholders whose support would be indispensable. Fair-minded observers should remain open to the ironic possibility that, at some point, nonprofit financing could prevent the IMPEX from achieving the scale necessary to engender third-stage funding. As the Kennedy School's David Gergen has observed, "The issue is how do we solve problems, now what form the vehicle takes." If it turns out that "creating a for-profit is the only way. . .to get to scale," so be it.[18]

This is not mere conjecture. Pierre Omidyar, eBay founder and philanthrocapitalist extraordinaire, estimated that the market for microfinance capital runs to $60 billion: "There is not enough nonprofit and aid capital in the world to get microfinance to the scale it could achieve. Relying on nonprofit capital, not self-sustaining business models, is a big mistake."[19] If the IMPEX could channel significantly more funding at significantly lower cost, some of that surplus value could be used to fund the infrastructure itself in the form of fees for nonprofits wanting to be listed on the exchange and institutional funders and other investors wanting to subscribe to proprietary IMPEX-based research products.

Also, the nonprofit/for-profit calculus can change over time:

A big opportunity for philanthropists may be to back ideas that, if they succeed, would profitably solve social problems, but which have a higher risk of failure than commercial providers of capital, including venture capitalists, are willing to bear. Bearing the risk of ascertaining whether the idea can be pursued profitably is well suited to philanthropy. If the idea is a dud the money can be counted as a donation to the cause of increasing human knowledge; if it only works as a nonprofit, philanthropists can choose to keep funding it; whilst if it succeeds, the philanthrocapitalists can let for-profit investors take it to scale while they, having played a crucial catalytic role, can put their philanthropic risk capital to work elsewhere.[20]

The foregoing discussion about design parameters for the IMPEX suggests a number of broad areas of responsibility for the managing entity:

- Establish and enforce eligibility standards.
- Lead marketing campaigns to galvanize a large ("thick"), diverse, informed, and active community of traders and to educate investors about the benefits of performance-based giving.
- Define stocks that meet Gebert's standards of clarity, precision, value, duration, sensitivity, and actionability.
- Publish market prospectuses and supplementary background information that foster orderly, informed, and fair trading.
- Conduct well-run markets (including lab experiments and pilot projects) with attractive incentives and manage the administration of awards when markets close.
- Organize and work with a cross-sector coalition of stakeholders, distribution partners, complementers, and strategic allies to nurture an ecosystem (discussed further in Chapter 9) of performance-driven philanthropy.
- Publish and sponsor reports and analyses that impartially explain the market results and offer lessons learned to promote the further development and utility of the IMPEX.
- Serve as an impartial intermediary among nonprofits competing for funding.

- Raise seed funding for the IMPEX and develop a financing plan for it to become self-sustaining.

Climbing Off the Drawing Board

I propose a three-stage IMPEX development process as a way of maximizing the chances for success. Each stage has distinct objectives and faces separate challenges and risks, which should be marked by clear boundaries between each stage. Exhibit 8.2 provides a summary.

Exhibit 8.2   Three Stages of IMPEX Development.

Stage	Objectives	Risks	Requirements
Lab Experiment	Proof of concept: demonstrate how prediction markets aggregate information, create dynamic price signals, and produce ordinal rankings	Poor experimental design; confusing process or interface; ambiguous or unconvincing results	Closed participation; skilled prediction market partners; fictional stocks and data; cogent presentation of results
Pilot Project	Feasibility demonstration with small number of volunteer stocks under controlled conditions	Poor design; inactive trading; confusing or ambiguous results that investors don't find compelling	Strong sponsors; appropriate forum; credible reporting and analysis
Rollout	Assess prospects for widespread uptake by social impact investors	Weak trader community; ineffective marketing effort; detractor hostility; too many stocks; confusing or ambiguous results; inadequate partners; cost; management complexity	Robust coalition of support; controlled growth; critical mass; viable ecosystem

Notes

1. Steven Johnson, *Emergence: The Connected Lives of Ants, Brains, Cities, and Software* (New York: Scribner 2001), p. 233.

2. Ajit Kambil and Eric van Heck, *Making Markets* (Boston: Harvard Business Press 2002), p. 17.

3. Allen Grossman, "Philanthropic Social Capital Markets: Performance Driven Philanthropy," Social Enterprise Series 12, Harvard Business School, 1999, p. 12, www.hbs.edu/socialenterprise/pdf/SE12SocialCapitalMarkets.pdf.

4. Carol Gebert, "Prediction Markets—A Guide to Practical Adoption in the Pharmaceutical Industry," *Foresight* 9 (Spring 2008): 27.

5. Matthew Bishop and Michael Green, *Philanthrocapitalism: How the Rich Can Save the World* (London: Bloomsbury Press, 2008), p. 113.

6. University of Iowa Health Prediction Markets, Avian Influenza, http://fluprediction.uiowa.edu/fluhome/Market_AvianInfluenza.html.

7. Ibid.

8. C. Slamka, W. Jank, and B. Skiera, "Prediction Markets for Long-Term and Non-Occurring Outcome Forecasting: A Comparison of Pay-off Mechanisms," WeB 2008, *Seventh Workshop on e-Business*, 13 Dec. 2008, Paris, France, www.im.uni-karlsruhe.de/web2008/WeB2008-Program.pdf; Andreas Graefe and Christof Weinhardt, "Long-Term Forecasting with Prediction Markets: A Field Experiment on Applicability and Expert Confidence," *Journal of Prediction Markets* 2, no. 2 (September 2008): 71–91, www.ingentaconnect.com/content/ubpl/jpm/2008/00000002/00000002/art00005.

9. Bishop and Green, *Philanthrocapitalists,* p. 80.

10. Google Trends, www.google.com/trends?q=intrade&ctab=0&geo=all&date=all&sort=0, search conducted by the author on Nov. 29, 2008.

11. Jon Pratt, "The Future of the Infrastructure," *Nonprofit Quarterly* 12, Special Issue, "Infrastructure" (2004): 17.

12. E. S. Rosenbloom and William Notz, "Statistical Tests of Real-Money versus Play-Money Prediction Markets," *Electronic Markets* 16, no. 1 (2006), www.informaworld.com/smpp/content~content=a741440857~db=all~order=page; Stefan Luckner, "A Field Experiment on Monetary Incentives in Prediction Markets," www.betforgood.com/events/pm2007/papers/Luckner_Incentives.pdf.

13. Emile Servan-Schreiber, Justin Wolfers, David M. Pennock, and Brian Galebach, "Prediction Markets: Does Money Matter?" *Electronic Markets* 14, no. 3 (September 2004), www.newsfutures.com/pdf/Does_money_matter.pdf.

14. Bernd H. Ankenbrand and Caroline Rudzinski, "Description & Analysis of Markets," MOSAIG oHG, Research Project, Information Markets, Report 1 (October 2005): 7, www.mosaig.com/downloads/Description_of_Information_Markets_2005-12-18.pdf.

15. Frequently Asked Questions about the University of Iowa Health Prediction Markets, http://fluprediction.uiowa.edu/fluhome/FAQ.html#q11.

16. Servan-Schreiber, et al., "Prediction Markets."

17. Tammy Hobbs Miracky, Amy Lieb, and Mia Kulla, "The SoCap Way: A Window into the Awards' Methodology," 12 Sept. 2008, www.fastcompany.com/social/2008/articles/methodology.html.

18. "Q&A: David Gergen," *Stanford Social Innovation Review* (Fall 2008): 21, www.ssireview.org/images/articles/2008FA_QA_gergen.pdf.

19. Bishop and Green, *Philanthrocapitalism*, p. 117.

20. Ibid., pp. 132–134.

Chapter 9

Crossing the
Fundraising Chasm

The whole is more than the sum of its parts.

—Aristotle

A prediction market that ranks nonprofit performance does not a virtual stock market make. By itself, a prediction market is just a widget, a gizmo of little or no value until it is plugged into a system of complementary components. Just as a microprocessor can't do much until it's soldered onto a circuit board and the circuit board is plugged into a computer, so does the Impact Index (IMPEX) need to be incorporated into an integrated network dedicated to enabling results-driven philanthropy.

As discussed in Chapter 8, the core functions of the IMPEX would be, first, to provide a place where many informed traders can express their opinions about the performance of participating nonprofits, and, second, to dynamically aggregate those opinions and rank them in the order that reflects the market's consensus. I contend that such a performance-ranking engine has been a crucial missing piece of an effective nonprofit capital market.

But it is by no means the only piece missing from the puzzle. As Joel Kurtzman observed in *How the Markets Really Work,* "the world of money also requires dozens of 'specialist' communities that in the aggregate constitute the larger global financial community."[1] While the community of specialists that would be needed to form a nonprofit capital market worthy of the name would bear little resemblance to the complex labyrinth known as "Wall Street," there is an identifiable group of essential network players without which the IMPEX could not accomplish much.

As explained earlier, the achievement of transformative social impact requires not just incremental increases in the "scale" of nonprofit organizations but an exponential leap from risk-tolerant niche markets to risk-averse mainstream markets. For example, innovative charter schools that are improving the educational prospects of thousands of students will not be able to grow organically within a reasonable period of time to supplant the inadequate education received by millions of students in underperforming traditional public schools. At some point, charter and other innovative schools must adopt Geoffrey Moore's "whole product strategy" to devise a fully fledged modern public school system capable of "crossing the chasm" from a small group of "visionary" and "early adopter" school districts to a vastly larger and far more conservative and skeptical group of "early majority pragmatists" who control tens of thousands of failing schools.

The *sine qua non* of a viable whole product solution is the ability to overcome the skepticism of conservative mainstream decision makers. The whole product solution comprises "all the other complementary products and services needed to fulfill the promised value proposition." Otherwise, "the compelling reason to buy is not addressed satisfactorily and the market does not emerge."[2] In philanthropy, the compelling reason to consider IMPEX rankings would be the prospect of making it much easier to find and fund mid-cap social enterprises that offer the best chances of producing transformative social impact.

Devising a whole product solution for results-driven giving involves searching for a "new normal" in which "over time, small pockets of self-interested philanthropists, choosing to boost their own impact, will catalyze system change because it has become easier to do philanthropy in the new way: connected, cooperatively, learning, and adapting."[3] The key, then, to making the nonprofit sector hospitable to third-stage funding is providing a compelling answer to this question:

> What set of integrated product and service features need to be in place to persuade social impact investors to incorporate IMPEX rankings into their philanthropic decisions?

I believe the prerequisites of a functioning market for nonprofit growth capital fall into five primary categories:

1. Growth-ready mid-caps
2. Social impact investors
3. Performance information
4. A social network of traders
5. A virtual stock market platform

Having discussed the first two in earlier chapters, I'll explore the last three here.

Performance Measurement

Perhaps no subject relating to the nonprofit sector has received more attention from academics and practitioners than performance measurement. It is an important, challenging, and frustrating subject on which a great deal of useful and creative work has been done. Having first studied performance evaluation some 30 years ago, I feel confident in saying that all the foundational work has been done. There won't be a "eureka!" breakthrough where someone finally figures out the one true way to gauge nonprofit effectiveness.

Indeed, I would venture to say that we know virtually everything there is to know about measuring the performance of nonprofit organizations with only two exceptions: (1) How can we compare nonprofits with different missions or approaches, and (2) how can we make actionable performance assessments common practice for growth-ready mid-caps and readily available to all prospective donors? These are nontrivial questions that have effectively stumped an awful lot of smart people who want to help nonprofits become more effective by providing easier access to funding.

As to the comparability question, it's surpassingly difficult to make rational choices among social investment opportunities when there's no universal benchmark such as profit, and the differences outweigh the similarities. And there are as many excellent and practicable models for performance evaluation as there are reasons for not adopting them: we don't have the staff or the expertise, it's too expensive, it takes too long, we don't have the data, our funders don't care, the results are inconclusive, and so on.

With the rise of venture philanthropy and social entrepreneurship, there has certainly been a noticeable up-tick in the adoption of outcomes measurement, but keep in mind that those advances still represent only a tiny part of the social sector. Having seen so many unsuccessful efforts to introduce performance evaluation into the practice of both nonprofit management and nonprofit funding, I have become convinced that, by itself, no amount of exhortation will significantly increase the adoption of performance measurement by mid-caps across the board in a way that would usher in an enlightened era of results-based giving.

Instead, we need to see the problem in an entirely new light. The problem isn't that the available methodologies aren't good enough; in fact, there are quite a few excellent approaches, many of which are in the public domain. The problem is that, practically speaking, there's no persuasive reason to make the effort or incur the cost. Neither nonprofits nor philanthropists will incorporate performance evaluation into their work until they decide it's in their vital interest to do so.

Remember, with very few exceptions, funding isn't connected to performance. Almost all fundraising depends entirely on building relationships and telling engaging stories. Every mid-cap nonprofit is adept at those skills, and every funder, whether private, public, or institutional, implicitly accepts them as an adequate basis for deciding whom to fund. Even when foundations condition grants on performance reporting, they're satisfied with explanations of how the recipient spent the money, not what the expenditures accomplished.

This situation, which virtually everyone deplores, is not caused by laziness or indifference. Rather, it's just another structural mismatch endemic to nonprofit capital markets:

- Traditional nonprofit funding—that is, money that's too small, too short, too restricted, and too time-consuming to raise—doesn't require performance data, so funders don't demand it and nonprofits don't supply it.

- Yet growth capital—that is, much larger infusions of multiyear, unrestricted funding used for the development of organizational capacity rather than additional program services that produce direct and immediate client benefits—is inconceivable without impact information.

Why would a social entrepreneur divert limited resources to impact assessment if there were no prospects it would increase funding? How could an investor who wanted to maximize the impact of her giving possibly put more golden eggs in fewer impact-producing baskets if she had no way to distinguish one basket from another? The result: there's no performance data to attract growth capital, and there's no growth capital to induce performance measurement. Until we fix that Catch-22, performance evaluation will not become an integral part of social enterprise.

Society could tolerate this mismatch when philanthropy was just palliative. But when many of the country's most basic public institutions have become chronically ineffectual for the last four decades, and inequality and immobility among the underclass have expanded and become increasingly entrenched, the social sector must find a way to connect funding and performance. Only when demonstrably superior performance can reliably attract substantially increased funding can transformational change occur.

The nonproliferation of third-stage funding and performance measurement isn't a chicken-and-egg problem. Neither can wait for the other to arrive; both have to show up simultaneously, or we'll have neither, as we do today.

I want to call attention to a recent blog entry by Ken Berger, the president and CEO of the nation's largest evaluator of nonprofits, Charity Navigator. As one of its "10 Best Practices of Savvy Donors," Charity Navigator recommends starting a dialogue to investigate a charity's programmatic results:

Although it takes some effort on their part to assess a charity's programmatic impact, donors who are committed to advancing real change believe that it is worth their time. Before they make a contribution, they talk with the charity to learn about its accomplishments, goals and challenges. These donors are prepared to walk away from any charity that is unable or unwilling to participate in this type of conversation.[4]

With all due respect, framing performing measurement as an activity that "takes some effort" but that "savvy" donors do because they "believe that it is worth their time" is like suggesting that consumers who switch to energy-efficient light bulbs can materially slow climate change. Isolated, voluntary efforts will never be enough. As we've seen, systemic problems require systemic solutions, not well-intentioned, small-scale adjustments that don't disrupt prevailing behaviors.

Berger is well aware that much criticism has been directed at Charity Navigator for overemphasizing legitimate but potentially misleading measures such as "administrative expenses" and "fundraising efficiency." In the past, Charity Navigator had been guilty of failing to take this problem seriously or to face up to its consequences. Berger, who joined Charity Navigator in 2008, deserves praise for his serious commitment to rectifying that situation:

> Over our six plus years, we have come to the conclusion that some donors are not taking the additional steps we recommend to assess outcomes and are relying almost entirely on our ratings. In addition, while we assume that financially strong organizations are far more likely to be effective in their outcomes, it may not always be the case. Alternatively, charities with mediocre financial strength may not necessarily have mediocre outcomes. Therefore, to help donors know with greater certainty which charities are achieving program results, we are exploring integrating outcome measurement into our rating system.

> As a first step, we have begun conversations with a variety of experts in the field to see the current state of such measurement tools. In large measure, from what I have seen so far, it appears that the field is in its infancy and we will have to do some heavy lifting to get a meaningful tool that can be broad enough to evaluate all categories of charities, while not becoming overwhelmingly cumbersome and complicated. In other words, this is going to take us some time to develop. It could be years rather than months. In the meanwhile, we have a number of

other efforts we will be making along the way to get the ball rolling. I will give you the details of these efforts in future blog entries.

Another challenge that leads us to the conclusion that developing this tool will take time is the fact that there is no standardized data source from a third party to get the information (like the IRS 990 that we use for financial analysis). Therefore, we will probably need to gather the information directly from the charities we evaluate. To say that many of them will not be thrilled by such a prospect is an understatement! However, at the end of the day, I think that most will welcome this expansion of our rating system with the hopes that it will more comprehensively capture what they do and how they do it. It will also further our core mission of providing guidance to donors on making intelligent giving decisions.

The leadership of Charity Navigator believes it is well worth the challenges it entails and as a result we are setting a goal over time of offering an expanded rating system to more comprehensively evaluate nonprofits and separate great organizations from the rest. We look forward to collaborating with our colleagues who are working on this issue to improve the state of charitable giving.[5]

Although we do have fledgling innovations in both performance reporting and growth capital, they're incapable of unlocking the Catch-22 because they're not connected to each other. If only there were some kind of organizing mechanism that could bring them together in a spirit of "complementary innovation."

Platform Leadership

The failure of the social sector to coordinate interdependent assets and create a whole that exceeds the sum of its parts results from an absence of what Professors Michael A. Cusumano and Annabelle Gawer call "platform leadership": "the ability of a company to drive innovation around a particular platform technology at the broad industry level." The object is to multiply value by working together: "the more people who use platform products, the more incentives there are for complement producers to introduce more complementary products, causing a virtuous cycle."[6]

Apple's iPhone is a classic technology platform. Apple distributes a free software development kit (SDK) to registered programmers who want to create low-cost applications (apps) for the iPhone, which Apple then distributes and promotes:

> The iPhone Developer Program provides a complete and integrated process for developing, debugging, and distributing your free, commercial, or in-house applications for iPhone and iPod touch. Complete with development resources, real-world testing on iPhone, and distribution on the App Store, you have everything you need to go from code to customer.[7]

One of the country's premier venture capitalists, Kleiner Perkins Caulfield & Beyers, has created a $100 million "iFund" dedicated to finding and funding companies working on the most promising apps. As of January 2009, iPhone customers had downloaded more than 500 million apps from among some 15,000 choices available directly on their portable devices[8] (see Exhibit 9.1). Apple establishes minimum design and compatibility requirements for participating developers to follow, but it does not dictate what products will be offered. Instead, as the platform owner, it creates an environment in which complementary innovation can flourish.

As explained earlier in the book, the nonprofit sector as a whole has a great deal of both money and innovation, but too little available information about too many organizations. The result is capital fragmentation that squelches growth. None of the stakeholders has enough horsepower on its own to impose order on this chaos, but some kind of realignment could release all of that pent-up potential energy. While command-and-control authority is neither feasible nor desirable, the conditions are ripe for platform leadership:

> Most platform leaders do not have the capabilities or resources to create complete systems by making all the complements themselves. They need to collaborate. The combined efforts of platform leaders and complementary innovators increase the potential size of the pie for everyone.[9]

It is doubtful that the IMPEX could amass all of the resources internally needed to build and grow a virtual nonprofit stock market that could connect large numbers of growth-capital investors with large numbers of

Exhibit 9.1   iPhone 3G. 15,000 apps. And counting.
Source: Apple iPhone, www.apple.com/iphone/.

growth-ready mid-caps. But it might be able to convene a powerful coalition of complementary actors that could achieve a critical mass of support for performance-based philanthropy. The challenge would be to develop an organization focused on filling in the gaps rather than encroaching on the turf of established firms whose participation and innovation would be required to build a platform for nurturing the growth of social enterprise:

> Determining the scope of the company—that is, which complements to make in-house and which to leave to external companies—is probably the most important decision.... Platform producers should not develop their own complements if they lack the technical, organizational or financial capabilities to compete in the relevant markets.

Inasmuch as "consensus among industry players depends on one company driving the process ... platform leaders should be industry enablers—helping others innovate in ever better ways around the platform." As a "platform producer," the role of IMPEX.org would be to "create an internal organization that allows it to manage relationships with complementors effectively."

Intriguing sketches are starting to emerge of what an intermediated nonprofit capital market might look like. REDF's Cynthia Gair has envisioned a co-funding model that shifts the fundraising burden from grantees to intermediaries in a way that involves nonprofits only after committed funders have been identified and selected (see Exhibit 9.2). Carla Dearing, Associate Vice President for Strategic Initiatives at University of Louisville, Office of Health Affairs, has outlined a more comprehensive framework for a market connecting sources and uses of donated funds, in which intermediaries offer financial products through market mechanisms housed within a managed infrastructure environment (see Exhibit 9.3).

The IMPEX.org could exercise platform leadership to organize an effective whole product solution that would be capable of crossing the fundraising chasm. Among other things, the platform would be dedicated to bringing about systemic change by generating the kind of rich performance data that third-stage funders would need to evaluate the risks of providing nonprofit growth capital to potentially thousands of growth-ready mid-caps.

Information Retrieval

I'll close by offering an abbreviated illustration of what an Impact Index platform might look like. At the center, of course, playing an intermediating role, would be IMPEX.org, which would be responsible for the activities described in Chapter 8, such as establishing eligibility standards, defining predictions stocks, and conducting markets as well as facilitating complementary innovation among diverse stakeholders. Rather than invent its own trading technology, IMPEX.org could invite such established prediction market providers as Inkling Markets or Consensus Point to act as host.

To create the kind of crowd from which wisdom might be drawn, the platform would need thriving communities of traders and investors. Many social networks, including Facebook and LinkedIn, already support charity-related connections among their millions of members. For example, the independently developed Causes application on Facebook, which "lets you start and join the causes you care about," had nearly

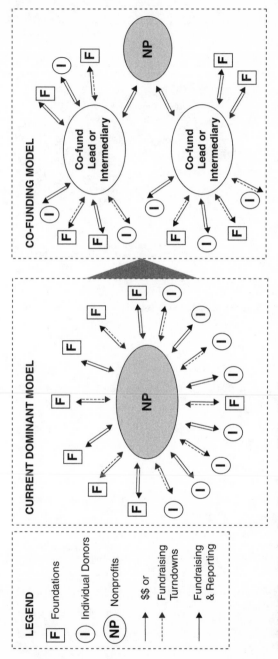

Exhibit 9.2 Co-funding Impact on Nonprofit Grantees

Source: Cynthia Gair, "Roadmap #1: Strategic Co-Funding," Out of Philanthropy's Funding Maze, REDF, p. 10.

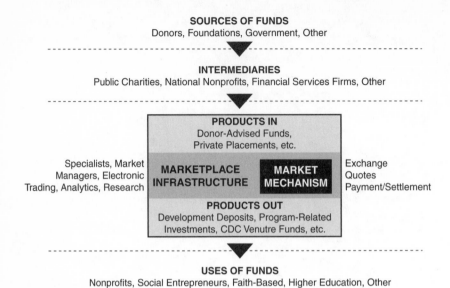

Exhibit 9.3   Social Capital Market Framework
Source: Adapted from Carla Dearing, "Social Capital Marketplace: Exploring the Relationship between Sources and Uses of Capital in the Social Sector," 15 January 2008.

13.9 million monthly users as of January 2009.[10] LinkedIn has a utility application built on the OpenSocial development platform called Polls that allows users to "leverage the wisdom of millions of business professionals."[11] In addition to inviting large numbers of potential traders to bring their knowledge of thousands of nonprofit organizations to the party, these massive networks could host Web widgets and apps that would allow network members to trade without even leaving those sites.

On the investor side, professional financial advisors could play a vital part in helping the IMPEX platform stimulate performance-driven giving. High-net-worth individuals and family foundations often rely on investment managers for advice about philanthropy, a subject about which they generally know very little. *Forces for Good* authors Leslie R. Crutchfield and Heather McLeod Grant assert that "philanthropists are hungrier than ever for concise, well-researched information that can help them achieve greater social change."[12] But as William Zabel, a leading trusts and estates lawyer, has observed, "most philanthropy is tax-motivated."[13]

The surging growth of national donor-advised funds, which simplify and reduce the transaction costs of methodical giving, exemplifies the kind of financial innovation that is poised to leverage market-based investment guidance. The president of Schwab Charitable certainly sounds like the kind of early-majority pragmatist who might consider the potential benefits of the Impact Index:

> National donor-advised funds are in a unique position as aggregators of more than 100,000 donors and $20 billion in assets poised to be granted. . . . I invite my peers in the sector to brainstorm creative ways to make charitable giving an even more information-driven, efficient system in which capital flows to charity are not driven by serendipity and reputation—as is often the case now—but by results.[14]

What if the same research tools that these advisors regularly use to inform their financial investment recommendations were available to evaluate philanthropic investments? That's the business model of another prospective IMPEX complementor, Root Cause's Social Impact Research project:

> Social Impact Research focuses exclusively on the needs of social impact investors and those who advise them. SIR aggregates, analyzes, and disseminates the best information available about social issues and the performance of nonprofit organizations so that advisors are able to support their clients make better informed philanthropic decisions.

> Modeled after private sector equity research firms, Social Impact Research offers advisors workshops, research reports, and philanthropic portfolio analysis reports. The products apply the quality of analysis and actionable investment insight available to private sector investors to assess the opportunities and risks facing organizations working within the most challenging social sectors.[15]

Social Impact Research is just one example of a diverse and emerging independent-research industry that could achieve liftoff as an integral part of a social capital marketplace. Others include growing numbers of academic research centers (e.g., the Center for the Advancement of Social Entrepreneurship at Duke University, Indiana University's Center on High Impact Philanthropy); private sector research (e.g., Forrester); social sector research (e.g., New Philanthropy Capital); government watchdogs (e.g., the Government Accountability Office); for-profit and nonprofit think tanks (e.g., the Heritage Foundation, the Monitor Group, the Urban Institute); rating agencies and organizations (e.g., Charity Navigator, Guidestar, Wise Giving Alliance); online donor rankings (e.g., GlobalGiving, GreatNonprofits, SocialMarkets); and evaluation consultants (e.g., Mathematica). With tens of billions of dollars looking for promising mid-cap investment opportunities, performance-based philanthropy should create fertile ground for professional research and advisory services.

While we're thinking about strategic partners, let's not forget the importance of cross-sector initiatives. One way to bring government and corporate players to the IMPEX table would be to involve coalition builders such as America Forward, which New Profit, Inc. launched "to create the conditions in which leaders from across sectors and at all levels work with social entrepreneurs to help solve our country's most pressing domestic problems." In one fell swoop, America Forward would bring to the table a coalition of more than 70 organizations with programs in all 50 states that collectively serve more than 10 million people with combined budgets of more than $400 million.[16]

Last but not least, there's this company called "Google" whose mission is "to organize the world's information and make it universally accessible and useful." I won't even try to enumerate the contributions that Google could make to the IMPEX platform, with one exception. Until quite recently, Google's philanthropic venture had an initiative called SME, which it formed to "fuel the growth of small and medium-sized enterprises" by helping to "increase the flow of capital to 'the missing middle' by tackling some of the root causes that prevent these firms from becoming profitable investment opportunities."[17]

Google.org announced in December 2008 that it was putting the SME initiative on hold to focus on other philanthropic initiatives.[18] Perhaps the IMPEX could entice Google.org back into the game. Taken together, these complementary components evoke a practicable whole product (see Exhibit 9.4) whose development could stimulate third-stage funding and guide its allocation to more productive uses. Such an intelligent system also could substantially shift the financing initiative from effective mid-caps that need growth funding to those who have it. In a phrase, the IMPEX could foster "smart money" for the social sector.

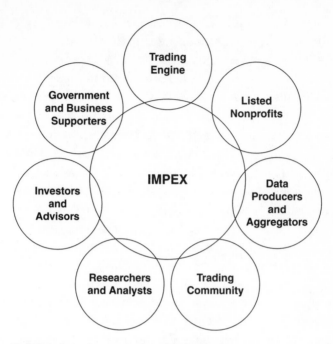

Exhibit 9.4   Impact Index Whole Product

We Know

Newsweek's Jonathan Alter wrote recently, "[T]he challenge is not to find what works for at-risk kids—we know that by now—but how to replicate it."[19] This is the stubborn predicament facing the nonprofit sector today. We have the necessary ingredients—unprecedented amounts of money, proven innovations, effective organizations, and passionate public engagement. Yet we still haven't been able to scale solutions that are large enough to make a real and lasting difference.

We do know what works. The aptly named Center for What Works and the Urban Institute have published—at no charge—performance benchmarks of successful program interventions in 14 areas of social need: Adult Education; Advocacy; Affordable Housing; Assisted Living; Business Assistance; Community Organizing; Emergency Shelter; Employment Training; Health Risk Reduction; Performing Arts; Prisoner Re-entry; Transitional Shelter; Youth Mentoring; and Youth Tutoring.[20]

The heroic research team at New Philanthropy Capital in London has published—at no charge—more than two dozen rigorous reports on all sorts of successful charitable efforts: Child Abuse; Community Organisations; Divided Communities; Domestic Violence; Financial Exclusion; Homelessness; Older People; Prisoners and Ex-Prisoners; Refugees and Asylum Seekers; Violence Against Women; Careers Guidance; Education Overview; Literacy; Mentoring; Out of School Hours Activities; Special Educational Needs; Truancy & Exclusion; Autism; Mental Health of Children and Young People; Children with Terminal Conditions; Cancer; Disabled Children; HIV/AIDS; Mental Health; Palliative Care; Environment Overview; and International Giving.[21]

These academic centers and research institutes provide the meta-analysis needed to systematically narrow the overwhelming number of available social investments down to manageable ranges for deeper examination. This is a wheel that mature philanthropists don't have to reinvent. Just as social entrepreneurs have operationalized tremendous innovation capable of advancing social progress, so have these researchers developed and applied innovative models for assessing potential impact. The approach adopted by the Center for High Impact Philanthropy at the University of Pennsylvania's School of Social Policy & Practice (Exhibit 9.5) illustrates the kind of disciplined thinking that could inform third-stage funding orchestrated through the IMPEX.

SOURCES OF INFORMATION

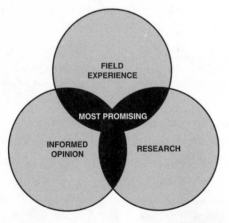

FIELD EXPERIENCE
- Practitioner insights
- Performance assessments
- In-depth case studies

INFORMED OPINION
- Expert opinion
- Stakeholder input
- Policy analyses

RESEARCH
- Randomized controlled trials and quasi-experimental studies
- Modeled analyses (e.g., cost-effectiveness)

Exhibit 9.5 Multiperspective, Evidence-Informed Approach
Source: Hilary J. Rhodes, Kathleen Noonan, and Katherina Rosqueta, "Pathways to Student Success: A Guide to Translating Good Intentions into Meaningful Impact," Center for High Impact Philanthropy, School of Social Policy & Practice, University of Pennsylvania, December 2008, p. 7, www.impact.upenn.edu/Pathways-CompleteGuide.htm.

One of the primary reasons we don't know how to replicate social innovations that work is because the nonprofits that solved these puzzles can't get third-stage funding to take on $100 million problems. And one of the primary reasons they don't have such funding is that social investors can't find them. That's the starting point for replication: finding and funding; matching money with performance.

But a consensus is emerging about ways in which capital markets can be enhanced to marshal growth capital and guide aggregated funding to its most productive destinations. A 2008 study prepared by the William and Flora Hewlett Foundation and Mckinsey & Company advances the now-familiar hypothesis that "access to high-quality information will lead donors to allocate funds more strategically to organizations doing the best work." Recognizing that "the nonprofit marketplace lacks the robust flow of timely, accurate information that is a hallmark of high-performing markets such as stock exchanges, commodity markets, or eBay," the study offers an integrated "nonprofit marketplace information framework" (see Exhibit 9.6) and a resonant blueprint for action:

- Improving the supply of information assessing nonprofit organizational and operational performance (How well is the organization run?) and social impact (To what extent is the organization achieving its intended goals and outcomes?)
- Increasing donor demand for nonprofit performance and impact information

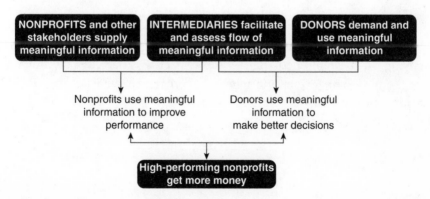

Exhibit 9.6   Nonprofit Marketplace Information Framework
Source: Maisie O'Flanagan, Jacob Harold, and Paul Brest, "The Nonprofit Marketplace: Bridging the Information Gap in Philanthropy," McKinsey & Company and William and Flora Hewlett Foundation, Exhibit 2, p. 11, www.givingmarketplaces.org/materials/whitepaper.pdf.

- Strengthening intermediary organizations that facilitate inter-actions between donors and nonprofits, provide value-adding services, and help improve donor decision making and nonprofit performance

In Chapter 1, I recounted the hypothetical funding nightmare that REDF's Cynthia Gair laid out about StepUp to Solar, Inc., a fictional nonprofit that helped runaway teens. But Gair also imagined how capital market intermediation could facilitate a more satisfying outcome:

> How will Strategic Co-Funding change the paths to capital for our example organization, and for the nonprofits it represents? Though runaway teenagers will probably still need help, the organizations they turn to, like our original example, StepUp to Solar, Inc., won't have to waste precious staff time on hunts through a maze of unclear and deadend funding options. In tomorrow's philanthropy, StepUp's new five-year plan will pave the way. The organization's local youth services intermediary will contribute guidance and information to the plan, and will take it to several appropriate funder groups. Seeing that StepUp is moving out of one longtime funder's early growth stage sweetspot, a replacement grant commitment will be lined up with a funding con-sortium that specializes in mature regional organizations. More debt may be appropriate at that point, so two local banks and the regional Community Development Financial Institution (CDFI) will be con-tacted. Two or three funder groups will express interest and will begin reviewing StepUp's plan. Three months later, the organization will have secured commitments for its next five years of youth services.[22]

An Aaron Bacall cartoon in the *New Yorker* shows a businessman talking on the phone, saying, "We're expecting stocks to rally but we don't know which ones and when."[23] Perhaps, in the case of growth-ready mid-cap social enterprises, we can figure that out together.

Notes

1. Joel Kurtzman, *How the Markets Really Work* (New York: Crown Business 2002), pp. 73–74.
2. Paul Wiefels, *The Chasm Companion* (New York: HarperBusiness, 2002), p. 112.

3. Katherine Fulton and Andrew Blau, "Cultivating Change in Philanthropy," Monitor Group, 2005, p. 25.

4. www.charitynavigator.org/index.cfm?bay=content.view&cpid=419.

5. www.kenscommentary.org/2008/12/measure-of-outcome.html.

6. Michael A. Cusumano and Annabelle Gawer, "The Elements of Platform Leadership," *MIT Sloan Management Review* 43, no. 3 (Spring 2002): 58.

7. Apple Developer Connection, "iPhone Developer Program, The Fastest Path from Code to Customer," http://developer.apple.com/iPhone/program/.

8. Christian Zibreg, "An iPhone Record: 500 Million App Store downloads," *TG Daily,* 16 Jan. 2009, www.tgdaily.com/content/view/41063/140/.

9. Cusumano and Gower, "Elements of Platform Leadership."

10. www.facebook.com/apps/application.php?id=2318966938.

11. www.linkedin.com/opensocialInstallation/preview?_ch_panel_id=1&_applicationId=1900.

12. Leslie R. Crutchfield and Heather McLeod Grant, *Forces for Good: The Six Practices of High-Impact Nonprofits* (San Francisco: Jossey-Bass, 2008), p. 4.

13. Quoted in Matthew Bishop and Michael Green, *Philanthrocapitalism: How the Rich Can Save the World* (London: Bloomsbury Press, 2008), p. 43.

14. Kim Wright-Violich, "We've Arrived. Now What? The Rise of National Donor-Advised Funds," *Stanford Social Innovation Review* (Summer 2008), www.ssireview.org/articles/entry/weve_arrived_now_what/.

15. www.socialimpactresearch.org.

16. http://americaforward.org/section/about.

17. "Google.org Announces Core Initiatives to Combat Climate Change, Poverty and Emerging Threats," press release, 17 Jan. 2008, www.google.com/intl/en/press/pressrel/20080117_googleorg.html.

18. "Sharpening Our Focus in Global Development," http://blog.google.org/2008/12/sharpening-our-focus-in-global.html.

19. Jonathan Alter, "Bill Gates Goes to School," *Newsweek*, 15 Dec. 2008, p. 42, www.newsweek.com/id/172572.

20. Center for What Works and Urban Institute, "Outcomes and Indicators of Nonprofit Success," www.whatworks.org/displaycommon.cfm?an=4.

21. New Philanthropy Capital, "Research Reports," www.philanthropycapital.org/research/research_reports/default.aspx.

22. Cynthia Gair, "Roadmap #1: Strategic Co-Funding," Out of Philanthropy's Funding Maze, REDF, p. 4.

23. Aaron Bacall, Cartoon, Cartoonbank.com, www.cartoonbank.com/product_details.asp?sid=23664.

Acknowledgments

I want to start by thanking George Overholser, Managing Director of NFF Capital Partners, and Clara Miller, CEO of the Nonprofit Finance Fund, both of whom unwittingly started me off on this long march. When I first began to consider advancing on the nonprofit sector, it was Clara's writings that opened my eyes to what she aptly called, "The Looking Glass World of Nonprofit Money." Since then, she has been supportive with her time and encouragement.

Almost everything in this book (other than the prediction market angle) traces back to something George Overholser invented, wrote about, or discussed with me. George, whom New Profit appropriately named its "Unsung Hero" of 2005, was exceptionally generous with his comments on drafts and his steadfast encouragement.

Many others listened to my fevered rants, read drafts, and offered helpful comments. Chris Meyer of Monitor Networks convinced me I wasn't a lunatic and not only suggested that I write an article for the *Harvard Business Review,* but successfully heaved it over their transom. I thank Gardiner Morse at HBR for his remarkable editorial skill in transforming a 2,500-word draft into a better 500-word article. Kim Syman and Vanessa Kirsch, respectively Managing Partner and CEO of New Profit, Inc., schooled me on the nonprofit sector, venture philanthropy, and social entrepreneurship. Heiner Baumann, formerly Chief Learning Officer of New Profit and now Executive Director, Grants, at the Children's Investment Fund Foundation in London, taught me about the need for late-stage capital funding.

Andrew Wolk, CEO of Root Cause, and Colette Stanzler, Director of Root Cause's Social Impact Research initiative, have been great colleagues and instrumental in shaping much of my thinking. Martin Brookes, CEO of New Philanthropy Capital, also of London, introduced me to the value of independent research in this difficult sector and made me appreciate the importance of free publication to all.

Allan Benamer and Jeff Tuller of SocialMarkets.org pushed back on many of my half-baked ideas and made me think harder. Adam Siegel at Inkling Markets was very encouraging about the idea of a virtual nonprofit stock market and provided invaluable help in figuring out how prediction markets could be adapted to that end. Thanks to Carla Dearing and Caroline Heine for inviting me to the Social Capital Markets meeting in New York and all they taught me there, and to another attendee, Perla Ni, for introducing me (and the world) to Great Nonprofits.

I've had the privilege of getting to know a number of "thought leaders" who influenced my thinking. They include Chuck Harris, Lincoln Caplan, and Thomas Hyland of SeaChange Capital Partners; Lucy Bernholz of Blueprint Research & Design, Inc., and author of the first book on this subject, *Creating Philanthropic Capital Markets: The Deliberate Evolution*; William Foster of the Bridgespan Group, who really gets this stuff; and Kathy Buechel, Visiting Practitioner at the Hauser Center for Nonprofit Organizations at Harvard University and former president of the Alcoa Foundation, who got me right away. Carol Gebert was an early pioneer of prediction markets at Eli Lilly, who kindly shared her grand perspective with me. A special thanks to Jerr Boschee, *eminence grise* of social enterprise, for allowing me to take my ideas out for a spin with two classes of his inspiring graduate students at Carnegie-Mellon.

Many colleagues and friends offered encouragement and kept me caffeinated, including the peripatetic F.J. Gould and our partner-in-crime, John Kelley; the effervescent Anne Ellinger of BolderGiving; the very fine consultant, Barry Horwitz; Erika Eurkus, Senior Director of Capital & Brand Development at ACCION USA, who kindly invited me to discuss my ideas with her colleagues, Jodi Hullinger and Dean Elson; Emily

McCann, who puts the Chief in Chief Operating Officer at Citizen Schools; Jen Cohen, soon-to-be Doctor of Philosophy; Emma Williams, super-mom and super-Business Manager at Cradles to Crayons; Joseph Wiinikka-Lydon of Jumpstart; former colleagues and enduring pals Steve McClain and Stuart Montaldo; and my oldest friends, Rick and Kerry Shea.

A special note of appreciation to Paul F. Levy, CEO of Beth Israel–Deaconess Medical Center and my former boss at the Massachusetts Water Resources Authority, for his no-holds-barred comments on an earlier draft that began, "I am sorry to say that I don't get it." You just can't buy that kind of candor.

Much appreciation to the great folks at John Wiley & Sons, including Senior Editor Susan McDermott for seeing the merit of my proposal and making it all happen; Development Editor Judy Howarth for all the heavy lifting and guidance; Senior Editorial Assistant Brandon Dust, for getting it done; and Natasha Andrews-Noel, Senior Production Editor, for her blue pencil.

I don't have the words to thank James Weinberg of Commongood Careers and Laura Gassner Otting of Nonprofit Professionals Advisory Group and author of the exceptional book, *Change Your Career: Transitioning to the Nonprofit Sector* (Kaplan, 2008), for all the support they've given me.

I wish to particularly thank the Steven H. Goldberg & Janet L. Klein Retirement Fund and the Massachusetts Unemployment Compensation Fund for their generous financial support.

And for enduring this Ahabian quest, special thanks and love to my favorite wife, Janet Louise Klein, and my two magnificent sons, Will and Addy.

Index

McCambridge, Ruth, 89 n.
McClurg, Jim, xxv, xxx n.
McKinsey & Company, 8, 75, 166
    n., 174, 275
measurement
    levels of, 233
        interval, 233
        nominal, 233
        ordinal, 233
        ratio, 233
    statistical significance, 233,
        238 n.
    uncertainty reduction, 232
Media Predict, 225
Meehan, William F., 39 n., 40 n.,
    212 n.
MGM, 225
Microsoft, 223, 225, 230
Microsoft PredictionPoint,
    226
mid cap. See social enterprises,
    mid–cap
middle class, 48, 69
Miller, Clara, 7, 21, 38 n., 39 n.,
    40 n., 42 n., 213 n.
Miller, Matt, xix, xx n.
Miracky, Tammy Hobbs, 258 n.
MIT Center for Coordination
    Science, 226
mobility
    downward, 62
    immobility, 54, 58, 59
    social and economic, 52–53,
        55, 59, 61, 69, 132
Monitor Group, xxxi, 25, 82, 89
    n., 123, 130 n., 202, 252,
    272, 277 n.

Moore, Geoffrey, 105–120, 115,
    116, 117, 130 n., 146,
    175, 260. *See also Crossing
    the Chasm*
Morgenson, Gretchen, 213
Morton, John E., 85
Motorola, 225, 229
Motwani, Rajeev, 239 n.
murder. *See* homicide
Myrdal, Gunnar, 136

Nation at Risk, A, 52
"Nation Still at Risk, A," 52
National Anti–Hunger
    Organizations, 22, 42 n.
National Center on Education
    and the Economy, 88 n.
National Commission on
    Excellence in Education,
    52, 85 n.
National Foundation for Infantile
    Paralysis, 49
national service. *See* Volunteers.
Nature Conservancy, 127
Neckerman, Kathryn, 86 n.
Nelson, Forrest D., 237 n.
NetFlix, 139
Network for Good, 232
Neumann, George R., 237 n.
New Deal, 64, 84 n.
New Commission on the Skills of
    the American Workforce,
    80, 82, 88 n.
New Leaders for New Schools,
    81
New Philanthropy Capital, 271,
    273–274, 277 n.

Tuan, Melinda, 38 n.
Tziralis, Georgios, 227, 237 n.

underclass, American 43–89, 98,
   131, 169
   mid caps and, 18
   not too strong a word, 57
   permanent, 29, 58
   See also Self–sufficiency
unemployment, 58
United Way, 8, 17, 19, 28, 40 n.,
   42 n., 124
University of Iowa, 224
University of Michigan, 127
unsustainability, 58
Urban Institute, The, 61, 141,
   165 n., 238 n., 272, 273,
   277 n.
U.S. Centers for Disease Control
   and Prevention, 225
US Futures Exchange, 225
U.S. News & World Report,
   235–236, 239 n.

value
   cash versus in–kind, 203–206
   difficulty of measurement, 201
   financial versus social, 200, 202
   price and, 198
   social impact and, 201
value chain, 74
van Heck, Eric, 238 n., 257 n.
venture philanthropy
   as multi–stage funding, 122,
      174
   as transformative innovation,
      123

model(s), 5, 9–10, 96, 176
rise of performance
   measurement, 262
second–stage funding and, 25,
   173
social entrepreneurs and, 4, 28,
   103
See also, New Profit, Inc.,
   Venture Philanthropy
   Partners
Venture Philanthropy Partners
   (VPP), 5, 10, 18, 25, 39
   n., 40 n., 75, 123, 129 n.,
   153, 166 n.
virtual stock market. *See* Stock
   market, nonprofit
Voltaire, 191
volunteers, 232

Waldron, Rob, 80, 81, 84, 89 n.
Wall Street Journal Political
   Market, 225
Wallace Foundation, 83
Wanner, Eric, 86 n.
Web 2.0, 157
Weiss, Marcus, 38 n.
welfare, 62, 87 n.
Whitman, Glen, 233, 238 n.
whole product(s), 112, 115, 117,
   175, 242
   defined, 115
   Impact Index, 273
   intermediation and, 146
   model, 117, 119
   nonprofit infrastructure and,
      150, 260
whole value system, 74

Wiefels, Paul, 110, 130 n., 188 n.,
    276 n.
Wikipedia, 146, 166 n.
William J. Clinton Foundation,
    89 n.
William and Flora Hewlett
    Foundation, 109, 275
Winfrey, Oprah, 24
Winograd, Terry, 239 n.
wisdom of crowds xx, 209–212,
    214, 224, 241, 249, 268
Wisdom of Crowds, The, 35, 42 n.,
    211, 214 n.
Wise Giving Alliance, 16, 272
Wolfers, Justin, 257 n.
Wolk, Andrew, 134, 178, 203,
    213 n.
Wood, Arthur, 129 n., 166 n.

workforce development, 82, 116,
    118
Wright–Violich, Kim, 277 n.

Xpree, 226
X Prize Foundation, 244
Xu, Zeyu, 37 n.

Yahoo, 122
Yankelovich, Daniel, 201
Year Up, 12, 82, 151
Youth Villages, 23

Zabel, William, 270
Zangrando, Joanna Schneider,
    46
Zangrando, Robert L., 46, 84 n.
Zocalo, 226